Peer-Assisted Learning in
ACADEMIC LIBRARIES

Peer-Assisted Learning in
ACADEMIC LIBRARIES

Erin Rinto, John Watts, and Rosan Mitola, Editors

Foreword by Patricia Iannuzzi

LIBRARIES UNLIMITED™
An Imprint of ABC-CLIO, LLC
Santa Barbara, California • Denver, Colorado

Library of Congress Cataloging-in-Publication Data

Names: Rinto, Erin, editor. | Watts, John (Librarian), editor. | Mitola, Rosan, editor.
Title: Peer-assisted learning in academic libraries / Erin Rinto, John Watts, and Rosan Mitola, editors ; foreword by Patricia Iannuzzi.
Description: Santa Barbara, California : Libraries Unlimited, an Imprint of ABC-CLIO, LLC, [2017] | Includes bibliographical references and index.
Identifiers: LCCN 2017026075 (print) | LCCN 2017001567 (ebook) | ISBN 9781440846892 (ebook) | ISBN 9781440846885 (acid-free paper)
Subjects: LCSH: Student library assistants—United States—Case studies. | Peer teaching—United States—Case studies. | Academic libraries—Relations with faculty and curriculum—United States—Case studies. | Mentoring in library science—United States—Case studies. | Research—Study and teaching (Higher)—Case studies. | Information literacy—Study and teaching (Higher)—United States—Case studies. | Library orientation for college students—United States—Case studies. | Libraries and colleges—United States—Case studies.
Classification: LCC Z682.4.S89 (print) | LCC Z682.4.S89 P44 2017 (ebook) | DDC 025.5/6770973—dc23
LC record available at https://lccn.loc.gov/2017026075

ISBN: 978-1-4408-4688-5
EISBN: 978-1-4408-4689-2

21 20 19 18 17 1 2 3 4 5

This book is also available as an eBook.

Libraries Unlimited
An Imprint of ABC-CLIO, LLC

ABC-CLIO, LLC
130 Cremona Drive, P.O. Box 1911
Santa Barbara, California 93116–1911
www.abc-clio.com

This book is printed on acid-free paper ∞

Manufactured in the United States of America

We dedicate this book to
Flora and Stuart Mason,
whose vision and generosity made this program possible,
and the past, present, and future Mason Undergraduate Peer Research Coaches.

Contents

Foreword

I have spent more than 30 years of my career framing academic libraries as partners in student learning: modeling action on various campuses, sharing strategies within our profession, and working on advocacy and curricular reform within higher education arenas ranging from professional associations to regional accreditation groups to private foundations. More than ever, I am convinced that academic libraries are uniquely positioned to contribute to student learning in and out of the classroom.

Our early efforts in articulating and embedding information literacy learning outcomes that overlap and integrate with critical thinking and oral and written communication have created a generation of librarians participating in campus conversations about student learning. We teach, we partner with classroom instructors on course and assignment design, and we intentionally design learning spaces and experiences outside of the classroom. We are likely the only unit on campus that contributes to student learning through both curricular and co-curricular experiences. We provide one-on-one instruction at service points, turning routine questions into teachable moments for guided inquiry. We employ pedagogy of place in reshaping our physical and virtual spaces to encourage a variety of student learning styles and preferences, supporting group and individual learning. We use our classrooms for formal instruction sessions and topical workshops, and we use our computer spaces to guide students as producers of their own knowledge, employing digital tools and techniques and practicing all the literacies that accompany them.

I have long supported the research claiming that teaching is the highest form of learning, which means that peer-assisted teaching and learning is a win–win environment for both peer leaders and peer learners. When you consider the library as creator and facilitator of intentionally designed peer learning experiences, you have a trifecta—a three-way winning combination for the peer leaders, the peer learners, and the library!

The diversity of learning experiences created by libraries provides many opportunities to embed peer learning into those environments, and I have experimented with these practices for more than 25 years. Over time, I have experienced a series of "aha" moments, leading to further experimentation and innovation. In some cases, I designed experiences to encourage and nurture peer learning among students as our users. In other situations, I created programs for library student employees who were trained, mentored, and supported to function as peer teachers. One of my first experiences was almost unintentional, back in the late 1980s when technological innovation in the form of CD-ROM and locally hosted databases were made available to students and other library users for the first time. The role of librarians as intermediaries to information was removed, and users were catapulted into the role of direct consumer. I hired my first "student rovers" in those years to extend the reference reach into the computer help space and provide peer assistance with technology applications. But I noticed something from those first peer leaders: they excelled academically because they learned how to do research and they were extensively trained and provided opportunities for continual learning. They even began to bring back stories of introducing their classroom instructors to the latest databases acquired by the libraries.

The CD-ROM era quickly gave way to the Internet. These were difficult transition years for generations of library users, classroom faculty, and even librarians. Library anxiety was real, especially in first-generation college students, returning students who completed their education before the Internet, and international students adjusting to cultural and procedural differences in library environments. It was quickly obvious that students were more likely to ask for help from another student, than from an authority figure behind a desk.

Almost overnight, the passive study spaces provided by libraries to complement collections were morphing into learning spaces as computers proliferated and peers were used to extend the one-on-one instruction provided at reference desks and other service points. Almost unintentionally, libraries were extending their impact on co-curricular student learning, not just through new services provided by student employees, but to the student employees themselves.

So my journey of experimentation started with student rovers to extend the library reach and connect with peers as the Internet evolved. It continued when I realized that the literature on the challenges of transitioning to college can be addressed through peer learning opportunities. My efforts further expanded when I intentionally designed programs for student employees to give them needed academic skills and train them as peer mentors to other students. And when I became a dean and was able to craft case statements for library donors, I had the freedom to pursue the notion of creating an endowed program for student employees: an intentionally designed peer coach program.

How often have we noticed that students who work in libraries are often good students? The literature on student employees on campus is beginning to bear that out, and the research on student learning provides clues as to the reason why. Students who have adult guides outside of the classroom perform better. Students who work on campus and do not need to juggle off campus jobs with schoolwork perform better. Students who learn library research skills possess transferable skills that help them in their academic work. What better way to provide a value-added educational experience for our students than to have them work in libraries, becoming more adept at our resources and services, and, in turn, extending their own learning through peer mentoring? As is reflected in this book, libraries are uniquely positioned to provide many, varied opportunities for peer learning. And doing so not only benefits our students, but also adds depth and complexity to our planning and assessment of how we contribute to student success.

Imagine the benefits of training our student employees as peers to other students. We can develop academic and library research skills, interpersonal and communication skills, and cultural skills. We can create experiences for them to learn alongside their peers as they negotiate their questions and guide them to resources, services, tools, and processes. We can create and support opportunities for students to learn from each other as we:

- mentor and train student employees in the wide range of interpersonal, technical, academic, and library skills, contributing to their own success even as they engage in peer learning;
- train students as assistants in the classroom alongside librarians;
- train students as rovers or on help desks in learning commons, guiding peers in the intricacies of library resources and services;
- develop students as library ambassadors at new student orientation sessions, at recruitment events, or in residence halls, providing a familiar, friendly, and approachable face of the library;
- teach students how to interview their peers in order to conduct informal assessments; and
- train students to provide assistance and instruction for the variety of technical tools offered by the library.

Some of you reading this book may be wondering how to make a case to your administration about why your library should allocate precious resources to intentionally design and assess peer-assisted learning activities. Resources should always be aligned with priorities, and library priorities should always be aligned with those of the campus. You need only review your campus strategic plan to learn what matters to your President and Provost. And it is highly likely that student retention and academic success are near the top of the list. We can and do make a difference in these areas. But all too often, because of the myriad activities and programs and projects we engage in, the fact that we make a difference is often not as obvious as it should be. It is most important for a library to weave its varied student learning activities together to form a strategic plan for adding value to the teaching and learning mission of the university. The varied ways that libraries support peer learning need to be intentionally planned and assessed for impact, providing evidence of our contributions to student success.

One final consideration. In this book, you will read a chapter by several library faculty at the University of Nevada, Las Vegas, who are involved in our Mason Undergraduate Peer Research Coach Program. Notice the naming. Campus fund-raisers all too frequently point out that donors prefer to give scholarships as they want to "make a difference" in the life of an individual student, and that libraries don't have students, so they can't raise funds to help students pay for their education. That's not exactly true. Fund-raisers also say that donors do not want to give money to support student employees as they are part of routine operations. That's not exactly true, either. I was able to connect a donor interested in making a difference in the individual life of a student with the concept of student employment. The result is a talented cohort of mentored library student ambassadors who work as research coaches in and out of the classroom and who become, from the experience, some of our most promising alumni. We CAN have our own brand of scholarships through this donor-funded program that contributes to the academic success of the Peer Coaches as well as the students they work with. And donors have the privilege of contributing to the education and academic success of real students who work in the library, and receive special mentoring and training throughout their time with us. Donors can see and interact with specific students that they fund, benefiting from the relationship and the joy of watching these students grow and learn. The library benefits from a cohort of specially trained students who extend the library's reach, who excel academically, and who demonstrate the value of creating a peer learning experience. And if the program builds in assessment measures, there is evidence of the impact of student learning beyond the classroom, through the library.

Peer learning experiences provide a pathway for libraries to expand their teaching and learning mission, not just to campus stakeholders, but also to the broader community of friends who support the university. And best of all, we make learning special for our students. I will bet on it every time!

Patricia Iannuzzi

Introduction

Consider the last time you learned something new. Was it from a webinar? A conference presentation? A conversation with your colleagues in the hallway outside your offices? As librarians, we are used to learning with and from one another. Collaborating, discussing, and experimenting with our peers are natural extensions of our profession. Indeed, these kinds of informal learning interactions happen regularly in our personal lives as well—perhaps you learned a new recipe from a blog or picked up a new exercise technique from your brother or mastered a new mobile technology alongside a friend. It is in our nature to seek out one another for guidance and to share our own knowledge with others; Deanna Martin, founder of Supplemental Instruction, notes "as a social species, all of us take part in a wide range of peer learning experiences each day" (Martin, 2008, p. 3).

As academic librarians, we know that these peer learning interactions also happen for our students. We see them collaborating on group projects, comparing notes for an upcoming test, or simply working alongside one another at library workstations or in information literacy instruction sessions. But there are also more formal mechanisms by which peer learning can take place, and, as will be seen, higher education scholars and practitioners have produced a great deal of research on the best practices for formal peer learning and the benefits of these programs. In its most distilled form, peer learning consists of "people from similar social groupings who are not professional teachers helping each other to learn and learning themselves by teaching" (Topping, 1996, p. 322). On the one hand, the premise of peer-to-peer learning is simple: if we accept the fact that "undergraduate students speak the language of other undergraduates more distinctly than graduate students and professors," then it follows that an undergraduate who has mastered a concept—whether it be course-related subject matter, research strategies, or even the culture and mores of the college campus—is in a prime position to help other students also learn that concept or develop that skill set (Nelson, 1995, p. 45). But on the other hand, the great diversity of peer learning programs, their many formats and varied objectives, can give pause to practitioners considering implementing these programs: What exactly is peer learning? How do we know that it is effective? Is it worth the time and energy it takes to implement a new program or restructure an existing one? How would a program of this nature function in an academic library?

The purpose of this book is to explore the application of social learning interactions, captured under the umbrella term "peer-assisted learning" (PAL), in the context of academic libraries. In the following pages, case studies from a variety of academic institutions examine how PAL programs are utilized in three different areas of traditional library services: information literacy instruction (Chapters 1–5), co-curricular outreach (Chapters 6–9), and the provision of reference (Chapters 10–14). But in order to contextualize the excellent work of our chapter contributors, in this introduction we offer a more theoretical perspective on the issue of PAL. Specifically, we provide an explanation of the learning theories that inform PAL and provide rationale for why academic libraries should adopt this practice, including the benefits for the institution, the peer learners (defined here as the students receiving the help or service), and the peer leaders (the students providing the help or service).

Of particular interest to us is the impact PAL has on the peer leaders. The Association of American Colleges & Universities (AAC&U) has identified a list of High-Impact Practices (teaching and learning practices that have been shown to be beneficial for college students from many backgrounds), as well as an explanation of the characteristics that make these educational practices especially effective (Kuh, 2008). By placing examples of peer learning alongside these characteristics, we illustrate how PAL actually has many similarities with AAC&U's High-Impact Practices, and we posit that PAL programs are one way in which academic libraries can directly provide our students with meaningful and transformative educational experiences.

WHAT IS PEER-ASSISTED LEARNING?

Definition

Many scholars have defined peer-assisted learning (PAL) (Adam, Skalicky, & Brown, 2011; Bodemer, 2014; Boud, Cohen, & Sampson, 2001; Dancer, Morrison, & Tarr, 2015; Falchikov, 2001; Havnes, 2008), but the most commonly used definition of PAL comes from Topping and Ehly: "a group of strategies that involve the active and interactive mediation of learning through other learners who are not professional teachers" (2001, p. 113). More specifically, Topping notes that the learners in question should be "status equals or matched companions" (2005, p. 631). The basic idea is that the "helper," or peer leader, has knowledge and ability proximal to the knowledge and ability of the "helped," or peer learner, so that both parties find a measure of "cognitive challenge"—both the leader and learner are gaining from the interaction (Topping, 2005, p. 632). In addition, Topping and Ehly (2001) have identified certain hallmark characteristics of PAL:

- Through helping others learn, the helpers themselves also learn.
- The peer learning interaction is supplemental to professional teaching.
- The peer learning interaction is structured in such a way that all participants can improve in one or more areas.
- The peer learning interaction is available to all students.
- The peer learning interaction is established and facilitated by professional teachers.

It is important to note the role of the teacher in Topping and Ehly's model of a successful peer learning interaction. PAL does not replace traditional teaching methods or content delivery, the expertise of the teacher, or the role of the teacher in evaluating student performance. What it does do is rely on the teacher's competence and judgment to create scenarios or programs that allow students to lead each other through the learning process.

What then does PAL look like in practice? There are many peer learning scenarios that meet Topping and Ehly's definition, and they can be both course-integrated or take place outside of the classroom. Commonly used examples include peer tutoring, peer mentoring, peer teaching, collaborative learning, cooperative learning, group mentoring, peer assessment, reciprocal teaching, peer-assisted writing, and peer-assisted distance learning; formats can also vary: peer learning may be cross-year (students are of different academic levels), same-year (students are in the same course or academic year), many-to-one, one-to-one, fixed role (peer leader and peer learner retain their roles throughout the learning interaction), or reciprocal (peer leader and peer learner switch roles) (Bodemer, 2014; Falchikov, 2001; Havnes, Christiansen, Bjørk, & Hessevaagbakke, 2016; Topping, 1996). More formalized PAL programs include Supplemental Instruction (SI), Peer-Assisted Study Sessions (PASS), and Peer-Led Team Learning (PLTL) (for more information on these programs, see Dancer et al., 2015; Gafney & Varma-Nelson, 2008; and Martin, 2008).

The various PAL programs described in this book differ from more structured models, because, just as with the provision of most library services, they are more one-off in nature as opposed to being fully embedded in one course over an entire semester; interactions can be brief, even transactional, from the perspective of the peer learner. For the peer leaders, however, the PAL experience is often much more enduring, and it is for these students that we believe the true benefits of PAL are realized.

Learning Theories

PAL is generally accepted to be informed by the work of Jean Piaget and Lev Vygotsky, who have examined the impact of social learning theory (Christiansen, Bjørk, Havnes, & Hessevaagbakke, 2011). It is Vygotsky's concept of the "zone of proximal development," however, that has most impacted the study of PAL (Vygotsky, 1978). In addition to Vygotsky, PAL can also be understood through the lenses of communities of practice and seamless learning cultures.

Vygotsky defines the "zone of proximal development" as "the distance between the actual developmental level as determined by independent problem solving and the level of potential development as determined through problem solving under adult guidance or in collaboration with more capable peers" (Vygotsky, 1978, p. 96). The theory assumes that learning takes place through social interactions (Havnes, 2008). Topping, who has extensively studied PAL, notes that "supported (or 'scaffolded') exploration through social and cognitive interaction with a more experienced peer . . . remains a theoretical cornerstone of peer assisted learning" (Topping, 1996, p. 324). One way to conceptualize the zone of proximal development is the idea of stretching one's capacity—a student of lower ability reaches out and a student of higher ability reaches back. Together, they are able to attain new knowledge, more than what students could accomplish on their own. In essence, the more experienced students pull their peer into a new level of cognitive development. This learning theory is largely focused on the gains made by the learner, rather than the leader.

In addition, the concept of communities of practice also has some bearing on PAL. A community of practice, as defined by Wenger-Trayner and Wenger-Trayner (2015) is a "group of people who share a concern or a passion for something they do and learn how to do it better as they interact regularly" (p. 1). In peer learning situations, two communities are developed: peer leaders and peer learners (Adam et al., 2011). In the context of library-led PAL, which typically consists of peers helping one another in more of a drop-in, or one-on-one, model, a true community of practice does not exist, at least not in the way it would for a semester-long course in which students work together on a weekly or daily basis. But the peer leaders themselves may form a community of practice, especially if peer leaders are hired and trained in cohorts. Wenger notes that the community should have the following characteristics, many of which also apply to peer learning contexts: the community should involve "engagement and action"—as opposed to passive participation (1998, p. 73); the members should be diverse and bring their own skills and experiences to the larger group; the community should work toward the goals of the larger institution; and there should be a "regime of mutual accountability and shared repertoire" (p. 81). When cohorts or teams of peer leaders are trained together, they can resemble Wenger's communities—they are active participants working together to support the mission of their library or institution, each bringing their own skills, knowledge, and experiences to the table, and holding each other responsible for delivering high-quality service. In addition, in a community of practice, "members interact and negotiate new meaning"—the students form a community of *learners* (Wenger, 1998, p. 102). Members in the community learn from and with one another, and they can then teach what they have learned to other peer learners, bringing them deeper into the university community (Adam et al., 2011).

Finally, the theory of seamless learning culture can inform our understanding of PAL. The premise of seamless learning is that students also learn outside of the classroom and that the institution should "fully capitalize on how and where students learn best" (Bell, 2000, p. 46). Learning does not take place only during normal business hours or in classrooms, but rather when students are properly situated for learning—when they are ready to apply what they have learned and put it into practice—which may happen in the residence hall, as part of an internship, or during a study abroad experience (Bell, 2000). Seamless learning can be realized through PAL programs, in which students learn from one another in more point-of-need situations, without the intervention of a professional teacher.

PAL in Academic Libraries

Higher education in general has embraced the notion of PAL—Supplemental Instruction alone exists in over 1,500 colleges and universities around the world—but what about academic libraries? What has our profession done in the way of utilizing PAL as a means of providing traditional library services? While these practices have been in place since the 1970s (if not earlier), academic librarians have not produced a great deal of literature on formal PAL programs, though studies do indeed exist (Bodemer, 2014; O'Kelly, Garrison, Merry, & Torreano, 2015). The purpose here is not to provide a history of all PAL programs in academic libraries, but rather to highlight some patterns in how PAL is typically integrated into library services (for a thorough treatment of the history of PAL in academic libraries, see Bodemer, 2014).

The most commonly cited example of peer learning in library contexts occurs in the provision of reference services; Bodemer notes that there have been "sporadic attempts" in utilizing PAL at the reference desk since the 1970s (2014, p. 165). The most typical manifestation of this practice is having students sit at the desk alongside (or near to) a professional librarian and working in a "triage" capacity, answering basic or directional questions and referring more advanced questions to the librarian. Specific examples of this model include the University of Southern California's Leavey Library, where student navigational assistants provided round-the-clock basic reference and computer help and were trained on how and when to refer questions (Crockett, McDaniel, & Remy, 2002). At

Coastal Carolina University's Kimbel Library, student assistants were, at one point, staffing the desk at all available hours, as well as handling chat reference. Over time, however, the model changed (due to the evolving nature of the library's service points); the current model limits the student assistants to "first-tier" questions, while all other questions are referred to a librarian (Faix, 2014).

There are far fewer examples of PAL in information literacy instruction; Bodemer points out that when peer leaders are integrated into the classroom, it is typically in a "peripheral role" as opposed to leading sessions on their own (2014, p. 169). Peer leaders might facilitate group work, co-teach alongside a librarian, or assist in the preparation of instructional materials. One exception comes from the University of Windsor, in which the library took a "teaching-the-teacher" approach: upper-division students were trained to facilitate student groups in a first-year course. A librarian worked with the peer mentors to improve their own research skills so that they could, in turn, assist the first-year students in a problem-based learning project. The emphasis of the mentor training was on how to model effective research strategies; rather than being tool-based in nature, mentors were taught to think critically about information (Bolton, Pugliese, & Singleton-Jackson, 2009). The study found that students preferred asking their mentors for help (rather than the librarian), so this approach helped improve student projects (Bolton et al., 2009).

In a similar vein, there are few cases of utilizing PAL in co-curricular outreach. While student employees *are* commonly used to promote the library at outreach events and to market the library to fellow students (MacAdam & Nichols, 1988; Mathews, 2009; Millet & Chamberlain, 2007), it is important here to remember Topping and Ehly's definition of PAL—especially the "active and interactive mediation of learning" piece (2001, p. 113). For true PAL to take place, there needs to be a learning interaction that enhances the cognitive development of both the learner and the leader. These learning scenarios seem to occur less frequently in the library outreach literature, though some examples can be gleaned. At Trinity University in San Antonio, campus peer tutors were trained to work with students in first-year seminars and writing workshops in the hope that "peers could take [information literacy] instruction further by helping to foster positive attitudes toward the library and all its resources" (Millet & Chamberlain, 2007, p. 98). It is rare, however, to find studies in which outreach is part of a learning interaction.

So if PAL has been around, in its most formal models, for nearly half a century, why are there so relatively few examples of applications of this practice in a library setting? Though there are numerous benefits to PAL (as will be further outlined later), these programs are not without their challenges. There are difficulties librarians may face when adopting PAL programs: they can be time-consuming and staff-intensive, there are some questions about the efficacy of such programs, and PAL can sometimes give rise to librarian anxieties.

One disadvantage of PAL programs is that they can be extremely resource-intensive, especially at their outset and especially in terms of staff time and energy (Topping, 1996). Librarians are often already pressed for time (indeed, addressing this very issue can be a long-term benefit of PAL), so spending additional effort on properly researching, implementing, and situating a formal PAL program can feel daunting; as Adam, Skalicky, and Brown (2011) point out, "there is the potential to jump in atheoretically, or, once in, not to allocate sufficient time for reflection" (p. 17). As will be highlighted in many of our chapters, program implementation is often iterative, with time needed to reflect and restructure, and changes to the program may involve new mechanisms for training and preparing students. After assessing a PAL program in which students provided reference services, Brenza, Kowalsky, and Brush (2015) learned that "student assistants require more training to develop the perceptions we seek, [and] the next step in the training process is ongoing refinement and development of student skills aligned with shared goals and a common philosophy" (p. 733). In addition to the time it takes to properly plan, assess, and revise a PAL program, there are also challenges involved with the time-consuming nature of supervising student employees (a challenge not unique to PAL contexts). In her analysis of a student reference assistant program at Coastal Carolina University, Faix (2014) found challenges related to supervisory responsibilities, including addressing student behavioral issues (calling off, tardiness, violations of the dress code and cellphone/internet use policies), coaching students through professionalism, and communication problems, especially if students were working later hours when librarians were not present.

On a related note, one may also consider that staff attitudes toward and acceptance of PAL programs needs to be cultivated, and instilling this organizational culture can also take time. What happens when PAL is championed by enthusiastic staff who move on to other positions? Kingston University was an early adopter of PAL as an adaption of Supplemental Instruction, but after just a few years, the original program suffered because staff had moved on to other institutions (Longfellow, May, Burke, & Marks-Maran, 2008).

Another potential disadvantage of PAL programs is their efficacy. Are these programs actually worth the time and effort? Hammond, Bithell, Jones, and Bidgood (2010) explore this issue in their discussion of a same-year PAL program for first-year students. After evaluating the program for three years, the authors concluded that while the "majority of students agreed that PAL helped with social aspects of learning," the students did not feel that PAL contributed to "improved study skills or assignment preparation" (p. 201). Havnes et al. (2016) also caution against treating PAL as a panacea for improved student learning, noting that research indicates "peer learning is often organized and used by students in ways that run contrary to research-based knowledge about how interaction among peers can support learning" (p. 75). In general, the same features that make PAL a potentially powerful learning experience—that it is student-led—can also make it a challenging one; peer leaders are not professional teachers, and therefore may lack professionalism (Christiansen et al., 2011).

Finally, there are some challenges to be found in accepting the fact that if peer leaders are, in fact, the ones facilitating the learning interaction for their fellow students, we, as professional librarians, are not. There are certainly concerns to be had regarding the quality control of letting students take over many of our traditional responsibilities (Bodemer, 2014). This is not unique only to librarians—Topping notes that in any peer-led learning scenario, the "quality of tutoring from a peer may be a good deal inferior to that from a professional teacher . . . and the need for monitoring and quality control cannot be overstated" (1996, p. 325). But we would caution against letting this discomfort inhibit librarians from implementing PAL programs; as a profession, we have already been through many uncomfortable transitions. Campbell (2007), in a reprisal of his 1992 article on the impending changes to the practice of reference librarianship due to new technologies, notes that librarians' penchant for remaining in our comfort zones has "a limiting effect on [our] eagerness to embrace questions of change" (p. 22). Campbell's solution to overcoming this uneasiness is to focus on our "primary mission rather than the means by which it [is] carried out;" that if we maintain clarity about our goal and purpose, we can be "flexible with regard to how it is pursued" (p. 22). If Campbell's argument is applied to the adoption of PAL, we can see that if our primary purpose is to provide our students with excellent service, enhance their learning, and/or increase their access and usage of high-quality sources of information, then utilizing other undergraduates as the means of provision is just one other way of achieving our goals.

THE BENEFITS OF PAL FOR ACADEMIC LIBRARIES

Despite these challenges, there are myriad reasons for why academic libraries should not, in the words of Bodemer (2014), "miss this boat" (p. 176). As the state of higher education continues to evolve, librarians need to find ways to improve their services while simultaneously taking on new roles and responsibilities. PAL has been shown to benefit the institutions that adopt these practices, the peer learners who participate in these learning interactions, and the peer leaders who facilitate them.

Benefits to the Library

One practical benefit of PAL for academic libraries is resource allocation. Arco-Tirado, Fernández-Martín, and Fernández-Balboa (2011) argue that peer learning "offers a viable model to institutions of higher learning as to how to allocate their resources and organize their student support services" (pp. 782–783). For academic libraries, this can mean a restructuring of staff time; if well-trained students can work the reference desk, then professional librarians have more time to partner with faculty, assist with more extensive research consultations, or participate in assessment efforts. Indeed, it has been noted that many reference transactions do not require a professional degree to answer, and there are more specialist tasks to which librarians could be devoting their time (Faix, 2014).

Training peer leaders to provide reference, instruction, and outreach services can also lead to improved educational experiences for our students. It is important to consider that students are experts in their own right—they are experts at being students—and they are therefore "better placed to lead novice students towards becoming expert students" (Longfellow et al., 2008, p. 95). It has been acknowledged that students prefer to learn from one another rather than librarians, and that they may be more likely to ask a peer for assistance; utilizing PAL is one way to make sure "[students'] research needs are fully met" (Faix, 2014, p. 308).

Peer leaders can also benefit the library by improving the organization and implementation of its services and programs. They can provide librarians with a unique student perspective on the efficacy and format of various library initiatives. O'Kelly et al. (2015) point out that in their PAL program, the peer leaders "are regularly encouraged to share their own feedback and provide suggestions for improving the program" (p. 168). This student perspective can give us insight that can lead to better overall services for the undergraduate population at large.

Benefits to the Peer Learners

The literature on PAL has identified numerous benefits to the peer learners, including gains in the cognitive, affective, and social domains. Cognitive benefits for the learner include improved study skills; better understanding, retention, and transfer of subject knowledge; greater use of critical and creative thinking skills; more ownership over their learning; and increased willingness to engage in difficult tasks (Hammond et al., 2010; Han, Chung, & Nam, 2015; Hanson, Trolian, Paulsen, & Pascarella, 2016). More specifically, studies have demonstrated a positive correlation with PAL and improved examination scores and/or final course grades (Carr et al., 2016; Dancer et al., 2015; Han et al., 2015).

There are also established affective benefits of PAL on the peer learners. These benefits include increased confidence and self-esteem, lowered stress, and greater satisfaction with and positive attitudes toward their academic courses (Carr et al., 2016; Hanson et al., 2016; O'Kelly et al., 2015). As part of the Wabash National Study of Liberal Arts Education, Hanson et al. (2016) examined the longitudinal effects of peer learning on psychological well-being. The Wabash National Study seeks to examine the impact of a liberal arts education and includes a survey that students complete in their first and last years of college; one set of questions on the survey is directly related to peer learning interactions. A total of 1,792 students from 17 colleges and universities in 11 states completed the survey; the results indicated "a significant, positive influence of peer learning on the Ryff scale of psychological well-being" (Hanson et al., 2016, p. 191). In particular, aspects of well-being that were positively affected by peer learning interactions included autonomy (self-determination and independence), environmental mastery (the ability to manage the environment and make use of surrounding opportunities), personal growth, purpose in life, and self-acceptance (Hanson et al., 2016).

Finally, there are also social benefits of PAL for the peer learners. Most commonly indicated social benefits are increased social and communication skills, but there are also more nuanced social gains. A survey of students participating in a same-year PAL program found that students valued learning with other students, the opportunity to discuss concerns about the course or subject matter away from the professor, and learning about other students' viewpoints (Hammond et al., 2010). In a study of participants in a peer tutoring program for students with disabilities, it was found that the peer learners felt they gained friendships and new insight into campus life (Kowalsky & Fresko, 2002).

It is clear from these studies that PAL programs can benefit the learners who engage in these programs—they learn new skills and subject matter, feel more comfortable and confident, and have the opportunity to engage in meaningful social interactions with their peers. These cognitive, affective, and social gains provide convincing rationale for librarians considering PAL as a means of delivering library services—clearly students benefit from working with their peers.

Benefits to the Peer Leader

Just as with peer learners, peer leaders also have been found to gain in the cognitive, affective, and social domains. The greatest cognitive benefit of PAL on peer leaders is their own learning of the subject matter. As Topping noted, the adage "to teach is to learn twice" highlights the relationship between teaching and learning that takes place for peer leaders (Topping, 1996, p. 324). If peer leaders know they are responsible for helping their peers master the content, it provides them with great motivation to master that content themselves (Hodgson, Benson, & Brack, 2015; Topping, 1996). Many studies of the benefits for peer leaders echo the sentiment that peer leaders strengthen their own learning and understanding as a result of participating in PAL (Christiansen et al., 2011; Han et al., 2015; Hilsdon, 2014; Hodgson et al., 2015; Wawrzynski, LoConte, & Straker, 2011). In a library context, the content peer leaders are responsible for teaching others, namely, information literacy and research skills, leads to their own increased mastery and confidence in these areas (Faix, 2014; O'Kelly et al., 2015). In addition to subject knowledge, peer leaders have also been found to gain leadership, organizational, and communication skills; new knowledge and information about the university; and improved teaching skills, including simplifying and clarifying complex concepts (Beltman & Schaeben, 2012; Topping, 1996; Wawrzynski et al., 2011).

Among the most commonly cited affective benefits for peer leaders are increased self-confidence and self-efficacy; indeed nearly every study that examines the benefits of PAL on peer leaders identified gains in self-confidence (Beltman & Schaeben, 2012; Han et al., 2015; Hilsdon, 2014; O'Kelly et al., 2015; Wawrzynski et al., 2011). Other affective benefits include a sense of satisfaction from helping others and increased empathy (Beltman & Schaeben, 2012; Han et al., 2015; Hilsdon, 2014); gains in sensitivity to diversity (Kowalsky & Fresko, 2002; Wawrzynski et al., 2011); a more positive attitude toward learning (Han et al., 2015); and personal growth (Beltman & Schaeben, 2012). In addition, peer leaders working with disabled students indicated they had learned how to "cope successfully with difficulties," and felt more motivated to overcome obstacles—concepts they learned from working with their peers (Kowalsky & Fresko, 2002, p. 267).

There are also social benefits associated with being a peer leader. In their survey of peer mentors, Beltman and Schaeben (2012) found that students felt they had gained new friendships, that they enjoyed getting to know new students and networking with other mentors, and that they liked working with university staff. The notion of creating friendships was also echoed in Kowalsky and Fresko, who found that tutors of disabled students indicated they developed personal relationships and were exposed to "a new area of human experience" (2002 p. 267).

Though PAL is rife with opportunity for libraries and peer learners, the most compelling reason for implementing PAL may be the benefits these learning interactions have on the peer leaders. To be sure, the cognitive, affective, and social benefits identified in various studies point toward the impact PAL has on the peer leaders who facilitate learning experiences for their fellow students. But we believe there is much more to be gleaned regarding the benefits of PAL for peer leaders. The literature demonstrates that PAL, as is the case with established high-impact educational initiatives, has the potential to deeply enhance the personal and academic lives of the students involved. In order to demonstrate PAL's potential as a deep and transformative learning experience, we will now explore the features of PAL that overlap with AAC&U's High-Impact Practices.

PAL: A HIGHLY EFFECTIVE EDUCATIONAL PRACTICE

AAC&U has developed a list of High-Impact Practices, which consist of educational activities that "increase rates of student retention and student engagement" (Kuh, 2008, p. 9). The practices identified include first-year seminars and experiences, common intellectual experiences, learning communities, writing-intensive courses, collaborative assignments and projects, undergraduate research, diversity/global learning, service learning, community-based learning, internships, and capstone courses and projects (Kuh, 2008). In developing this list of ten High-Impact Practices, George Kuh's investigation included the identification of characteristics these practices share, features that make them especially effective. An exploration of Kuh's six characteristics (time and effort; faculty and peer interaction; diversity; formal and informal feedback; integration, synthesis, and application; and connection with the larger world), reveals that though PAL is not in and of itself one of AAC&U's ten High-Impact Practices, each of the features of effective educational practices described by Kuh apply to PAL (Kuh, 2008). By exploring each of the characteristics of effective educational practices through the lens of the various PAL programs presented in our book, we hope to show that PAL aligns with other high-impact practices in terms of its impact on the educational experiences of the peer leader.

Moreover, many of AAC&U's High-Impact Practices are difficult, or even impractical, for librarians to directly engage in. While we contribute to these practices in many essential ways—collaborating with faculty on course design, providing information literacy instruction for writing-intensive courses, supporting undergraduate research, and so on—we typically do not have the opportunity to fully take ownership of these initiatives. But a compelling aspect of PAL is that it transcends the curriculum—it does not need to be embedded in a course or tied to a degree program. And this means that librarians can directly engage in the provision of PAL—our student employees can become our peer leaders, and our services can become the peer-mediated learning interactions. We would offer then that implementing well-designed PAL programs is one way in which academic libraries can directly provide our students with meaningful and transformative educational experiences.

What follows next is an explanation of each of Kuh's characteristics of especially effective educational practices, coupled with practical examples from the PAL programs in our chapters. Our intent is to highlight that PAL does indeed provide a deep learning experience for peer leaders and that academic libraries have a wealth of possibilities for implementing these programs and impacting the learning experiences of our students.

1. Time and Effort

> The most important thing I've learned about myself in the past year is that I am able to interact with other students really well. I know how to collaborate with a student or librarian to find a solution to a problem in the classroom. Also, I've learned that I can rely on my critical thinking skills to find any solutions needed.
>
> (University of Nevada, Las Vegas, Peer Coach)

When describing educational practices that lead to deeper student learning, Kuh indicates that one hallmark is the time and effort students spend engaged in these activities: "These practices typically demand that students devote considerable time and effort to purposeful tasks; most require daily decisions that deepen students' investment in the activity as well as their commitment to their academic program and the college" (Kuh, 2008, p. 14). As will be seen throughout our chapters, PAL programs absolutely require a great deal of time and energy for the peer leaders involved; across the board, they are engaged in substantive work (teaching information literacy skills, answering research questions, and, in some cases, delivering course-related content in the areas of math and writing). In addition, peer leaders are extensively trained, are retained in their positions for the duration of their academic career, and are often required to reflect about the meaning of their work.

The training component of PAL cannot be overstated; it is essential that students are well-prepared for the demands of their position and are able to deliver high-quality learning experiences to their peers. Many programs provide an initial intensive period of training: Harvard College (Chapter 6) trains students over a five-week period; at California Polytechnic State University, San Luis Obispo (Chapter 2), peer leaders are trained over a full academic quarter; at the University of New Hampshire Manchester (Chapter 1), training is incorporated into a credit-bearing academic course. In addition, nearly all programs include a measure of ongoing training, in which students meet with each other and their supervisors on a regular basis. In these cases, peer leaders cannot be passive participants—they are immersed in the peer learning experience and form a community of learners.

Another indication of the substantial time and effort required by PAL is the longevity of the peer leader experience in such programs. Many chapters emphasize the retention of peer leaders; students are hired early in their academic careers with the aim that they will remain in the program until graduation. Indeed, academic persistence is a goal of some programs, such as the University of Texas at San Antonio (Chapter 8). Utah State University (Chapter 4) hires students in their first or second year and has been extremely successful at retaining students through graduation; Southern Illinois University Carbondale (Chapter 13) has been so effective at retaining students that it now intentionally hires students with staggered graduation years, so they don't all leave at once.

Finally, these PAL programs are often purposefully designed so that students find meaning in the work they do. At the University of Nevada, Las Vegas (Chapter 5), peer leaders complete weekly reflections about their experiences co-teaching information literacy instruction sessions; at Southern Illinois University Carbondale, peer leaders are asked to write a letter to incoming peer leaders regarding their time in the program and how it impacted their college experiences.

2. Faculty and Peer Interaction

> Through my experience as a Peer Coach, I gained lifelong friendships with my peers and colleagues, and met some great mentors.
>
> (University of Nevada, Las Vegas, Peer Coach)

A second feature of highly effective educational practices is that they involve extended contact with other peers and faculty: "The nature of these high-impact activities puts students in circumstances that essentially demand they interact with faculty and peers about substantive matters, typically over extended periods of time" (Kuh, 2008, p. 14). In the following chapters, there are myriad examples of these extended relationships. One feature shared nearly universally is the close mentoring relationship that librarians foster with peer leaders. There are also numerous instances of group learning—peer leaders often form cohorts that learn and work together.

Mentoring is an essential function of many PAL training programs. At Gettysburg College (Chapter 10), supervision duties are shared among a team of librarians, so that peer leaders receive more personalized coaching and feedback. At San Diego State University (Chapter 9), one-on-one mentoring between the peer leaders and their supervisor is utilized to help acclimate students to their new positions and get them up to speed on the technologies they will need to utilize on the job. Harvard College also employs a librarian mentor scheme that supports peer leaders both in their training and once they begin their outreach work. The benefit of these mentoring relationships is that though they are between professional librarians and peer leaders, they are reciprocal in nature, with librarians learning about new ideas and directions for the PAL program and peer mentors learning the more nuanced aspects of library services.

Group learning is another pattern that has emerged across the chapters. An essential feature of the training program at the University of Oregon (Chapter 3) is peer mentoring, in which senior peer leaders help train new peer leaders. At Utah State University, peer leaders are required to co-teach alongside a more experienced peer as part of their training; this is also the case at Cal Poly, San Luis Obispo, where peer leaders shadow their peers at the desk as well as observe and co-teach peer-led instruction sessions. These group-learning scenarios, in which more experienced peer leaders coach and guide students who are new to the program, result in a multitiered peer learning program, in which peer leaders are trained by students so that they can teach students.

3. Diversity

> My experience as a peer coach has provided me the opportunity to interact with more people of different backgrounds. It has diversified me in so many respects of learning more about different cultures and people.
>
> (University of Nevada, Las Vegas, Peer Coach)

An important feature of a highly effective educational practice is that it will encourage students to leave their comfort zones and connect with students from different backgrounds. Kuh writes that "participating in one or more of these activities increases the likelihood that students will experience diversity through contact with people who are different from themselves" (Kuh, 2008, p. 15). The PAL programs in our chapters encourage diversity in numerous ways; they support diversity within the peer leader cohort as well as through enabling peer leaders to engage with diverse populations of peer learners.

Diversity within peer leader cohorts takes place at Hope College (Chapter 14), where students are hired from a variety of majors; students are able to form relationships with students they may not otherwise have opportunities to connect with. Cal Poly, San Luis Obispo, also strives to include a diversity of majors so that students can work across disciplines. The University of Oregon includes peer leaders from diverse backgrounds including nontraditional college students and international students, and the PAL program at the University of Texas at San Antonio was created in order to offer employment to first-generation students or other students demographically at risk for not completing a college degree.

PAL also offers an opportunity for peer leaders to work with diverse populations across campus. At Indiana University of Pennsylvania (Chapter 7), peer leaders, by nature of their work, engage with a variety of audiences, including peers in the residence halls, full-time campus housing professionals, and campus librarians. The makerspace at San Diego State University is designed to enhance socioeconomic diversity through removing the barriers of cost and access to emerging technologies; peer learners and peer leaders alike have different experiences and skills that they bring to the table. At the University of Nevada, Las Vegas, part of the peer leader training is a cultural competency workshop, in which peer leaders learn about different kinds of identities and how to create an inclusive classroom environment.

4. Formal and Informal Feedback

> The assumption I had about teaching and learning [that has] been most confirmed for me in the past year is that practice makes perfect. I feel like I have improved dramatically and I think the biggest reason is practice in different classrooms and with different instructors.
>
> (University of Nevada, Las Vegas, Peer Coach)

The fourth characteristic of an effective educational practice is that students have access to constructive feedback about their work: "Even though the structures and settings of high-impact activities differ, students typically get frequent feedback about their performance in every one. . . . Indeed, because students perform in close proximity to supervisors or peers, feedback is almost continuous" (Kuh, 2008, p. 17). Unilaterally, the chapters in our book exemplify this characteristic, as the nature of PAL also reflects the importance of feedback. Topping (2005) notes "both helper and helped give feedback to each another, implicitly, and/or explicitly" (p. 638). Peer leaders have constant access to performance evaluation—be it formally (from their supervisors) or informally (through their work with peer learners or their fellow peer leaders).

Formal feedback is an opportunity for librarians to exercise some quality control over PAL programs. At Michigan State University (Chapter 12), peer leaders are required to submit work reports at the end of their shifts so that their supervisor can respond to questions or issues that arose. Indiana University Bloomington (Chapter 11) has a dual layer of feedback in which professional librarians and graduate students in the master of library science program provide formative feedback to undergraduate peer leaders; this can be both formal (through training sessions and mini reports peer leaders complete after research consults) and informal (when working alongside the graduate students). There are also many instances of group meetings or debriefs in which peer leaders discuss with their supervisor any difficult questions or interactions they have encountered (Harvard College; Utah State University; Cal Poly, San Luis Obispo; Hope College).

Informal feedback also frequently occurs, such as at Southern Illinois University Carbondale or Hope College, where peer mentors reverse-shadow librarians at the desk; as issues come up, the librarian and the peer leader can work through them together. At the University of Oregon and San Diego State University, peer leaders "check in" with their supervisors informally. Gettysburg College's "librarian buddy" system, in which peer leaders work alongside a librarian, is another way that students can receive formative feedback in the midst of their work.

There are also some opportunities for peer leaders to reflect on their performance. At the University of New Hampshire Manchester, peer leaders are observed by their supervisor, who provides them with written feedback; peer leaders respond to this feedback via reflective writing. At Cal Poly, San Luis Obispo, all instruction sessions include an evaluative component in which students in the class evaluate the session; peer leaders receive their own evaluations and often try to self-improve. As part of peer leader training at the University of Nevada, Las Vegas, we film peer leaders teaching a mock class session; peer leaders have the opportunity to watch themselves teach and reflect upon what changes they would like to make.

5. Integration, Synthesis, and Application

> Being a peer coach has allowed me to gain knowledge [about] the academic research process, which I was able to fully transfer to my class research projects and assignments. I was able to grasp a better understanding of the process of research, which was vital to the overall contribution of my academic career.
>
> (University of Nevada, Las Vegas, Peer Coach)

Another hallmark of an effective educational practice is whether or not it transfers to contexts outside of the initial learning experience. Kuh (2008) notes "participation in these activities provides opportunities for students to see how what they are learning works in different settings, on and off campus" (p. 17). This is an important facet of higher education in general; it is now accepted that students learn more in college than what is in their courses. Havnes (2008) argues that during these formative years, students "transform as social agents and form identities as learners, professionals, and, more widely, as members of society" (p. 194). PAL contributes to these deeper learning experiences and supports students' abilities to transfer their knowledge and skills to new situations (Topping, 1996). Our chapters reflect this notion, with many programs working to instill peer leaders with transferable skills.

In some cases, the improved research skills of peer leaders contributed to academic success in their own coursework. Harvard College found that the skills peer leaders learned through their work were not duplicated anywhere else in the curriculum and that these skills helped peer leaders complete their own research assignments. The University of New Hampshire Manchester also found that peer leaders perceived improvement in their research and writing skills as a result of their participation in the PAL program.

Other transferable skills were gained in the areas of interpersonal skills, self-confidence, and patience (Cal Poly, San Luis Obispo; University of Oregon; San Diego State University), and communication skills, problem solving, design-thinking, teamwork, and adaptability (San Diego State University). At the University of Nevada, Las Vegas, we also aim to gauge the transferability of skills gained by peer leaders through a series of reflection prompts; specifically, we found that peer leaders made connections between their experiences in the program and their academics, their personal lives, and their professional development.

6. Connection

> The peer coach program has made me more socially aware of my surroundings. Being socially aware has made me more politically correct and conscious about others in life. It has helped me in the workplace setting but also in everyday life.
>
> (University of Nevada, Las Vegas, Peer Coach)

The final characteristic of highly effective educational practices is that they should help students make connections with the world around them; Kuh (2008) argues that when students engage in these activities, they are able to "develop the ability to take the measure of events and actions and put them in perspective" (p. 17). Kuh goes on to state that we ideally aim to help students "understand themselves in relation to others and the larger world . . . and act with confidence for the betterment of the human condition" (p. 17). These are ambitious goals, but ones that can be realized through PAL programs. It is imperative that we consider our student employees as just that—students first, employees second. Through PAL, librarians have the chance to intentionally design and implement experiences that meet the criteria of these highly effective educational practices and create meaningful opportunities for students to learn from and with one another.

In conclusion, if PAL programs are compared against AAC&U's characteristics of highly effective educational activities, the similarities and overlaps between PAL and High-Impact Practices start to emerge. When PAL is viewed through the lens of Kuh's work, we can see how the peer leaders engaged in these programs are actually participating in a larger framework of best practices for student learning, retention, and persistence. The librarians who guide these programs are able to directly impact the educational experiences of the peer leaders by creating time-intensive meaningful work opportunities, by allowing peer leaders to engage in substantive mentoring and group learning, by increasing peer leaders' exposure to diversity, by providing peer leaders with timely formative feedback, and by helping peer leaders apply what they have learned in new contexts. Taken together, these programs can increase peer leaders' understanding of themselves and their place in the greater community.

A CALL TO ACTION

The aim of this introduction was to provide an overview of PAL, its theories and formats, its challenges and benefits, and the incredible potential it holds for academic librarians to provide students with a highly effective educational experience. In the following chapters, you will see many applications of how PAL plays out in practice: the impetus for these programs and how they contribute to the greater goals of the university or library, how programs were planned, how students were hired and trained, how the peer learning interactions took place, how programs were assessed, and the next steps for each program. There are incredible examples of how peer learning has been leveraged to increase the reach of librarians, enhance campus partnerships, and improve student learning. High-quality case studies have been selected from different kinds of institutions, with different motivations and goals, so that you may in fact see a reflection of your own institutional context and envision how PAL could function at your library. It is our hope that these case studies will inspire you to consider implementing a program of your own and that PAL will become an enduring characteristic of academic libraries.

REFERENCES

Adam, A., Skalicky, J., & Brown, N. (2011). Planning sustainable peer learning programs: An application and reflection. *The International Journal of the First Year in Higher Education, 2*(2), 9–22. doi:10.5204/intjfyhe.v2i2.81

Arco-Tirado, J. L., Fernández-Martín, F. D., & Fernández-Balboa, J. (2011). The impact of a peer-tutoring program on quality standards in higher education. *Higher Education, 62*(6), 773–788. doi:10.1007/s10734–011–9419-x

Bell, S. J. (2000). Creating learning libraries in support of seamless learning cultures. *College & Undergraduate Libraries, 6*(2), 45–58. doi:10.1300/J106v06n02_05

Beltman, S., & Schaeben, M. (2012). Institution-wide peer mentoring: Benefits for mentors. *The International Journal of the First Year in Higher Education, 3*(2), 33–44. doi:10.5204/intjfyhe.v3i2.124

Bodemer, B. B. (2014). They CAN and they SHOULD: Undergraduates providing peer reference and instruction. *College & Research Libraries, 75*(2), 162–178. doi:10.5860/crl12–411

Bolton, T., Pugliese, T., & Singleton-Jackson, J. (2009). Advancing the promotion of information literacy through peer-led learning. *Communications in Information Literacy, 3*(1), 20–30. Retrieved from http://www.comminfolit.org/index.php?journal=cil

Boud, D., Cohen, R., & Sampson, J. (2001). *Peer learning in higher education: Learning from and with each other*. London: Kogan Page.

Brenza, A., Kowalsky, M., & Brush, D. (2015). Perceptions of students working as library reference assistants at a university library. *Reference Services Review, 43*(4), 722–736. doi:10.1108/RSR-05–2015–0026

Campbell, J. D. (2007) Still shaking the conceptual foundations of reference: A perspective. *The Reference Librarian, 48*(2), 21–24. doi:10.1300/J120v48n02_05

Carr, S. E., Brand, G., Wei, L., Wright, H., Nicol, P., Metcalfe, H., . . . Foley, L. (2016). "Helping someone with a skill sharpens it in your own mind": A mixed method study exploring health professions students experiences of Peer Assisted Learning (PAL). *BMC Medical Education, 16*(1), 48–57. doi:10.1186/s12909-016-0566-8

Christiansen, B., Bjørk, I. T., Havnes, A., & Hessevaagbakke, E. (2011). Developing supervision skills through peer learning partnership. *Nurse Education in Practice, 11*(2), 104–108. doi:10.1016/j.nepr.2010.11.007

Crockett, C., McDaniel, S., & Remy, M. (2002). Integrating services in the information common: Toward a holistic library and computing environment. *Library Administration & Management, 16*(4), 181–186. Retrieved from https://journals.tdl.org/llm/index.php/llm

Dancer, D., Morrison, K., & Tarr, G. (2015). Measuring the effects of peer learning on students' academic achievement in first-year business statistics. *Studies in Higher Education, 40*(10), 1808–1828. doi:10.1080/03075079.2014.916671

Faix, A. (2014). Peer reference revisited: Evolution of a peer-reference model. *Reference Services Review, 42*(2), 305–319. doi:10.1108/RSR-07–2013–0039

Falchikov, N. (2001). *Learning together: Peer tutoring in higher education.* London, UK: RoutledgeFalmer.
Gafney, L., & Varma-Nelson, P. (2008). *Peer-led team learning: Evaluation, dissemination, and institutionalization of a college level initiative* [Springer Link version]. doi:10.1007/978-1-4020-6186-8
Hammond, J.A., Bithell, C.P., Jones, L., & Bidgood, P. (2010). A first year experience of student-directed peer-assisted learning. *Active Learning in Higher Education, 11*(3), 201–212. doi:10.1177/1469787410379683
Han, E., Chung, E., & Nam, K. (2015). Peer-assisted learning in a gross anatomy dissection course. *PLoS One, 10*(11): e0142988. doi:10.1371/journal.pone.0142988
Hanson, J.M., Trolian, T.L., Paulsen, M.B., & Pascarella, E.T. (2016). Evaluating the influence of peer learning on psychological well-being. *Teaching in Higher Education, 21*(2), 191–206. doi:10.1080/13562517.2015.1136274
Havnes, A. (2008). Peer-mediated learning beyond the curriculum. *Studies in Higher Education, 33*(2), 193–204. doi:10.1080/03075070801916344
Havnes, A., Christiansen, B., Bjørk, I.T., & Hessevaagbakke, E. (2016). Peer learning in higher education: Patterns of talk and interaction in skills centre simulation. *Learning, Culture and Social Interaction, 8*, 75–87. doi:10.1016/j.lcsi.2015.12.004
Hilsdon, J. (2014). Peer learning for change in higher education. *Innovations in Education and Teaching International, 51*(3), 244–254. doi:10.1080/14703297.2013.796709
Hodgson, Y., Benson, R., & Brack, C. (2015). Student conceptions of peer-assisted learning. *Journal of Further and Higher Education, 39*(4), 579–597. doi:10.1080/0309877X.2014.938262
Kowalsky, R., & Fresko, B. (2002). Peer tutoring for college students with disabilities. *Higher Education Research & Development, 21*(3), 259–271. doi:10.1080/0729436022000020760
Kuh, G.D. (2008). *High-impact educational practices: What they are, who has access to them, and why they matter.* Washington, DC: Association of American Colleges and Universities.
Longfellow, E., May, S., Burke, L., & Marks-Maran, D. (2008). "They had a way of helping that actually helped": A case study of a peer-assisted learning scheme. *Teaching in Higher Education, 13*(1), 93–105. doi:10.1080/13562510701794118
MacAdam, B., & Nichols, D.P. (1988). Peer information counseling at the University of Michigan Undergraduate Library. *Journal of Academic Librarianship, 14*(2), 80–81. Retrieved from http://www.journals.elsevier.com/the-journal-of-academic-librarianship/
Martin, D. (2008). Foreword. *Journal of Peer Learning, 1*(2), 3–5. Retrieved from http://ro.uow.edu.au/ajpl/vol1/iss1/
Mathews, B. (2009). *Marketing today's academic library: A bold new approach to communicating with students.* Chicago: American Library Association.
Millet, M.S., & Chamberlain, C. (2007). Word-of-mouth marketing using peer tutors. *The Serials Librarian, 53*(3), 95–105. doi:10.1300/J123v53n03_07
Nelson, R.R. (1995). Peer tutors at the collegiate level: Maneuvering within the zone of proximal development. *Journal of College Reading and Learning, 27*(1), 43–51. doi:10.1080/10790195.1996.10850030
O'Kelly, M., Garrison, J., Merry, B., & Torreano, J. (2015). Building a peer-learning service for students in an academic library. *portal: Libraries and the Academy, 15*(1), 163–182. doi:10.1353/pla.2015.0000
Topping, K.J. (1996). The effectiveness of peer tutoring in further and higher education: A typology and review of the literature. *Higher Education, 32*(3), 321–345. doi:10.1007/BF00138870
Topping, K.J. (2005). Trends in peer learning. *Educational Psychology, 25*(6), 631–645. doi:10.1080/01443410500345172
Topping, K.J., & Ehly, S.W. (2001). Peer assisted learning: A framework for consultation. *Journal of Educational and Psychological Consultation, 12*(2), 113–132. doi:10.1207/S1532768XJEPC1202_03
Vygotsky, L. S. (1978). *Mind and society: The development of higher psychological processes.* Cambridge, MA: Harvard University Press.
Wawrzynski, M.R., LoConte, C.L., & Straker, E.J. (2011). Learning outcomes for peer educators: The national survey on peer education. *New Directions for Student Services, 2011*(133), 17–27. doi:10.1002/ss.381
Wenger, E. (1998). *Communities of practice: Learning, meaning, and identity.* Cambridge, UK: Cambridge University Press.
Wenger-Trayner, E., & Wenger-Trayner, B. (2015). *Introduction to communities of practice: A brief overview of the concept and its uses.* Retrieved from http://wenger-trayner.com/introduction-to-communities-of-practice/

Part I

PEER-ASSISTED LEARNING IN INFORMATION LITERACY INSTRUCTION

1

The Research Mentor Program at the University of New Hampshire Manchester Library

Annie Donahue, Carolyn Gamtso, and Kim Donovan

The Research Mentor Program is a collaborative endeavor between the University of New Hampshire Manchester (UNH Manchester) Library, the Center for Academic Enrichment (CAE), and the First-Year Writing Program. The initial aim of the program was to create an opportunity to enhance peer-assisted learning across the entire research cycle by training peer writing tutors in basic information literacy skills, thus equipping them to holistically support first-year students in their composition courses. After 10 years of operation, the scope of the program has expanded beyond First-Year Writing courses to incorporate peer-assisted support for writing and research across the entire curriculum. Adaptation and evolution are the hallmarks of the program's success, beginning with the idea that sparked its development, through several curricula changes, to the current iteration that aligns with the Association of College and Research Libraries' (ACRL) *Framework for Information Literacy for Higher Education* (ACRL, 2015). This chapter offers a glimpse into the origin and evolution of the program, provides a review of the assessment and evaluation activities conducted, and culminates with a discussion of possibilities to further student success through peer-assisted learning.

INSTITUTIONAL CONTEXT

UNH Manchester is one of the six colleges that make up the state's flagship university, the University of New Hampshire. UNH Manchester is a commuter campus in the heart of the state's largest city and is located approximately 50 miles west of the residential campus, which is in Durham, New Hampshire. The College is completely housed in a recently renovated six-floor mill building within the city's downtown environs.

UNH Manchester students are a diverse set of individuals. Enrollment numbers average approximately 1,050 students per semester. The College offers 17 baccalaureate degrees with Biological Sciences, Business, Computer Information Systems, Psychology, and Mechanical Engineering Technology among the fastest growing programs. A snapshot of demographic data reveals that the average age of our students is 24 years, 50 percent are female and 50 percent are male, 87 percent of students attend full time, 85 percent of students are New Hampshire residents, and 55 percent of students live with family while the rest live on their own (UNH Manchester, 2013).

These students are often described as nontraditional because most are working a 30+ hour work week in addition to carrying a full-time course load. Many students are raising families and juggling school and work obligations, while others incorporate military service duties with their school and family responsibilities. The transfer population is significant, approximately 60 percent of each entering class, which adds to the academic diversity by creating a mix of students at varying levels of college preparedness with a broad range of skills requiring innovative approaches to supporting effective student learning. At UNH Manchester, we employ cross-departmental strategies to meet our students' needs.

One example of those cross-departmental approaches is the College's Learning Commons, which houses the library along with four additional units supporting student academic success: the Center for Academic Enrichment (CAE), the Office of Student Development and Involvement, the English for Speakers of Other Languages Program, and the Student IT Support team. The nature of our collective work with students lends itself to overlap, so opportunities for partnerships abound. The Research Mentor Program is a happy consequence of our collaborative culture, enacting a long-standing tradition of working together across units to support student success.

The UNH mission statement asserts that learning is its primary purpose, encouraging students to collaborate with faculty and other students on research and creative expression to advance knowledge (University of New Hampshire, 2016). The UNH Manchester Library's mission of "promoting academic success through personal attention and expert assistance" (UNH Manchester, 2016a) complements the CAE mission to "help underprepared students prepare, prepared students advance, and advanced students excel" (UNH Manchester, 2016b). By tapping into the benefits associated with peer-assisted learning approaches, the Research Mentor Program exemplifies these institutional goals by enabling all stakeholders—students, Research Mentors, librarians, CAE staff, and faculty—to gain new knowledge and advance learning.

BACKGROUND OF THE PROGRAM

The impetus for creating the Research Mentor Program was sparked by a poster presentation at an ACRL conference in spring 2003. The poster described a program whereby students were trained as library research assistants who then conducted evening and weekend drop-in sessions in the dormitories during times when the library was closed (Auer, Moeckel, & Presnell, 2003). This approach applied peer-assisted learning efforts to extend the library's reach to meet students' needs in a timely and convenient manner. Two aspects of this program appealed to us: (1) the peer-to-peer approach to advance learning and (2) the opportunity to support students at their point of need throughout the research cycle. UNH Manchester's commuter status made direct adoption of this program impossible; however, with some creative thinking a workable adaptation was devised.

UNH Manchester had (and continues to have) a highly effective peer tutoring program that adheres to the College Reading & Learning Association's (2015) criteria for International Tutor Training Certification. Housed in the CAE, peer-assisted learning is a hallmark of the program as it develops a cadre of peer math, science, and writing tutors each semester. One of the instruction librarians served as a peer writing tutor during her undergraduate years in the mid-1990s and experienced firsthand the reciprocal benefits of peer-assisted learning. There is significant scholarly evidence demonstrating that cooperative learning environments, similar to the tutoring dyad, impact cognitive development for both the tutor and the tutee (Conrady, 2007; Fallon, 2010; Griffin & Griffin, 1997; Langor, 2000; Nelson, 1995; Pobywajlo, 2004; Posa, 2011).

Capitalizing on the proven success of the peer tutoring program, the library and CAE staff worked collaboratively to adapt the idea presented at the conference into a cohesive approach that would work on a commuter campus. This approach involved training all peer writing tutors to incorporate basic information literacy skills as part of their tool kit when supporting first-year students with writing and research projects. Upon completion of the training, these peer writing tutors were designated as Research Mentors, and they worked alongside the instruction librarians in the First-Year Writing classroom to deliver effective information literacy instruction. Research Mentors also worked one-to-one with first-year students in writing tutorial sessions outside the classroom to address a variety of research concerns.

The students who participate as Research Mentors have demonstrated effective academic skills in their own course work. The CAE accepts recommendations from faculty for potential tutor applications each semester and holds recruiting forums in a central location on the campus to attract interested applicants. Eligible candidates should have completed the first semester of their first year and should meet the following criteria:

- Maintain a 3.0+ GPA
- Earn a minimum grade of B+ in any course they will tutor
- Complete the Tutor Development course
- Commit to a minimum of five hours per week of tutoring
- Provide a faculty recommendation
- Submit a writing sample

Interviews are conducted by the CAE professional staff and include an opportunity for candidates to demonstrate potential through a mock tutorial exercise. The final decision to hire all tutors (math tutors, science tutors, and Research Mentors) rests with the CAE staff. Some Research Mentors also train as math tutors or science tutors, but those instances are rare.

As with hiring decisions, the funding for math tutors, science tutors, and Research Mentors is firmly set within the CAE budget. Early in the Research Mentor Program, library funds were allocated to pay Research Mentors to participate in library-related activities, such as training sessions, instruction preparation meetings, and in-class instruction; however, once information literacy instruction was integrated into peer tutor training activities, it became too difficult to determine discrete library-related activities. The Research Mentor Program was crafted upon the principle that writing and research are integrated activities. Attempts to quantify Research Mentors' time to accommodate departmental budget structures seemed artificial, and a decision was made to centralize budget matters within the CAE.

The Research Mentor Program began in September 2003 on a small scale by incorporating three of the CAE's senior-level peer writing tutors. They trained directly with the instruction librarian, completing 10 hours of individualized training in basic reference and information literacy skills to earn the designation "research mentor" (White & Pobywajlo,

2005). These students were each assigned to a specific composition course. Throughout that fall semester, these Research Mentors attended each class, participating as assigned by the composition course professor and partnering with an instruction librarian during library instruction sessions to guide first-year students through the iterative processes of college research. In the classroom, the role of the Research Mentors varied from modeling good research skills by describing their own research practice to demonstrating specific library resources during a library instruction session and to actively engaging in group writing and research assignments. Outside of class during individual tutoring sessions, the Research Mentors guided first-year students through the entire research cycle, including brainstorming topic ideas; developing effective search strategies; evaluating sources; and crafting outlines through first drafts, rewrites, and final drafts; thereby demonstrating that writing and research are integrative processes (Fensom, McCarthy, Rundquist, Sherman, & White, 2006).

The construct of research as an integrated whole was one of the underlying assumptions shared by the library team and the CAE staff in developing the Research Mentor Program. Philosophically aligned with a student-centered collaborative approach to learning (Vygotsky, 1978), the UNH Manchester milieu was perfectly suited to this partnership that enhanced deep learning through peer-to-peer dyads, employed scaffolded instruction in multiple segments rather than a single one-shot session, and engendered a reciprocal learning environment for Research Mentors and tutees alike. Although the overarching goal of the program was to provide multifaceted support to students engaged in research across the disciplines, there were specific outcomes available to the Research Mentors who participated in the program. These shared program outcomes included opportunities to expand tutor roles, enhance writing skills, increase information literacy competencies, earn Master Tutor Certification through College Reading & Learning Association, and explore librarianship as a potential career.

TRAINING AND PREPARATION OF RESEARCH MENTORS

In the years since the program's inception in 2003, the Research Mentor training has successfully evolved in response to student and faculty feedback, research findings, and changing trends in information literacy pedagogy. The training has gone through three distinct iterations, all of which will be discussed in the following section.

In the first iteration, peer writing tutors were trained by the instruction librarian through a 10-week unit focused on the information literacy skills necessary for the successful completion of the First-Year Writing research paper. The tutors were prepared to help students with research skills during one-on-one tutorials, with a strong focus on helping students to refine topics through brainstorming techniques, to obtain background information by using reference sources, to develop effective Boolean search strings in online databases, and to evaluate the sources retrieved through those searches. Tutors were also incorporated into the librarian-led in-class information literacy sessions. To help them prepare for this in-class role, during training they practiced leading specific library instruction units, such as brainstorming exercises on topics and demonstrations of specific resources (Fensom et al., 2006; White & Pobywajlo, 2005). After the initial semester in 2003, in which three experienced tutors were handpicked for the program, all newly hired peer writing tutors participated in the Research Mentor training program as a cohort during their first semester as tutors. Upon completion of the training program, the tutors earned the designation "Research Mentor."

While the original training program adequately prepared the Research Mentors for their roles in the library instruction classroom and in one-on-one tutorials, the instruction librarian found it increasingly difficult to schedule the training sessions at a time when all the Research Mentors could attend. At times, she had to make up sessions with individual Research Mentors, which created a workload issue for her and affected the cohesiveness of the training curriculum. After discussing various solutions to the problem, the librarian and the CAE Director decided to fold the research mentor training into the existing CAE tutor training class, thus embarking on the second iteration of research mentor training.

All CAE peer tutors at UNH Manchester prepare for their role by enrolling in an academic course, Tutor Development (UMST 521), which can be taken for two or four credits; the three-hour per week course is taught by the CAE Writing Specialist and the Math/Science Specialist. The course includes a generic section, attended by all tutors, that introduces the novice tutors to universal pedagogical and tutoring philosophies and practices. During the second half of the course, the tutors break into two sections, with the math and science tutors joining the Math/Science Specialist and the writing tutors joining the Writing Specialist for discipline-specific discussions. For this iteration, the librarian and the CAE Director decided to add research mentor training to the writing section of the Tutor Development course. Together, they rewrote the course's curriculum to include research skills as part of the instruction on writing tutoring practices, thus firmly asserting information literacy as a skill necessary for critical thinking and writing fluency.

The core of the Research Mentor training sessions remained the same under the new delivery model, continuing to prepare the Research Mentors for work with students in one-to-one tutorials and in short units during the librarian's in-class library instruction sessions. However, through the Tutor Development course, the librarian had the time and flexibility to incorporate readings from the library literature to spur class conversation, and she added units to align with the curriculum of the general and writing sections of the course, including sections on library ethics, services to students with learning differences, and the educational needs of linguistically diverse populations. For example, after the Mentors discussed professional ethical standards during the generic section of the Tutor Development course, the librarian led a discussion of the *Library Bill of Rights* (American Library Association, 1996) and the American Library Association's *Code of Ethics* (American Library Association, 1997), and how those documents impacted the Research Mentors' professional interactions with students. After the mentors learned about how to work with students with learning differences during writing tutorials, the librarian asked them to read and discuss an article on universal design and library services (Chodock & Dolinger, 2009).

Using end-of-semester feedback as a catalyst for adapting the course, the librarian responded to the Research Mentors' desire for more actual research tutoring practice by adding a mock tutorial activity: she invited a colleague to visit the class to play the part of a student seeking assistance with a research paper. After several Research Mentors indicated that they wanted more experience exploring the online resources, the librarian developed a "faux" research assignment: the Research Mentors were given a research task and were asked to find articles and books to complete that task. The Research Mentors then turned in an annotated bibliography documenting their work and presented their research path to the entire class. In addition to these training activities, the Research Mentors continued to participate in library instruction sessions as well as tutorials. Their preparation for these information literacy sessions took place outside of the Tutor Development course through one-to-one consultations with instruction librarians, who included the Research Mentors as partners in class preparation and presentations (Gamtso et al., 2013).

In 2014, the instruction librarian decided to take a fresh look at the role of the Research Mentors in writing tutorials and in the classroom. Her decision coincided with a change in leadership at the CAE, as well as with the results of an original study of the Research Mentor Program that explored the impact of the program on the Research Mentors themselves. Through questionnaires and interviews, Research Mentors indicated that while they ultimately viewed their participation in the program as positively influencing their growth as students, researchers, and tutors, they initially felt intimidated and overwhelmed by their role as research guides. Their insights confirmed the trepidation the instruction librarian often sensed in novice Research Mentors whose concern about appearing to be "experts" at times made them unwilling to refer students to a librarian or to participate in library instruction sessions in the classroom. The librarian conferred with the new CAE Director, and together they reimagined the role of the Research Mentors: in one-to-one tutorials, the Research Mentors would assist students with refining topics, gaining contextual knowledge through reference sources, developing research questions and thesis statements, and evaluating sources. However, they would not directly assist students with navigating library resources, instead referring the students to a reference librarian for such guidance. They would also no longer lead in-class library instruction units, as these classroom demonstrations and discussions proved to be anxiety-provoking for many mentors.

The librarian and the CAE Director revamped the research mentor training to reflect the mentors' newly envisioned role. Moving away from the skill-based approach of the previous training, the librarian centered the library sessions in the Tutor Development course around the more conceptual *Framework for Information Literacy for Higher Education* (ACRL, 2015), with each session focusing on a particular frame. Her goal was to encourage the Research Mentors to delve beyond mere skill-based instruction in their tutorials and to use their unique position as peer guides in the research process to prompt their tutees to ask probing and meaningful questions about their topics, as well as to gain a real understanding of the issue's importance and of their own role in the conversation around that issue.

The new research mentor training—the third iteration since the Research Mentor Program's inception—consists of five sessions, each focused on one or two of the information literacy frames. The Research Mentors read the assigned frame outside of class, and each session begins with a general discussion of that frame and how the Research Mentors have incorporated the learning dispositions associated with the frame into their own research practices. Through class discussion, films, and small group activities, the librarian demonstrates to the Research Mentors how they can use their one-to-one tutorials to guide their tutees toward an understanding of the practices and dispositions. To spark classroom discussions, the librarian uses a series of videos developed by librarians at the University of Washington (University Libraries, 2016) focused on the information literacy frames, as well as several TED Talks that approach the concepts from novel, entertaining, or provocative perspectives (Goldacre, 2011; Lessig, 2007). All of the resources used in class are available on the UNH Manchester Library LibGuide for the course (http://libraryguides.unh.edu/c.php?g=326931&p=2190801).

The classroom activities for research mentor training are approached through the lens of a veteran researcher—the Research Mentor—using the Framework's information literacy threshold concepts (Townsend, Brunetti, & Hofer, 2011) to guide students as they develop the abilities and dispositions described in the Framework document. For example, after a discussion of the frame "Scholarship as Conversation," the librarian demonstrates to the mentors how leading students toward an understanding of the conversations surrounding their chosen topics can help them develop a research question. Together, the class follows the media coverage of a recent event from the first eyewitness reports on social media, through early news reports, to political commentary and peer-reviewed literature on the topic. The exercise highlights the many conversations that surround any issue, as well as the need to focus on a particular conversation in one's own research study. After a conversation about the frame "Research as Inquiry," the librarian and the mentors explore how to gain a broad understanding of a topic through hands-on research in online and print reference sources. The mentors discuss how guiding students through such resources can help them grasp the "big picture" surrounding a topic and can also help them choose a research focus. "Information Creation as a Process" introduces the mentors to information formats (such as popular magazines and peer-reviewed journals). This unit includes an exercise in which the mentors handle and assess a variety of source types (from print magazines to online blogs), analyzing the intellectual and physical processes behind each source's generation and production. The frame "Authority Is Constructed and Contextual" raises issues of source evaluation: students follow a particular conversation among scholars in a certain discipline, focusing on the credibility of the authors and the nature of the venues in which they are publishing their opinions. "Information Has Value" raises the issues of intellectual ownership and citation and how the mentors can help students navigate the pitfalls of unintended plagiarism. The semester concludes with mock tutorials, during which Research Mentors practice the techniques discussed throughout the semester by role-playing with a visiting librarian.

IMPLEMENTATION OF THE PROGRAM

The Research Mentors work one-to-one with students initially in First-Year Writing courses and, subsequently, in classes across the curriculum that assign research and writing. This class-based mentoring is an effective strategy that promotes collaboration and exciting developments in teaching and learning, ultimately resulting in improved research writing (Spigelman & Grobman, 2005).

When linked with the First-Year Writing classes, Research Mentors attend weekly classes and assist the instructor in applying concepts and lessons during class time. Outside of the classroom, Research Mentors are available on an appointment basis to work with First-Year Writing students in one-to-one sessions at any stage in the research process. Some First-Year Writing course instructors require their students to make a set number of appointments at designated intervals throughout the semester with the class-linked Research Mentor, while others may require students to meet with any Research Mentor or not require appointments with a Research Mentor at all. The practice of requiring scheduled tutorial sessions with a class-linked Research Mentor has been demonstrated as a best practice approach (Rendleman, 2013), resulting in a closer collaboration between the students and the Research Mentor. Student tutorials are limited to one-hour appointments per subject, but there is no limitation on the number of times a student may work with a Research Mentor across the semester. As the College's transfer admit numbers increase and our first-year admit numbers decrease, the work of the Research Mentor becomes more critical, especially in writing-intensive classes. Because transfer students often receive credit for composition courses taken at other academic institutions, it is difficult to assess their information literacy skill level when they arrive at UNH Manchester, or for the instruction librarian to address it adequately in an in-class session. The Research Mentors are able to work with any potential research problems at the point of need, personalizing the research assistance within the context of the writing-intensive course and the particular assignment.

During these tutorial appointments, Research Mentors may work with either initial research questions or paper drafts, as they receive training in both research and writing pedagogy practice, informing the work at varying steps along the research cycle (Ryan & Zimmerelli, 2010). It is important to note that because the Research Mentors no longer lead units in the library instruction sessions, these one-to-one tutorials constitute their primary interactions with the students and allow them to address issues with library research at the point of need. In the tutorials, the mentors apply the skills learned through their training to guide students toward the learning dispositions and knowledge practices outlined in the Framework. If a student comes to a tutorial without a focused topic, or if a student's paper draft reveals a lack of contextual knowledge, the mentor will help the student explore print and online reference sources to fill in that knowledge gap. If a tutee comes to a tutorial with a bibliography or with sources in hand, the mentor can help the student assess those sources by asking probing questions: Why is this source a good choice to support a particular argument? How does it fit into the conversation? While library skills such as the use of reference sources and the critical reading of those resources continue to fall into the Research Mentors' purview, many of their interactions with students now focus on honing the tutees' understanding of broader critical issues surrounding scholarly discourse and the nature of authority. The instruction librarians are responsible for guiding students through the fine points of database navigation, so the Research Mentors are clearly instructed to walk students to the reference librarian for database searching assistance when such intervention is needed. This practice affords the librarian an opportunity to include the research mentor in the reference interaction with the student, thus clearly demonstrating to the student that learning is a collaborative process.

In the course of their normal workload, Research Mentors are supervised and assessed by the CAE Director. Each semester, members of the CAE staff observe Research Mentors as they engage with students during tutorial appointments that occur within the Learning Commons. Research Mentors receive feedback from these observations and are required to provide thoughtful, reflective written responses to that feedback. Research Mentors must maintain a 3.0 GPA during the course of their service in order to continue in the program. Research Mentors' hourly pay rate is increased, commensurate to their experience and training levels in subsequent semesters.

The Research Mentor Program is enthusiastically supported by all library staff members at UNH Manchester. All of the instruction librarians participate in the program by visiting the Tutor Development class for mock tutorials and other training activities, and librarians work with the Research Mentors and the tutees at the reference desk when the Research Mentors walk there with students who need guidance with the databases. Indeed, a current library services supervisor worked as a Research Mentor while an undergraduate at the College; her experiences in this role and her training prepared her for her position in the library and gave her an appreciation for the program and for the work of the Research Mentors.

EVALUATION OF THE PROGRAM

Since the Research Mentor Program's inception, two distinct program evaluation studies have been conducted. Completed in June 2012, the first study sought to measure the impact of peer-assisted learning on information literacy skill development of first-year students who worked with a Research Mentor while enrolled in a First-Year Writing course. The second study, completed in June 2014, sought to determine the impact of reciprocal learning environments, created through tutoring dyads, on Research Mentors who participated in the program. Although each study demonstrated advancement of learning among the populations studied, areas for improvement were highlighted, which offered critical impetus for reviewing the tutor training curriculum and adapting the program for improvement.

Both studies were approved by the UNH Institutional Research Board (IRB). Participation in each study was voluntary. Online surveys were administered through SurveyMonkey, and data gathered through this method were anonymously submitted. Interview responses were anonymized to protect participant privacy. Each study utilized a mixed-methods approach, combining quantitative and qualitative aspects to gain a more holistic outcome. Results were disseminated to appropriate stakeholders, and a subset of each study's results was originally shared through professional conference presentations (Donahue, 2012, 2015b).

The first evaluation study was conducted over an 18-month timeframe with full support of the First-Year Writing Program faculty. A Research Mentor was assigned to each First-Year Writing course and Research Mentors attended classes throughout the semester as their own schedules permitted. The students in these First-Year Writing courses were either required or strongly encouraged to meet several times outside of class with the assigned research mentor, depending on the course instructor's pedagogical expectations. The evaluation study sought to determine the impact of this peer-assisted support on student learning and information literacy skills.

Each faculty member teaching one of the course sections provided class time for administration of the evaluation. The evaluation instrument was a pretest/posttest survey, utilizing a combination of fixed-choice and open-ended questions. The pretest was administered during the second week of class and the posttest was completed during the second to last week of class. The survey questions focused on three competencies of effective library research: (1) defining an information need, (2) crafting effective search strategies, and (3) evaluating resources. Three questions were constructed to measure each of the competencies identified earlier. Two questions were fixed-choice format, and one question allowed for an open-ended response. An example of the questions used to measure student knowledge regarding crafting effective search strategies is found in Figure 1.1.

Overall, the evaluation results were positive, and students demonstrated improved knowledge levels with respect to the three competencies measured. Results indicated that the rate of change from pretest to posttest scores increased on average 15 percent to 25 percent for two competencies, defining an information need and evaluating sources, and from 45 percent to 60 percent for creating effective search strategies. Students' improvement rates were higher for fixed-choice questions than for open-ended questions, suggesting that they were better able to recognize and identify the appropriate information literacy skill than to articulate that skill in their own research practice. This simple indirect assessment was a first step in program evaluation, providing key data to measure the impact of

Fixed-Choice	*Fixed-Choice*	*Open-Ended*
Imagine you are searching a library database for articles about forms of bullying among high school students. Choose the best search terms strategy from the examples below. A. High school students who are bullied B. Bullying C. Bullying and "high school students" D. Forms of bullying in high school E. I don't know	Mike is doing research for his paper on bullying and is looking for journal articles on the effects of bullying on the victim's mental health. He has searched one of the library's online databases using the keyword "bullying" and has gotten thousands of results, many of which are not relevant to his topic. Which choice below would be the best search strategy to narrow Mike's search and provide more relevant results? A. Bullying and schools B. Psychological effects of bullying on victims C. Mental health and bullying and the victim D. Students and suicide	In your research paper on bullying, you have decided to focus on the psychological effects experienced by victims of bullying in school. List the search terms you will use to find relevant results in an academic database.

Figure 1.1 Example of search strategy questions.

a peer-assisted learning construct on first-year students' ability to understand and to apply information literacy competencies when conducting college research (Donahue, 2015a).

The second evaluation study, conducted over a six-month timeframe, incorporated semi-structured interviews and a survey designed to measure Research Mentors' perceptions of their own learning growth. An invitation to participate in the study was sent to 58 Research Mentors who served between fall 2004 and spring 2013. Eighteen Research Mentors responded to the invitation, and a representative sample of eight was selected for participation. Each of the eight participants completed both the interview and the online survey components of the study. Interview questions asked participants to describe their role as Research Mentors working with students both one-to-one and in the classroom and with librarians during information literacy instruction sessions. Participants described activities that best prepared them for the role of research mentor and discussed the impact of participation in the Research Mentor Program on their own learning and development.

The survey was a modified version of the *Survey Regarding Satisfaction, Learning and Development of Peer Mentors in Higher Education* (Posa, 2011), requiring participants to rate their own knowledge and development growth on a five-point Likert scale from "strongly agree" to "strongly disagree." A sample of statements used to rate information literacy skills is found here:

- I use Boolean logic more effectively to construct search strategies when using the library databases.
- I am more confident using library databases for my research projects.
- I am better able to evaluate sources for use in my research projects.
- I have adapted my study skills in order to be more academically successful.
- I am more confident evaluating the sources found to complete my research projects.
- My ability to develop a focused research topic has improved.
- I feel that my involvement in the research mentor program has had *no* effect on my learning and development.

The results of this study were very encouraging and indicated that participants acknowledged a perceived increase in their writing and research skills following their service as Research Mentors. Furthermore, these participants attributed the increased knowledge to their participation in the program and the opportunity to learn from each other as members of a Tutor Development course cohort and from working one-to-one with their tutees both in the classroom and in the individual tutorial sessions. Another finding of the study, as noted earlier, revealed that novice Research Mentors experienced feelings of inadequacy because they believed they were expected by their tutees to be "experts" in writing and research matters. This outcome led to curricular revision in the information literacy component of the Tutor Development course and to a revision of Research Mentors' roles in the classroom and in tutorial sessions in order to mitigate these concerns.

IMPLICATIONS AND LESSONS LEARNED

The UNH Manchester Research Mentor Program has had demonstrable positive effects on the learning of both the Research Mentors themselves and the students they tutor. The program has also impacted library services at the College. Following are the key ways in which students, faculty, librarians, and CAE staff have been affected by the program:

- By training writing tutors in information literacy skills, the Research Mentor Program demonstrates to students and faculty alike the vital connection between quality academic research and quality academic writing.
- Reference and instruction librarians provide information literacy instruction through in-class or online library sessions, and through one-to-one interactions at the reference desk. Research Mentors expand the librarians' ability to teach students by reaching them at key points during the critical drafting process.
- The results of the program evaluation studies demonstrate that student learning is positively impacted by a peer-assisted learning approach to support research.
- Research Mentors have brought their skills to other disciplines outside of First-Year Writing through their tutoring with students in gateway, research methods, and upper-level courses. This expansion of their influence makes it essential for librarians and CAE staff to market the program to faculty members in the disciplines and to communicate how faculty can make good use of the research mentor's unique skills.
- The program has created strong student development opportunities for the Research Mentors, many of whom have discussed their work at professional conferences and in peer-reviewed journal articles.
- With careful preplanning to determine appropriate budget and reporting lines, a program can be developed that provides clear direction for Research Mentors about supervising and payroll issues. Our approach began with dual reporting and budget lines; which proved messy, and in time, we evolved to incorporate all recruitment, hiring, supervision, and payroll budgeting and reporting within one unit (the CAE), creating a smoother process for all.

One of the reasons the Research Mentor Program works rests in the strong collaborative relationship between the librarians and the professional staff of the CAE. This long-standing relationship had been cultivated many years before our units shared communal space in a Learning Commons. We recognized shared goals for supporting students' academic needs and sought out opportunities for working together to achieve our individual unit goals. We would strongly encourage librarians interested in this type of shared approach for supporting student research efforts to reach out to your institution's writing/tutoring center. Shared workshops and effective referral services can be beginning steps to a more cohesive collaboration. When we presented this program at various conferences over the past 10 years, we often heard writing center staff express a wish to work with their librarians in a similar fashion. We always suggested that they contact their library colleagues and make the first step. Our suggestion to our library colleagues reading this chapter remains the same: reach out to your writing center colleagues; take the first step and you will be glad you did.

NEXT STEPS

Since the reinvention of the research mentor training through the incorporation of the information literacy frames, Research Mentors have focused their work on one-to-one interactions with tutees in writing/research tutorials. The librarian and the CAE Director would like to bring them into the writing classroom again to assist with information literacy instruction. We envision the Research Mentors leading discussions of the frames and/or facilitating small group activities. Such an expanded role may be an "add on" chosen by Research Mentors for whom such classroom experience would be comfortable and beneficial.

The CAE Director would like to develop a more targeted evaluation of the Research Mentors' performance in tutorials relating to their application of the dispositions associated with the Framework learned during research mentor training. A third program evaluation study to measure student learning under this new Framework focus for information literacy instruction is needed. Crafting an authentic assessment to examine student learning will be a challenge, but working cooperatively across institutions may offer opportunities to find appropriate and effective solutions.

The Research Mentor Program has evolved during these past 12 years in response to user feedback, research findings, pedagogical innovation, professional trends, and programmatic changes of our institution. With each adaptation, the program has become a stronger mechanism for supporting students at all levels within the research cycle. It is our hope for the future that the Research Mentor Program will continue to be responsive and flexible to the academic needs of our community to advance student learning and achieve student success.

REFERENCES

American Library Association (1996). *Library bill of rights.* Retrieved from http://www.ala.org/advocacy/intfreedom/librarybill

American Library Association (1997). *Code of ethics of the American Library Association.* Retrieved from http://www.ala.org/advocacy/proethics/codeofethics/codeethics

Association of College and Research Libraries (2000). *Information literacy competency standards for higher education.* Retrieved from http://www.ala.org/acrl/standards/informationliteracycompetency

Association of College and Research Libraries (2015). *Framework for information literacy for higher education.* Retrieved from http://www.ala.org/acrl/standards/ilframeworkhttp://www.ala.org/acrl/standards/ilframeworkhttp://www.ala.org/acrl/standards/ilframework

Auer, N. J., Moeckel, N., & Presnell, J. (2003). *Peer tutors as information literacy advocates on campus.* Poster session presented at the ACRL 11th National Conference, Charlotte, NC.

Burgess, C. (2015). Teaching students, not standards: The new ACRL information literacy framework and threshold crossings for instructors. *Partnership: The Canadian Journal of Library and Information Practice and Research, 10*(1), 1–6. Retrieved from https://journal.lib.uoguelph.ca/index.php/perj/index#.V4gEMLgrKUk

Chodock, T., & Dolinger, E. (2009). Applying universal design to information literacy: Teaching students who learn differently at Landmark College. *Reference & User Services Quarterly 49*(1), 24–32. Retrieved from https://journals.ala.org/rusq/index

College Reading & Learning Association. (2015). *International tutor training program certification.* Retrieved from https://www.crla.net/index.php/certifications/ittpc-international-tutor-training-program

Conrady, L. L. (2007). *A phenomenological case study of mentoring outcomes: Benefiting the mentor in student development, self-esteem, and identity formation* (Doctoral dissertation). Retrieved from Dissertations Abstracts International (3324703).

Donahue, A. E. (2012, October). *Charting success: Using practical measures to assess student learning in a peer2peer model.* Paper presented at the ARL Library Assessment Conference, Charlottesville, VA.

Donahue, A. E. (2015b, July). *But what's in it for them? Understanding the effects of participation in the Research Mentor Program from the mentors' perspective.* Paper presented at the 11th Northumbria International Conference on Performance Measurement in Libraries and Information Services, Edinburgh, Scotland.

Donahue, A. E. (2015a). Charting success: Using practical measures to assess information literacy skills in the First-Year Writing course. *Evidence Based Library and Information Practice, 10*(2), 45–62. Retrieved from https://ejournals.library.ualberta.ca/index.php/EBLIP/index

Fallon, B. J. (2010). *The perceived, conceived, and lived experiences of 21st century peer writing Tutors* (Doctoral dissertation). Retrieved from Dissertation Abstracts International (3433440).

Fensom, G., McCarthy, R., Rundquist, K., Sherman, D., & White, C. B. (2006). Navigating research waters: The research mentor program at the University of New Hampshire at Manchester. *College & Undergraduate Libraries, 13*(2), 49–74. doi: 10.1300/J106v13n02_05

Gamtso, C. W., Blair Vogt, R., Chartier, N., Fensom, G., Glisson, N., Jefferson, J. & Sherman, D. (2013). Research mentoring: Expanding the role of writing tutors. *Writing Lab Newsletter, 38*(1–2), 10–13. Retrieved from https://wlnjournal.org/index.php

Goldacre, B. (2011). *Ben Goldacre: Battling bad science* [Video file]. Retrieved from https://www.ted.com/talks/ben_goldacre_battling_bad_science?language=en

Griffin, B. W. & Griffin, M. M. (1997). The effects of reciprocal peer tutoring on graduate students' achievement, test anxiety, and academic self-efficacy. *Journal of Experimental Education, 65*(3), 197–209. doi: 10.1080/00220973.1997.9943454

Langor, G. (2000). *Peer tutoring: What are its benefits to the tutor? Tutor perceptions of a peer tutoring experience in nursing education* (Doctoral dissertation). Retrieved from Dissertation Abstracts International (MQ55517).

Lessig, L. (2007). *Lawrence Lessig: Laws that choke creativity* [Video file]. Retrieved from https://www.ted.com/talks/larry_lessig_says_the_law_is_strangling_creativity?language=en

Nelson, R. R. (1995). Peer tutors at the collegiate level: Maneuvering within the zone of proximal development. *Journal of College Reading and Learning, 27*(1), 43–51. doi:10.1080/10790195.1996.10850030

Pobywajlo, M. C. (2004). *The role-taking experience of undergraduate peer tutors: A cognitive developmental approach* (Doctoral dissertation). Retrieved from Dissertation Abstracts International (3158680).

Posa, K. L. (2011). *A study of satisfaction and perceived learning and development of peer mentors in higher education* (Doctoral dissertation). Retrieved from Dissertation Abstracts International (3486693).

Rendleman, E. (2013, July). *Writing centers and mandatory visits: WPA-CompPile research bibliographies no. 22.* Retrieved from http://comppile.org/wpa/bibliographies/Bib22/Rendleman.pdf

Ryan, L., & Zimmerelli, L. (2010). *The Bedford guide for writing tutors* (5th ed.). Boston, MA: Bedford/St. Martin's.

Spigelman, C., & Grobman, L. (2005). *On location: Theory and practice in classroom-based writing tutoring.* Logan, UT: Utah State University Press.

Townsend, L., Brunetti, K., & Hofer, A.R. (2011). Threshold concepts and information literacy. *portal: Libraries and the Academy, 11*(3): 853–869. doi: 10.1353/pla.2011.0030

University of New Hampshire. (2016). *Mission and institutional identity.* Retrieved from http://www.unh.edu/president/mission

University of New Hampshire Manchester. (2013). *Fast facts*. Retrieved from http://manchester.unh.edu/about/fast-facts

University of New Hampshire Manchester. (2016a). *About the library*. Retrieved from http://manchester.unh.edu/library/about

University of New Hampshire Manchester. (2016b). *Center for Academic Enrichment*. Retrieved from http://manchester.unh.edu/student/center-academic-enrichment

University Libraries, University of Washington. (2016). *Research 101: A new approach to library tutorials*. Retrieved from http://guides.lib.uw.edu/c.php?g=342113&p=2302727

Vygotsky, L. S. (1978). *Mind in society: The development of higher psychological processes*. Cambridge, MA: Harvard University Press.

White, C. B., & Pobywajlo, M. (2005). A library, learning center, and classroom collaboration: A case study. In J. K. Elmborg & S. Hook (Eds.), *Centers for learning: Writing centers and libraries in collaboration* (pp. 175–203). Chicago, IL: Association of College & Research Libraries.

2

The LibRAT Program at Cal Poly, San Luis Obispo

Brett Bodemer

The LibRAT (Library Reference Assistance Technician) Program at Cal Poly's Robert E. Kennedy Library equips students to provide research help and lead lower-division instructional sessions. Launched as a pilot in 2010, the program continues to thrive. Since 2011, LibRATs have provided most of the coverage at Kennedy Library's Research Help Desk. Their eagerness and effectiveness in facilitating instructional sessions has also allowed the library to expand its lower-division instruction program from 60 sessions per year to over 200. The LibRAT program is a boon to the students who participate—they gain research skills, presentation skills, interpersonal skills, and an enriched collegiate experience by working shoulder to shoulder with students from different majors. The campus at large benefits through the efforts and skills of the LibRATs, who so naturally reach undergraduates in meaningful, relevant, and unassuming ways. We, the librarians at Kennedy also benefit, for in working with peer assistants so closely and in learning so much about them, we gain windows into the lives of our patrons, their peers.

INSTITUTIONAL CONTEXT

California Polytechnic State University (Cal Poly) in San Luis Obispo is one of 23 California State University institutions, a statewide system primarily serving California's undergraduate higher education needs. Undergraduates account for 95 percent of Cal Poly's enrollment, with in-state residents totaling 88 percent. Equidistant from the populous conurbations of San Francisco and Los Angeles, students from the immediately surrounding area represent only a small fraction of the enrollment, and first-year students are required to live on campus. Remote in locale and situated in a city of less than 50,000 people, Cal Poly is, in essence, the antithesis of a commuter college.

So what is the draw? Educationally, Cal Poly has a long-standing ethos of incorporating learn-by-doing pedagogy into coursework. This prepares graduates for immediate entry into professional positions at desirable salaries. The blend of hands-on pedagogy and immediate professional readiness, combined with the relatively low cost of a state university, has contributed to *U.S. News & World Report*'s ranking of Cal Poly as the best public-master's university in the west for the last 23 years (University News, 2015). In

2014, it even rated Cal Poly as the 10th overall best university in the west among institutions that do not confer doctorates, and *Business Insider* joined the media bandwagon that same year by ranking Cal Poly at 40th on its nationwide listing of the "Smartest Public Colleges in America" (Wai & Goudreau, 2014). With particular strengths in engineering, agriculture, and architecture, admission into Cal Poly is highly competitive, and entering students must apply for admission not only into the university but also into their chosen major. As a rule, then, students at Cal Poly are highly motivated, have chosen to attend *this* institution, and do not shy away from learn-by-doing pedagogy that often involves working together in groups.

Cal Poly's express mission is both polytechnic and comprehensive: polytechnic in promoting the application of theory to practice and comprehensive in providing a balanced education in the arts, sciences, and technology. Both aspects of this mission are accomplished through experiential learning in which students, staff, and faculty are partners in discovery (California Polytechnic State University, 2015). Critical Thinking and Lifelong Learning comprise two of seven formal University Learning Objectives, and both of these encompass salient elements of information literacy as defined not only by academic librarianship but also by accrediting agencies such as the Western Association of Schools and Colleges.

The Robert E. Kennedy Library is the sole campus library, and it directly supports these learning objectives and the university's mission through outreach, instruction, and consultation. What perhaps differentiates Kennedy Library's efforts in this arena is the way in which we have deliberately embraced Cal Poly's learn-by-doing ethos. Through engaging students as partners in both reference and instruction, we have not only learned more about our ever-changing patrons, but also nurtured an instructional program that reaches thousands of students each year. Through our intense earn-and-learn-by-doing program, our peer assistants, not only gain knowledge of information resources, but also develop interpersonal skills, teaching skills, and increased confidence. Through our program, we contribute directly to accomplishing the university's mission at the individual scale of our peer assistants, but more impressively, in concert with these assistants, we contribute to accomplishing that mission in the student body at large. When the Robert E. Kennedy Library received the Association of College and Research Libraries' (ACRL) Excellence in Academic Libraries Award in 2014, the ACRL panel specifically noted the success of our peer assistant program (ACRL, 2014).

BACKGROUND OF THE PROGRAM

The LibRAT (Library Reference Assistance Technician) Program at Robert E. Kennedy Library was first piloted as a modest experiment in peer reference in 2010. It has since grown into a thriving program in which peer assistants (LibRATs) provide the primary coverage at our Research Help Desk and also lead over 100 information literacy instruction sessions per year. And when I say lead, I do not mean co-teach or assist a librarian—I mean lead—solo, with no librarian hovering in sight. Our typical peer assistant cohort is small, with six to seven seasoned LibRATs and two to four LibRATs in training. Each student is typically scheduled between eight and 12 hours per week at the Research Help Desk, and is also expected to lead between eight and 12 instructional sessions per quarter. This blend of regular and irregular hours keeps the LibRATs financially, intellectually, and socially engaged, and their continuous engagement is a key to the program's success. As time and skills allow, we also involve LibRATs in a number of other activities—contributing to instructional design, creating instructional materials, and even creating online jeopardy games for the benefit of student employees in other public-facing library departments.

It would only be honest to admit that the original pilot was a flop and that the eventual addition of instruction to the LibRAT portfolio was more opportunistic than strategic. In 2009, we conceived of a program to embed peer assistants in the residence halls where they lived. In 2010, we selected and trained five students in various majors to do so, and though the students were thoroughly trained, they received pitifully few questions in the residence halls. In 2011, we recommissioned them at the Research Help Desk, where they flourished and proved to have an insatiable appetite for learning and providing service. In an unrelated initiative, Kennedy Library had also launched an ambitious lower-division instruction program aimed at English composition and communication speech courses. These courses all had research components and large numbers of sections. This lower-division information literacy program was immediately successful and by 2011 had already exceeded the sustainable teaching capacity of the Kennedy librarians. Enter the LibRATs. They had proven extremely adept at research help and triage when relocated to the Research Help Desk. How might they do with instruction, we wondered? Two LibRATs enthusiastically embraced the opportunity, and after one experimental quarter, all the rest were on board as well. With a cohort of LibRATs and librarians poised to teach, we were instantly able to meet the burgeoning demand for instructional sessions. The LibRATs' embrace of teaching and Kennedy Library's commitment to peer learning in instructional settings resulted in the hiring of a new Foundational Experiences Librarian whose primary focus is the design and delivery of the lower-division instruction that relies so heavily on LibRATs. Our LibRATs now have two coaches, one for reference and one for instruction, who act in seamless concert to further enrich the experiences of our LibRATs and our campus population at large.

The primary key to success for our program is hiring the right students. We aim to hire first-year students who have a service disposition and who collectively embody the disciplinary breadth of the student population. The latter point we learned from our first cohort who had been specifically hired from different majors. We quickly and repeatedly saw how the individual subject expertise of the students strengthened the knowledge of the cohort as a whole. As one example, our first Business major created a list of key resources for other LibRATs to use when helping students driven to the desk by a complex marketing assignment. As a student who had recently taken the course and successfully completed the assignment, she knew exactly which resources were most helpful. Other examples abound, ranging from the use of software to the finding of primary sources, and to this day, we continue to weigh a balance of majors as an important factor in our hiring.

Trumping majors, and perhaps all other considerations, however, is the matter of disposition. In programs like this, it is imperative to hire students who are friendly, helpful by nature, and eager to learn. The two librarians who now team together to coach and manage the LibRATs (the Reference Coordinator and the Foundational Experiences Librarian) apply informal vetting measures. We painstakingly scout for direct evidence of disposition and indirect evidence as suggested by previous volunteer work and service industry jobs. The required combination of cover letter, résumé, and online application provides initial written screening samples, and e-mail responses to interview invitations provide more. For applicants who make it to the interview round, we describe the position at length to gauge their listening skills, and last of all, we probe for reflections on previous service positions.

When an interviewee remarks, "I hate stupid questions," one can be sure that this is *not* an ideal candidate. When an already well-spoken candidate remarks "The teaching aspect of the job really appeals to me because I want to get better at public speaking," this signals that this may indeed be a good fit for a LibRAT position. See Appendix 2–1 for LibRAT Interview Worksheet.

The goals of our LibRAT program are fairly simple, and should be considered not as ordinal or hierarchical but as intertwined. One goal is to contribute to student learning at Cal Poly by leveraging the social advantages of peer learning. Another is to enhance the learning and collegiate experience of the students we hire. The fact that several LibRAT Program alumni have sent us e-mails signed "LibRAT for life" tells us we are making positive impacts in this area. Another salient goal is to establish multidirectional learning, so that we can learn deeply from our students and apply what we learn to better engage the student population at large.

TRAINING AND PREPARATION OF LIBRATS

The two main components of the LibRAT portfolio, reference and instruction, reinforce student skills and confidence in both areas. Reference training grounds the peer assistants in the knowledge and use of library services, databases, catalogs, and other basic information resources frequently needed by our patrons. We hire and train in small cohorts, typically at the beginning of winter quarter, and the first phase of reference training lasts approximately a full quarter. It comprises two hours per week in group training sessions with the Reference Coordinator, and two additional hours per week shadowing seasoned LibRATs at the Research Help Desk. During group training, it is important to create opportunities for social bonding, and relying on exercises such as team treasure hunts not only helps the students learn, but also helps them become comfortable with one another. Similarly, when new LibRATs shadow seasoned LibRATs at the desk and learn from them, the relationships formed encourage and perpetuate a continuity of group mission and identity. The second phase of LibRAT reference training is permanent and involves all the LibRATs in continuous learning. This consists of weekly reading and annotation of reference logs and "refreshers," which take the form of periodic worksheets (often designed by LibRATs for LibRATs) and annual group "refreshers" in the fall.

Our instructional training reinforces our reference training, with an emphasis on particular conceptual elements, but it also introduces an entirely new element by inspiring and nurturing the presentation and facilitation skills of our peer assistants. As with our reference training, it relies heavily on learn-by-doing pedagogy. Launched concurrently with reference training, instruction training is very carefully scaffolded. In its initial phase, the new LibRATs meet weekly with the Foundational Experiences Librarian, who grounds them in principles of authenticity, encouraging them to bring their personalities to the sessions they will facilitate. As they begin to observe sessions led by librarians and seasoned LibRATs, they continue weekly meetings with the Foundational Experiences Librarian, where they flesh out learning objectives and conceptual components and where they further discuss effective strategies for asking questions and generating participant engagement. Next, the trainees co-teach with either a librarian or a seasoned LibRAT. Only after co-teaching and demonstrating the ability to articulate the conceptual elements of the sessions do the new LibRATs lead sessions on their own.

As with reference training, the second phase of instruction training extends over the rest of the LibRATs' tenure, and consists of continuous learning, engaging in quarterly teaching observations of other LibRATs, and working intensively with the Foundational Experiences Librarian when changes are made to lesson plans for any of the three session modules we offer. In order to support LibRAT understanding and delivery of instruction, learning objects, training materials, and even screencasts are all housed in our university's learning management system, Moodle, to which the peer assistants can refer at any time. Annual meetings at the launch of fall quarter serve as a chance to generate enthusiasm, review any changes in the instructional design, and solicit multidirectional feedback. As with other aspects of the program, the LibRATs provide input and have even helped create important features of the library sessions.

A word of caution: anyone contemplating the launch of a peer reference *and* instruction program may not want to emulate our model of concurrent reference and instruction training. We can only follow this model now because we have established a solid base of peer assistant expertise and can lean heavily on the seasoned LibRATs in our training, who act as both mentors and models. In our experience, it is not until LibRATs have been in the program for a full year that we are fully confident in their level of accomplishment in reference, so adding instruction too early is likely to prove counterproductive without the example of peers to support their learning. For any new program entailing both reference and instruction, it may indeed be best to have librarians intensively ground the first cohort of peer assistants in reference provision before integrating them into instruction.

IMPLEMENTATION OF THE PROGRAM

The Research Help Desk duties of a LibRAT are probably typical of reference desks in academic libraries. LibRATs open and close the desk, reshelve current periodicals, tidy the general vicinity, and assist patrons with computers, printers, scanners, and microfilm machines. They answer the full spectrum of questions from directional to genuine research inquiries. After 4:00 p.m. on weekdays and during weekend shifts, they also provide online chat coverage while staffing the desk. On a weekly basis they annotate and initial the printout of recorded reference transactions. As needed, and drawing on their various skill sets, students engage in other activities, including contributing to video content and signage, and even creating in-house learning objects for library student employees in other departments.

Because our lower-division information literacy sessions are timed to coincide with assignments, teaching opportunities for our peer assistants come in peaks and valleys. Some weeks there is little or no demand, but other weeks the demand is huge, with sessions scheduled as early as seven in the morning and as late as eight at night. The Foundational Experiences Librarian tries to distribute the teaching load evenly, but student schedules and instructional demand can mean that LibRATs teach twice on a given day.

We offer a menu of three instructional sessions, and instructional faculty may request the modules in any combination. The first, which is most common early in an academic quarter, is called the Orientation Workshop, and it leverages technology through a treasure hunt deployed via the GooseChase app. The content of this session and the choice of technology were devised collaboratively by the Foundational Experiences Librarian and one of our very seasoned LibRATs. As with the other modules, the peer assistants begin each session by directing participants to *Research 101: Your Research Survival Guide*, a LibGuide designed specifically to facilitate all the instruction delivered through our lower-division information literacy program. LibRATs start at the "Orientation" tab of this guide, play a clip from the *Big Bang Theory* about scavenger hunts, and then demonstrate some basic navigation of the library website and the catalog. Immediately afterward, the LibRATs direct the participants to download the GooseChase app on their personal phones, and send the students out in teams to pursue a set of predetermined "missions." GooseChase routes photos of "completed" missions submitted by students to a leaderboard that the LibRAT moderates. When all the students return, a winner is declared, and a class-wide debriefing follows.

One of the most frequently requested modules that LibRATs facilitate is called Research Workshop A. The LibRATs begin this workshop by introducing themselves, reviewing learning outcomes with the participants, and sharing some key things to know about the library website. They then direct the participants to the "Use the Best Sources" tab on the *Research 101* LibGuide. This tab houses presentation slides pertaining to types of information sources as well as issues of credibility and ethos that LibRATs discuss before handing out photocopies of three "mystery" articles. With crucial identifying information blacked out, copies of all articles go to teams of two or three students who try to gauge what type of sources they are (i.e., magazine article, peer-reviewed article, book chapter). The teams read, confer, and then write up their results on whiteboards, at which point the LibRAT facilitates class-wide discussion. The first activity is kept to a strict timeline, allowing sufficient time for the second activity of Research Workshop A. This second activity is preceded by a demonstration of basic functionalities of *Academic Search Premier* by the LibRAT, after which student teams are directed to find a peer-reviewed article on a prescribed topic. The teams search through *Academic Search Premier* to identify what they take to be a peer-reviewed article and enter the citation into a Google form that is linked on the *Research 101* LibGuide. Again, the LibRAT facilitates a class-wide discussion of the posted results. After reminders about the various forms of help (Research Help Desk, chat, and college librarians), the LibRAT concludes the session by inviting participants to enter responses into an online survey that solicits participant perceptions of the session's content, design, and delivery.

Our LibRATs also lead one other module though with less frequency than either the Orientation Workshop or Research Workshop A. Research Workshop B is intended as a sequel to A. Although it includes a quick review of information evaluation and database searching, it is primarily a venue for providing "guide-on-the-side" help to participants as they search for materials for their upcoming papers or speeches. On occasion, two peer assistants (both Engineering majors) facilitate sessions for a lower-division technical writing course. This really brings their status as peers to bear, as both these students were themselves at one time enrolled in this course.

In addition to these reference and teaching activities, part of the day in the life of a LibRAT involves communication with the two supervisors, often in relation to scheduling. We use Google Calendars for both the desk and teaching activities, and coordinate available times to cover the teaching. However, with so many sessions (often over 100 in a quarter), session assignments and confirmation of assignments can be tricky at times. Anyone starting such a program should anticipate spending a lot of time managing a schedule.

Although the LibRATs have two supervisors, one for reference and one for instruction, we ensure that our shared view of the program is holistic, with both domains truly belonging to one sphere and one position. The two supervisors work closely together on budgeting, scheduling, and training so that the natural synergy of reference and instruction reaffirm each other. With two supervisors collaborating so well, we are able to expend more time and energy on bolstering reference and in adding further nuance and complexity to the instructional program.

EVALUATION OF THE PROGRAM

Assessment of peer reference is embedded in the continuous and formative reference training gained through reading and annotating weekly printouts of reference and chat transactions as recorded in an online Google form. The Reference Coordinator and all the LibRATs read through the transactions each week, annotating the printout when they spy a weakness or offering a better solution than the one given. Examination of these transactions suggests areas where further training is needed. No names are attached to the online entries, which encourages honesty in reporting the transactions, and issues in provision that appear are addressed to the group at large. When issues of inappropriate desk comportment arise, which on rare occasion they do, the Reference Coordinator reminds the group as a whole, but also addresses the individual peer assistant in private.

The use of this online reference form, initially instituted for monitoring the quality of LibRAT transactions, now ingests entries from all reference providers, including special collections, data services, and college librarians. With this diverse data encompassed in a single spreadsheet, Kennedy Library is able to generate a holistic view of the place of LibRATs within the entire reference ecosystem. For the last three years, LibRATs have answered the greatest number of questions, but have spent far less time per transaction. This is exactly what we are seeking: simpler, shorter questions satisfied at the Research Help Desk or via chat, and longer, more in-depth consultations taking place away from the desk. It is no exaggeration to say that the need to constantly assess the performance of our LibRATs has actually made us better at assessing our entire reference program.

Our assessment of LibRATs as instructional leaders, as is the case with reference, is not a discrete activity but is also embedded in ongoing formative assessment. In fact, assessment of our lower-division instruction program and assessment of the LibRATs as session leaders go hand in hand. Because the LibRATs lead so many of our sessions, this is a given—if they fail, the program fails; if they succeed, the program succeeds. Our assessment methods enable us to glean information that speaks to the design of the instruction sessions as well as specific information regarding the effectiveness of the delivery. Scheduled observations of LibRAT-led sessions by the Foundational Experiences Librarian provide some of this data, and can be leveraged to enhance performance. But we also gather continuous formative assessment data through a Google form that session leaders (librarians and LibRATs alike) administer to participants at the end of each session. For formative assessment of session delivery, we rely heavily on required responses to 1, 3, and 4, of the following Likert scale statements:

1. The workshop gave me a solid understanding of the material presented.
2. The activities covered in this workshop will help me with my assignment or research.
3. The workshop leader presented information in a way that I could understand.
4. The workshop leader encouraged and responded to questions.

Responses to statements 1 and 3 render an idea of the session leader's effectiveness while responses to statements 3 and 4 yield information about the teaching demeanor of the session leaders. All peer assistants are given access to the results and can "compete" against themselves to get even better scores. Alternatively, if scores are low, self-intervention or intervention by the instructional supervisor can be made. Our LibRATs score consistently high on these questions, and often higher than librarians on prompt 3: "The workshop leader presented information in a way that I could understand." This is where peer learning should leverage its strength—students communicating to students.

One informal way we evaluate the program is by gathering written reflections from the LibRATs themselves. We did this after the pilot cohort's first quarter in the residence halls and have done it periodically since. It was in that first set of reflections that we came to fully realize how little most first-years and second-years knew about the library, and this knowledge served to solidify our commitment to the lower-division instruction program and to peer learning. As most of the LibRATs are with us for several years, we gather the reflections at long intervals, but in reading them, we get a sense of the program's various impacts on their collegiate experience. These include learning research tools, giving presentations, making long-standing friendships with students from other majors, and the sheer camaraderie of being a LibRAT. Even after their graduating from Cal Poly, we have seen significant lasting impacts. A first-generation LibRAT landed a position at a law library while pursuing her JD and performed high-level work as a legal research assistant for her internship. Another LibRAT is currently pursuing a PhD in animal science and she included her online LibRAT teaching evaluations as part of her application to the program. Three other LibRATs have obtained degrees in librarianship. Of these, one has a tenure-track faculty library position, another works as an information architect in the private sector, and a third recently landed a position as a Young Adult librarian at the Los Angeles Public Library.

IMPLICATIONS AND LESSONS LEARNED

The LibRATs have immensely expanded the ability of our library to provide services. Through their dedicated and informed contributions to the related domains of research help and instruction, they have provided indispensable support for our ambitious initiatives. However impressive these contributions are, though, it is still not the greatest value they bring to our organization. Through the close relationships we forge with them, through valuing their input, and through our multidirectional learning, the LibRATs have become living windows into the lives of our patrons. Through them we learn about perceptions and behaviors across the spectrum of student experience. To name a possibly mundane example, we are even able to detect shifts in technology use. Where earlier generations of LibRATs relied on the Facebook page they had created to get timely responses for scheduling shift changes, the current cohort instead resorts to a text-message group. As a more significant example, we have learned from the LibRATs that the first-year new student orientation at the lead-off to fall quarter is so overwhelming and chock-full of information that the library stands little to gain through heavy exertions in that arena, even though to librarians it seems like a logical and promising opportunity. By trusting these students and having their trust, we continue to develop services, instruction sessions, and materials that resonate well with our patrons, their peers.

NEXT STEPS

As our LibRAT program rolls into the future, we expect that it will continue to conform to the contours of the possible, the effective, and the useful. Our librarians are currently striving to create a meaningful and appropriate definition for what information literacy should be at *this* undergraduate polytechnic institution. That definition will in turn generate specific outcomes. To support these outcomes, current and next-generation LibRATs will likely get more exposure to information visualization tools, strategies for finding data sets, and media-editing experience. From an instructional standpoint, it is possible that we have finally reached the capacity for face-to-face delivery of sessions, as we are on a pace to exceed more than 250 requests this year. The Foundational Experience Librarian is devising ways to create online surrogates or complements for in-person instruction, and you can bet that partners in the creation of those learning objects will be the current and next generation of ever-morphing and ever-learning LibRATs. Whatever path the future holds, our steps will continue to be informed by the abiding principles of multidirectional learning, continuity of purpose, and flexibility.

REFERENCES

Association of College and Research Libraries. (2014, January, 24). *2014 ACRL excellence in academic libraries award winners.* Retrieved from http://www.acrl.ala.org/acrlinsider/archives/8227

California Polytechnic State University. (2015). *2015–2017 catalog.* Retrieved from http://www.catalog.calpoly.edu/universitylearningobjectives

Hines, S. S. (2007). Outpost reference: Meeting patrons on their own ground. *PNLA Quarterly, 72*(1), 12–13.

University News and Information, California Polytechnic State University. (2015, September). *Cal Poly is the best in the west for 23rd consecutive year.* Retrieved from http://calpolynews.calpoly.edu/news_releases/2015/September/usnews.html

Wai, J., & Goudreau, J. (2014, October). The 104 smartest public colleges in America. *Business Insider.* Retrieved from http://www.businessinsider.com/smartest-public-colleges-in-america-2014–10

APPENDIX 2–1: LIBRAT INTERVIEW WORKSHEET

Interviewee name ______________________________

Major ______________________________

Expected graduation date ______________________________

1) *Probing for: interests/articulacy.*
What specifically attracted you to the LibRAT position?

2) *Probing for: teamwork skills/sense of place on teams.*
Tell us about your experience working on teams.

3) *Probing for: availability/level of engagement. (Note: engaged is optimal, but extensively engaged is concerning for scheduling.)*
What kinds of activities are you involved in on campus?

4) *Probing for: service disposition.*
Have you ever had a customer service job? What did you like best about it? What did you like least?

5) *Probing for: comfort in front of groups.*
What experience do you have doing public presentations and how do you feel about that part of the position?

6) *Determining: availability.*
Will you be able to begin training this quarter with on-the-job training? Yes/No

7) *Probing for: engagement, acuity, surfacing of personal priorities.*
Do you have any questions for us?

3

The Mathlete Program at the University of Oregon Libraries

Genevieve Schaack and Annie Zeidman-Karpinski

This chapter examines the University of Oregon's math homework help program, which is entirely staffed by students working for the Libraries. These student employees, called Mathletes, provide drop-in homework help for all underclass mathematics courses in the reading room of the Math Library. The program has proved successful, with patron participation far exceeding initial projections. However, the real success of the program has been what the Mathletes themselves have gained as peer-to-peer instructors, through meaningful work experience and a supportive community. In this chapter, we will describe our program and the training process, both of which emphasize mentoring, communication, and problem solving. In order to ascertain the benefits of peer-assisted learning on the Mathletes, we conducted a qualitative and quantitative survey assessment of our program. Results of this assessment reveal that the work has meaning above and beyond the amount that students earn as an hourly wage. Finally, this program has been a wonderful way to connect the Library to an underserved academic department as well as the greater campus community.

INSTITUTIONAL CONTEXT

The University of Oregon is the flagship school for the state of Oregon. It is a residential campus, home to approximately 20,000 undergraduates and 3,500 graduate students. Located in Eugene, Oregon, long considered a hotbed of counterculture activity, today the campus has a popular athletic program and an active fraternity and sorority scene. The library system at the University of Oregon consists of the Knight Library, which serves as the main administrative hub and Social Science and Humanities repository, as well as the Art and Architecture, Law, Science, Marine Biology, and Mathematics branches. We are the only Association of Research Libraries member in the state, and we support both undergraduate learning and the rigorous research expected of an Association of American Universities institution.

The Mathematics and Science Libraries, while housed in separate buildings, share management, staff, and student employees. While the Science Library was seeing increasingly steady use, the Math Library was not. Math is housed in one of the oldest buildings on campus. In 2009, a seismic retrofit of the building prompted a redesign of the Math Library. It reopened in 2011 with many enhancements, but without a clear purpose for the new space. We knew we wanted to build a student-centered library that reflected the libraries' mission statement and strategic plan of being "an essential partner" in enriching "the student learning experience" as well as take advantage of the building's central campus location (University of Oregon Libraries, n.d.). The Head of the Science and Math Libraries was supportive of new ideas and gave the Math Librarian and Library Manager free rein to explore options for the new library. Initially, we considered offering needed services, such as student computer support, or staffing it with a math department graduate student teaching assistant. However, these options were determined to be too difficult to fund or operate, and they did not meet our students' greatest need. Math classes—college algebra, general university math, and first-year calculus—are among the most failed courses at the University of Oregon. Math requirements are important for all majors and are especially important for retention in science-related fields of study. When we reopened the Math Library, there were limited options for math homework help on campus. Thus, we decided to focus our new space on peer-to-peer math tutoring.

BACKGROUND OF THE PROGRAM

Student employees work at both the Science Library and the Math Library. Prior to the redesign of the Math Library, these student employees had no particular background in math and were sent to keep the space open, but with little to do and minimal supervision. Even when we knew the students weren't reporting for their shifts promptly, we didn't have the staff to fix the issues. In order to solve this problem as well as to provide a useful service, we considered new leadership opportunities for our student employees. When the Math Library reopened in 2011, we focused on three main outcomes. First, we wanted to provide meaningful work for student employees. We also hoped to help undergraduates with the 100- and 200-level math courses that they so often struggle with. Finally, we wanted our new program to improve our relationship with the Math Department and the campus community. The peer-to-peer math homework help program, subsequently called the Mathlete program, was our opportunity to address these goals.

In order to staff the Mathlete program, we hired a group of undergraduates with sufficient math coursework and an interest in peer-to-peer instruction. Due to the specific requirements of math tutoring, most of the Mathletes were recruited and hired specifically for these new positions. When we started, we hired only undergraduates majoring in math, most of whom were also prepared, via a training course in the Math Department, to help run discussion sections for the large introductory 105, 106, 107 math sequence. Working around their schedules required that, right at the outset, we also hire at least one nonmath major. As the program grew and we could no longer count on hiring the majority of Mathletes from the Math Department, we asked other departments and specific professors to recommend students looking for on-campus work to fill our ranks. Whatever their major, interested students must have succeeded at college-level calculus and/or discrete math.

In addition to hiring students with sufficient math coursework, we also try to include students from diverse backgrounds. By striving for diversity amongst our Mathletes, we are creating a more inclusive space. Due to the unique skills needed for these positions, we are authorized to hire students even if they don't have a Federal Work Study award as part of their financial aid package. In the rest of the library system, it's unusual to be able to hire student employees unless they have Federal Work Study to help pay their salary. As a result of our relative flexibility, our Mathletes represent a diverse range of students. Our Mathletes have been fairly evenly divided along gender lines. We have had international students, all of whom have extremely strong English language skills. We have also had a large number of what our campus calls nontraditional students. Most of them are in their mid- to late twenties (or older) and they did not come directly from high school. At one point, over half of the Mathletes working for us had dropped out of either high school or college before returning. We found that this population brought a unique perspective to our program, were hard-working problem solvers, and were sympathetic to the students seeking help, in part because they were representative of the students they were helping.

In order to become a Mathlete, students fill out an application and take part in a lengthy interview process. The length of the application and interview emphasizes the importance of time management and communication skills for these positions. The application includes information about their coursework, schedule availability, and four short-answer questions about libraries and helping with math homework. Most students who complete the application have the chance to interview for a position. The interview takes about an hour and involves a short tour, and then a lengthy conversation about the library, the patrons, and our expectations. During this hour, we discuss the importance of communication and what we expect from them as Mathletes in terms of leadership skills and the need for problem solving in both the subject area of math and the workplace. The interview concludes with a demonstration of how the student would explain a math problem to the librarian, who plays the role of a confused student. The interviewees are given a list of math problems and they decide which one to solve as a way to demonstrate their tutoring skills. Most choose the problem that seems easiest to explain, but very few applicants reach the correct answer for one reason or another. It is always interesting to see how they go about asking for background information, how they involve the pretend student, and which problem they choose to solve. Many applicants do a good job showing us they understand the material and know something about teaching it. Students who interview successfully are eligible for hire. In cases where we don't hire a student, and there have been a few, either there was a problem with their ability to explain the math clearly or they were simply too nervous for us to get a sense of how they would interact with patrons.

Over time, the popularity of the Mathlete services meant that we needed to hire more students than we originally anticipated and our original student budget was wholly inadequate. While library administration was able to increase our student budget to an extent, eventually the program outgrew even these additional funds. Library administration suggested we talk to the Math Department. Our administrators joined us in presenting the data we had gathered, illustrating our need for more math tutors to the chair of the Math Department. At the time, our choices were to limit the number of students we helped or employ more students, but only if the Math Department was able to fund the additional positions. Since that meeting, we have been partially financially supported by the Math Department. Each year we ask the Math Department for the supplemental funds and see if it has the resources to commit to the program. If the department changes its level of support for financial reasons, we would have to consider restricting the amount of help available to students who come to the library.

TRAINING AND PREPARATION OF PEER MENTORS

Our Mathlete training program emphasizes mentoring, communication, and problem solving, some of the cornerstones for effective peer-to-peer tutoring in STEM (Bowling,

Doyle, Taylor, & Antes, 2015). This training comes not only from library staff but also from more senior Mathletes and the Math Department as well. There are training exercises and shadowing hours that must be completed before a Mathlete is considered ready to work the reading room, as well as long-term training that involves multidirectional feedback and ongoing education. We are confident that in addition to fostering the community that supports the students needing help and the students providing the help, these skills are transferable to whatever work or schooling they may undertake after leaving employment with us.

Mentoring takes place at the start of the training program, as we encourage Mathletes to teach and learn from each other. One of the first things we ask the new employees to do shortly after starting is to observe a more experienced coworker for an hour. The new employees arrange a time when they can shadow the other Mathlete. The observer is paid for their time and they are expected to watch what happens, but not help the patrons. This requires that the new student take control of planning and reporting back to their supervisors. After the observation, they send the librarian an e-mail outlining something they observed that they liked, something that could be improved on, and something they saw that they might incorporate into in their own practice as a Mathlete. They might also reflect on their own teaching style, often for the first time. While the returning student gets the experience of being a leader, the new student must plan the interaction and reflect on what they saw. We like that it establishes a relationship where the more seasoned students mentor the new hires. This is a flexible activity and can be done at any time, but we encourage students to do this soon after starting. At our group meetings, we announce or remind students about this task and send an e-mail to the returning Mathletes confirming that they are now expected to serve as a role model and trainer. Mathletes must depend on each other to keep the program running smoothly. We build in chances, like the observation, to develop this trust.

To emphasize professional communication and to capitalize on the hard-earned lessons learned while on the job, we asked graduating Mathletes to write down what they considered best practices for staffing the tutoring space. Based on their experiences, they developed a set of guidelines for the library space. Currently it includes tips like the following: keep moving, encourage patrons to work together, and don't be afraid to ask for help. Periodically we ask the current Mathletes to reread the document to see if it needs updating. We also have the new Mathletes read this document and comment on it since it is full of practical advice from seasoned colleagues. All of this training uses written forms of communication to pass along useful lessons from Mathletes and staff who help keep the space running well. It also models how we expect students to communicate professionally on the job.

Our hiring practices and subsequent training show how much we value the ability to problem-solve in math and in the workplace. Problem solving has multiple meanings in the Mathlete program. Other programs hire students who take a class and do well in it as tutors for that specific class. Because math builds on itself in a logical order, we prefer to hire students who know more math than is necessary to help with lower-division homework. From the beginning, we ask Mathletes to help with homework problems they might not be familiar with. In addition to the math problems they help their peers with, we ask the students at the Math Library to figure out how to resolve issues in the library as they arise. As staff, we are available for support, but we actively encourage students to gain independence in both math and workplace problem solving.

To provide more opportunities for students to learn about the wider world of math problem solving and to strengthen relationships with the Math Department, we have begun requiring the Mathletes to attend a Math Department lecture or event. This helps expand the student's training in mathematical thinking and difficult problems. We were able to secure gift money to pay for this additional expense. Although this is not necessarily directly work related, we ask that the students attend a talk and let us know what they think. The librarian sends out e-mails about appropriate venues and opportunities. In addition to the educational value of the events, we hope that by having our students participate in the departmental functions we have fostered stronger ties between the students, the Math Department, and the University of Oregon Libraries.

To reinforce Mathletes' training and to provide ongoing support, the librarian meets with each Mathlete, usually informally, to discuss setting goals for the term. The goals have run a wide range of possibilities, far beyond the scope of daily work assignments. Mathletes ask for various types of guidance; we have reminded students to get more sleep, encouraged them not to smoke cigarettes, helped them connect with faculty members doing work that they are interested in, and checked in on their progress toward studying for the GREs. Some of the Mathletes respond enthusiastically to the goal-setting offer, while others would rather be left alone; goal setting is entirely optional, but provides an additional facet to the ongoing community building and mentorship of our program.

IMPLEMENTATION OF THE PROGRAM

Math tutoring is a drop-in service, meaning that the tutors do not know what material they will be responsible for on a given day. Help is provided on a round-robin basis; a Mathlete sits with a student for approximately 3–10 minutes, the length of time to answer a single question, before moving on to the next student. That student may be in a completely different class in addition to having a different learning style. Rapidly switching between material and presentation style requires a high level of mental flexibility on behalf of the Mathlete. While juggling the above tasks, Mathletes are still responsible for all regular library circulation and organizational duties.

From almost the beginning, we have needed to expand our service as much as possible to the meet the need for help. Originally, we anticipated that 10 student work hours per day would suffice during the fall, winter, and spring terms with a decrease to perhaps 4–6 student work hours per day during the summer term. At the Math Department's request, we initially concentrated on helping specifically with 100-level (and lower) classes. However, we quickly found an incredible demand for more help than we expected to give. One issue is that, outside of instructor office hours and private tutors, there are very limited resources available on campus for students at the 200 level. In addition, the class series we meant to specialize in, University Mathematics: Math 105, 106, and 107, is a large lecture class for students who are not ready for college algebra or do not intend to take any further math. This course sequence does not have any coverage at the only other tutoring center on campus, the Undergraduate Studies–sponsored Teaching Learning Center (a separate multisubject tutoring center on campus with whom we share information but are not affiliated). In order to support the demand in the room at any given time, we had to increase the number of Mathletes, which in turn required us to think about and develop systems for the student employees to share tasks, communicate clearly, and be responsible for keeping the peer instruction working smoothly.

Beyond the simple problem of volume, we also had another problem: nearly all higher-level math classes are scheduled in the same blocks of time. When the student employees submitted their class schedules, we found that most of them were completely unavailable for some of these blocks, since they were generally taking at least one math class each term. So another consideration was that in order to have continuous coverage, we had to hire at least a few nonmath majors. Since we had already encountered the volume problem, this alleviated another concern, which was that there would not be enough interested math majors to staff our space.

Scheduling has been an opportunity to help students learn the importance of following directions and organizing their time, both of which are important job skills post-graduation. Students submit their term schedules to the Math and Science Library Manager toward the end of the previous term or near the start of fall term. She carefully develops a 10-week schedule that has Mathletes working at least one two- to three-hour shift at the Science Library as well as time at the Math Library. All students must also sign up and work some part of finals week. The schedules reflect both student preferences and their availability. There is therefore tremendous variability in terms of the number of hours worked by each Mathlete, which is okay, as long as the spaces are adequately staffed. One of our challenges has been communicating clearly to each student how important it is to work within the rules of our system. After a few difficult students, we found that dismissing students if they could not work with us was important for our sanity and for the morale of the group as a whole. While schedule management seems mundane, we know that it is important for the long-term success of the program, and it has the added benefit of teaching Mathletes important time management skills.

Upon arriving for the start of a shift, the Mathletes will check in with whomever they are relieving of duty or whom they'll be working with that day. Mathletes check in about the status of library operational duties (such as making sure circulation requests have been met), as well as the needs of students awaiting help. They also strategize for the shift ahead, which may involve checking the syllabi of various math courses—if a 500-person lecture class has a calculus midterm, we can expect a serious spike in requests for help. The Mathletes work together to figure out the best approach for dividing up the duties of a given shift. Some Mathletes are stronger in a particular type of math, while some are more comfortable working lecture-style with large groups, all working on the same problems. In addition, Mathletes need to attend to the operations of the Math Library, including circulation, shelving, and light cleaning duties.

When answering other students' questions, the first step the Mathlete takes is to listen. Pinpointing precisely where the student is having trouble allows the Mathlete to better explain the problem and alleviates possible frustrations down the road. Typically, Mathletes ask guiding questions in order to steer the students to the solution of the problem, rather than just giving them the answer or working the problem out for them. While this approach takes a bit longer, it is more effective in teaching students how to approach problems independently.

By providing math help in a dynamic and welcoming space, the Mathletes increase their own understanding of mathematical concepts as they explain them to other students. By being responsible for so much, they benefit from countless leadership opportunities, improve their communication skills, and have many chances to learn about problem solving. While they are working, the Mathletes are given a great deal of autonomy to shape what they do while being held accountable for their work by their fellow Mathletes as well as the patrons who are counting on them.

EVALUATION OF THE PROGRAM

> The power of tutoring derives from two of its main features: adapting to the individual learner's cognitive needs and the emotional benefits of the tutor–tutee relationship. (Karsenty, 2010)

Earlier studies about tutoring centers, specifically in math, suggest that the students who use them aren't usually doing particularly well in their classes. Therefore, it is difficult to evaluate how much math tutoring improves grades. However, studies suggest that because homework help improves student satisfaction, tutoring likely pays for itself in goodwill and student retention (Gillard, Robathan, & Wilson, 2011; Xu, Hartman, Uribe, & Mencke, 2001). Missing from these studies, however, is a discussion of the benefits of tutoring to the students *providing* the service.

While the Mathlete program collects traditional data including patron counts and student feedback, we wanted to investigate the benefits for the Mathletes themselves. To this end, a survey was constructed that sought both qualitative and quantitative assessments of Mathletes' opportunities to learn on the job, satisfaction levels, and work-type preferences. We began by asking about the Mathletes' self-reported satisfaction levels. The mean satisfaction level was significantly higher at the Math Library than at the Science Library. We have the rare opportunity in this analysis to have a control group among student employees; while all Mathletes work at both the Math and Science Libraries, the Science Library maintains a pool of student assistants who work solely there. Without exception, student employees of both libraries rated their satisfaction level with their work at the Math Library at least equal to, if not greater than, their satisfaction level with work performed at the Science Library. In the case of students employed only at the Science Library, overall satisfaction was still lower. What this does not tell us, however, is the specific cause of that increased satisfaction.

In the open-ended, descriptive questions about on-the-job learning, students cited increased self-confidence and patience as by-products of the opportunity to engage frequently with foundational math skills, which then led to deeper overall understanding of advanced material. There is also the benefit of working closely in one's field of study. One student employee preferred the work at the Math Library, despite a pay cut in comparison to their off-campus job, because it alleviated some of the cognitive dissonance of juggling work and school, allowing students a work opportunity that is more closely tied to and in support of their studies.

The survey also assigned a quantitative value to opportunities to learn while on the job, contrasting the work done at both the Math and Science Libraries. In order to quantify opportunities to learn, a somewhat fuzzy concept at best, we used college credit as a proxy, piggybacking on the quantification that the university itself performs in associating course credit hours to amount learned. Students were asked to equate the amount they learned at work to the equivalent in course credit hours. These were adjusted for the number of hours individuals worked in a semester and then multiplied by the cost of an undergraduate credit hour at the University of Oregon. Students felt that they had the opportunity to learn what was worth the equivalent of an additional $2.00 *every hour* on the job, when averaged. If we are to look at this as a percentage of wages, then they account for 17.6 percent increase in perceived benefit to the Mathletes for work completed in comparison to wages alone. These findings are all excellent indicators of how much these positions provided for the peer tutors themselves.

Whenever possible, we conduct exit interviews with students who leave. We will do these interviews at the library or off campus at a nearby coffee shop; usually this is a one-on-one conversation with open-ended questions that ask the student to reflect on what worked, what could be improved, and their final thoughts upon exiting the program. We have gathered a great deal of useful information from these conversations. These exit interviews also model several important aspects of employment. They provide the students a chance to consider their experience, and it shows that their employer is interested in their ideas and the lessons they have learned. It also provides a sense of closure and a way to say farewell on good terms. Finally, we hope that by showing students how to leave gracefully, they will visit when they can and remember us fondly.

In addition to the benefits the Mathletes derive from peer-to-peer tutoring, the students at the University of Oregon clearly see our service as useful to their studies. Of all undergraduate students currently enrolled in math classes at the University of Oregon, we see 20 percent of them for tutoring at the Math Library. Weekday homework help sign-ins indicated that there were on average 15–20 patrons present at any time. Keep in mind that many people sign in and remain for hours asking questions and working with friends and classmates. One sign of our success has been the number of students who return to the Math Library for help with math-related problems. Although our evidence is entirely anecdotal, we have been asked to help with math concepts in fields as diverse as physics, sociology, finance, business, biology, and psychology. Because we think of ourselves as a community of logical thinkers, we are willing to help when we can.

IMPLICATIONS AND LESSONS LEARNED

Even though our program strives to foster excellent communication, this does not always happen in practice. Solving problems with such a close-knit community of students working in such a high-profile and busy environment can be complicated. While the positions demand the use of problem-solving skills and leadership, the Mathletes do not want to report others for not doing their jobs. We have had issues with students missing shifts, showing up late, and having mental health issues that prevented them from working at full capacity, and a student who had a difficult time reading patron social cues. In most cases, when the supervisors find out about the problem, we make a point of closely observing what is happening and attempt to assess it with as much neutrality as possible. Usually, we have a short conversation with the problematic Mathlete and outline an action plan and time to check in and observe. All of the students get at least one more chance after these conversations. They are asked to correct the problematic behavior and we try very hard to help them improve. Despite our efforts, some of the students have either decided to leave or been asked to leave when they are unable to self-correct.

Far more often, we help Mathletes succeed through regular informal check-ins. These allow for students to let us know what is on their minds and to try to address any issues before they become a crisis. We know how important this is because when we had a vacancy in the supervisor position, student morale was low and small problems with job performance went unchecked. Since then, our new supervisor has been diligent about maintaining best practices. With the return of regular check-ins, we have seen a marked improvement with the student employees and the sense of community in the Math Library.

While we are pleased that our peer-to-peer tutoring helps so many students, we think that the real value of the program is for the Mathletes themselves. Meaningful student employment has a positive effect on retention rates, but we also see that this type of work helps student employees increase their confidence and desire to both teach *and* learn (Stern, 2014). The nature of peer-to-peer work like the Mathlete program means that these students take on greater leadership responsibilities, work better independently, and allow us to offer a program that is beyond the scope of most library student employees. The program fosters a rich relationship between the student assistants and staff, which more closely resembles post-university work environments. This mentoring relationship is mutually rewarding for the student employees and the library staff. Our program has worked hardest to develop the relationships of tutor–tutor, tutor–tutee, and tutor–staff, and it is from these relationships that we amplify the benefits of a peer-assisted learning program. Creating a library staff position, or at least officially dedicating staff time, to developing and supporting these relationships is a vital step in ensuring the quality of our program is maintained and Mathletes get the most out of their jobs.

NEXT STEPS

One task that we would like to undertake is to provide more training for career-readiness. Aside from the exit interviews, the libraries don't do as much as we would like to help students transition to post-graduation life. We hope that while they are working for us they are acquiring useful real-world skills, including valuable ones about communicating with their supervisors and coworkers and learning how to be responsible for their work shifts. In order to support this goal, all student supervisors try to complete annual evaluations for their students. This is a work in progress and it is time-consuming. We also want to help Mathletes be mindful of what skills they want to have upon graduation. To this end, we now ask students write down what they hope a letter of recommendation from their supervisor would contain when they graduate. By knowing their end goals, we have a chance to give our students the experiences they would find valuable for securing a job or attending graduate school.

Bolstered by the success of the Mathlete program, as the Science Library completes its rebuild in fall 2016, it will embark on similar collaborations with departments within the Sciences, using the newly remodeled space to house several subject-specific tutoring spaces. Navigating this expansion will be an exciting challenge, though it will be of the utmost importance to ensure that these new programs do not expand so quickly that the quality of services diminishes, or the important aspects of mentorship are lost.

What started out as a directive to revitalize the Math Library has turned into a tremendous opportunity. We expected to help the students struggling in math classes with their homework and hoped to provide students with well-paying campus employment. What we didn't expect was that the Mathletes would get so much more out of these jobs. We also didn't realize how much effort library staff would need to put into training Mathletes, coordinating their schedules, and helping them grow in meaningful ways. Though it is a great deal of work, it has also been one of the most rewarding programs that we have been involved in. This program shows the value of an academic library as an employer who can facilitate undergraduate peer-to-peer learning. We instill in our students practical skills as well as teach them values that they take with them when they graduate. In turn, the Mathletes make our library an energetic and exciting space of engaged problem solvers of all kinds. Ultimately, the Mathlete program is so much more than math tutoring—it is a student-led community that affords our students a safe place to grow.

REFERENCES

Bowling, B., Doyle, M., Taylor, J., & Antes, A. (2015). Professionalizing the role of peer leaders in STEM. *Journal of STEM Education: Innovations & Research, 16*(2), 30–39. Retrieved from http://jstem.org/index.php?journal=JSTEM

Gillard, J., Robathan, K., & Wilson, R. (2011). Measuring the effectiveness of a mathematics support service: An email survey. *Teaching Mathematics and Its Applications, 30*(1), 43–52. Retrieved from http://teamat.oxfordjournals.org/

Karsenty, R. (2010). Nonprofessional mathematics tutoring for low-achieving students in secondary schools: A case study. *Educational Studies in Mathematics, 74*(1), 1–21. doi:10.1007/s10649–009–9223-z

Stern, G. M. (2014). Part-time job program for Latinos boosts college success. *Education Digest, 79*(9), 55–58. Retrieved from https://www.eddigest.com/index.php

University of Oregon Libraries. (n.d.). *UO libraries mission values and strategic directions.* Retrieved from https://library.uoregon.edu/general/about/mission

Xu, Y., Hartman, S., Uribe, G., & Mencke, R. (2001). The effects of peer tutoring on undergraduate students' final examination scores in mathematics. *Journal of College Reading and Learning, 32*(1), 22–31. doi:10.1080/10790195.2001.10850123

4

Library Peer Mentors at Utah State University

Pamela Martin

This chapter outlines the Library Peer Mentor Program at Utah State University (USU), highlighting how peer-assisted learning is utilized in library instruction. Started in 2004, this program supports the course-integrated instruction efforts of the Merrill-Cazier Library. History of the program, training and management of the student employees, and lessons learned from over ten years of experience are discussed.

INSTITUTIONAL CONTEXT

Utah State University (USU) is a public, land-grant research university in Logan, Utah. While we have additional, smaller campuses sprinkled throughout the state as well as a large online student population, the Logan campus undergraduate enrollment is 16,000. Our undergraduate students are fairly young (22.3 average age) and predominately white and Mormon. USU is a residential campus with most students (over 80%) living away from home, often either in student housing or very close to campus. The Merrill-Cazier Library opened in 2005 and is a very busy building. Our 2015 fall semester gate count was 417,816, though it is worth noting that some of this traffic can be attributed to a handful of classrooms in the library.

The Library Peer Mentor Program at USU supports the library's mission of supporting "inquiry, discovery, and engagement by providing access to quality resources, and by facilitating the use of information in teaching, learning, and research" (Utah State University, 2014). The Library Peer Mentor Program is housed in the Reference and Instruction Department, and Library Peer Mentors serve on the frontlines of the library, both in the classroom and on the information desk, and help their fellow students access library materials and engage in research.

USU values and enhances the undergraduate experience through two programs: Undergraduate Research Fellows and Undergraduate Teaching Fellows. Students actively participate in these programs across all academic departments at USU and gain valuable experience outside the classroom, either assisting in labs and research studies as Research Fellows or helping professors teach college-level courses as Teaching Fellows. On campus,

Undergraduate Teaching Fellows teach, mentor, and tutor students in select classes, and the Library Peer Mentors are part of this program.

BACKGROUND OF THE PROGRAM

The Library Peer Mentor Program began at USU in 2004. The goal of the program was to extend the reach of librarians and "use peer teaching as a way to engage students and make them more comfortable using USU Libraries" (Holliday & Nordgren, 2005, p. 282). This purpose remains the same today. The Reference and Instruction Department has employed three to five Library Peer Mentors per year since 2004, with occasionally one Library Peer Mentor working in Special Collections. The Library Peer Mentors assist instruction librarians in the classroom, provide a few hours of research help on the information desk per week, and work on special projects as assigned by librarians. Like the purpose of the program, these three areas of focus have remained largely unchanged for the past decade.

Since its inception, the Library Peer Mentor Program has been funded by USU's Undergraduate Teaching Fellows Program, which provides undergraduates with paid teaching assistantship opportunities across campus. This program is housed in the Provost's Office, and all USU departments are invited to apply annually for Teaching Fellows funds. The library reapplies for this funding each year and has been successful in continuously attaining funds, though Reference and Instruction has had to occasionally supplement Library Peer Mentor wages with departmental coffers. In nonlibrary departments, an Undergraduate Teaching Fellow will serve as a teaching assistant to one class for a semester and receive a stipend. In the library, Library Peer Mentors are paid hourly wages. Though Library Peer Mentors hold many of the same responsibilities as other Teaching Fellows (teaching classes, supporting students, developing teaching materials, etc.), they assist in many different classes in addition to working on the information desk and in the office.

Since we offer no for-credit information literacy class at USU, but embed library instruction throughout the curriculum, Library Peer Mentors are involved with myriad classes throughout each semester. Library Peer Mentors pick up library instruction sessions as requested and as they fit into their own schedule, sometimes helping with sessions outside their normally scheduled work hours. For any given session, they might co-teach with librarians or fellow Library Peer Mentors, assist library instructors in the classroom, or teach on their own. Since library instruction requests can come in at any time, Library Peer Mentors need to be flexible. Instruction duties take precedence over any other duties during their work day.

For many years, the Library Peer Mentor Program was coordinated by different librarians in the Reference and Instruction Department who agreed to take on extra supervisory duties. However, this arrangement eventually proved problematic. Without these duties written into a librarian's job description or yearly goals, management of the Library Peer Mentor Program lagged. In busy times, when our office is occupied with consultations, meetings, and classes, no librarian had time to schedule work for Library Peer Mentors, who were often left idle in the office. Formal meetings and scheduled group trainings became less frequent and nearly nonexistent. To remedy this, in September 2013, the library created the position of Coordinator for Outreach and Peer Learning within the Reference and Instruction Department. I serve in this position, which includes specific duties to oversee, train, and coordinate the Library Peer Mentor Program.

Since Library Peer Mentors need extensive training to be comfortable representing the library on the information desk, as well as in front of classes, we try to recruit and retain lower-division students (second semester first-year students or sophomores). This helps minimize the time spent orienting new Library Peer Mentors to the library, as we have been tremendously successful in retaining Library Peer Mentors. In my 11 years at USU, I can only remember one Library Peer Mentor who quit before graduation, and it was because this student transferred to another college. Students must meet a minimum GPA requirement and submit a short essay to apply for the position, and incomplete applications are not considered. We look for students with an interest in the library and—perhaps more importantly—a healthy dose of intellectual curiosity since Library Peer Mentors help patrons do research on a variety of topics.

TRAINING AND PREPARATION OF LIBRARY PEER MENTORS

When the Library Peer Mentor Program began, there was extensive training and weekly meetings; however, after a few years, weekly meetings and trainings dissolved as the department's instruction duties increased and management of the Library Peer Mentor Program changed hands. As the new Coordinator for Outreach and Peer Learning, I reinstated the weekly meetings and developed a more rigorous training schedule. I believe that for Library Peer Mentors to be effective, they must constantly learn about the library and our ever-changing services and materials. Training includes group meetings, as well as one-on-one meetings (especially while orienting new Library Peer Mentors), and takes place both on the job and in scheduled training sessions.

Orientation to the job includes reviewing basic materials for the Merrill-Cazier Library, taking a tour of the building, and reading foundational literature on reference, instruction, and information literacy. This literature includes a list of jargon used in the Merill-Cazier Library, the *Information Literacy Competency Standards* (Association of College and Research Libraries, 2000) and *Framework* (Association of College and Research Libraries, 2016), textbook chapters on conducting the reference interview (Ross, 2002), and current innovations in information literacy (Fister, 2013). In addition, Library Peer Mentors read through the library's database of public LibAnswers, which contains frequently asked questions they will need to be able to answer about the building and the library's services. While orienting to the library, Library Peer Mentors start to shadow librarians on the information desk and observe library instruction sessions. Through these observations, all librarians help train the Library Peer Mentors on the job. Newly hired Library Peer Mentors are not required to work the information desk alone for a month or to lead their own classes in the first semester of their employment.

During their first semester, I periodically give new Library Peer Mentors quizzes that require them to explore different parts of the library and contain commonly asked research questions, such as the location of a book, pulling items from our automated retrieval network, or an e-journal's accessibility off campus. These exercises require students to think about keywords, search strategies, and how to best fill patrons' needs. Students are given specific instructions for the quizzes, encouraging them to work both independently and collaboratively with other Peer Mentors and librarians. After the quizzes are completed and e-mailed to me, we then sit down together one-on-one to discuss the questions. Library Peer Mentors are asked: Could you have done this differently? What are some other keywords and search strategies we can consider? Why did you choose that path to answer the patron's question? For a sample quiz, see Appendix 4–1.

Ongoing training (outside of orientation to the library) consists mostly of weekly meetings where we discuss many different issues. These meetings are designed to be helpful both with the traditional reference work on the information desk and in the classroom. Library instructors often request Library Peer Mentors as teaching assistants so they can provide more individual help in a short class period. Library instruction sessions at USU almost always include a hands-on component, and students are given time to conduct library research while Peer Mentors provide research assistance. Library Peer Mentors must be comfortable not only conducting reference interviews in these classroom settings (surrounded by dozens of peers) but also initiating these interactions with students. Because students can often be quick to refuse an offer of assistance in the classroom, Library Peer Mentors are taught how to approach students with open-ended questions ("What are you working on?" or "What are you interested in researching?") to open up a dialog with the students, rather than just offering help to each student. We also conduct weekly research help role-playing in our meetings to prevent Mentors from getting flustered during these interactions.

While they usually serve as teaching assistants in sessions, Library Peer Mentors also occasionally co-teach with librarians and teach classes on their own. If co-teaching or leading a class, Library Peer Mentor training will differ depending on the nature of the class and the Library Peer Mentor's role in the classroom. To prepare for library instruction sessions where they teach or co-teach, Library Peer Mentors might meet with the library teaching partner or attend training sessions specifically designed for the upcoming class. Lesson plans are discussed and fine-tuned, and Library Peer Mentors are given the opportunity to practice the lesson both in front of librarians and in front of fellow Library Peer Mentors. By the time Library Peer Mentors lead their own classes, they have also usually observed many library sessions, both as strict observers and as teaching assistants, hopefully picking up tips and tricks along the way.

Our weekly training meetings are sometimes highly structured, while in other instances, meetings may be more open to allow for discussion with Library Peer Mentors and to encourage them to share any questions or concerns they may have. Occasionally Library Peer Mentors teach a mock session, and the other Library Peer Mentors and I critique their performance. Often I will invite other librarians—the Government Documents Librarian, the Head of Digital Initiatives, the Coordinator of Instruction—to speak with Library Peer Mentors about their areas of the library. Once a year, we use a meeting to take a tour of special collections. At most of the meetings, there is time to discuss any out of the ordinary or difficult interactions in classes or on the information desk. In fact, Library Peer Mentors are required to bring at least one tough question they received over the week and use it to role-play with me and their fellow Library Peer Mentors. The Library Peer Mentors fielding the question must work through whatever question they are given on a projected screen, so other Library Peer Mentors can both critique and learn from this experience. I also take part in this practice, demonstrating not only how to search but also what to do if they become "stumped." Weekly role-playing serves as great preparation for the classroom, as sorting out difficult reference questions in front of a knowledgeable audience (consisting of fellow Library Peer Mentors and their boss) can be just as intimidating as teaching a session. These role-playing sessions serve as opportunities to brainstorm search strategies and learn from each other. Occasionally, when I hear confusion from Library Peer Mentors about a library service or resource, or (heavens forbid!) complaints about Library Peer Mentors, I create new content-specific quizzes that all Library Peer

Mentors must complete. After the quizzes are turned in, we cover the content in our next weekly meeting.

Library Peer Mentors are also given self-guided work, broken down into four 3-week periods, each semester. This self-guided work schedule is loosely adapted from Zollinger and Huff's "Lean, Mean Training Machine" (2013). The first and last weeks of the semester are intentionally not included in the self-guided work, since student schedules can fluctuate in these weeks. Self-guided work serves as additional ongoing training that Library Peer Mentors can complete independently. A large bulletin board, complete with gold stars, is used to keep track of the self-guided work, and if Library Peer Mentors accomplish all tasks, they are given a small reward at the end of the semester (usually a gift certificate). During each period Library Peer Mentors must complete each of the following tasks: quality control, database exploration, interview, and reference reading. These tasks are designed to both help the Reference and Instruction Department and expand Library Peer Mentors' library knowledge.

Quality control might include checking online library tools for typos, missing links, or outdated instructions and screen captures. Depending on departmental needs that semester, Library Peer Mentors might check LibGuides, LibAnswers, tutorials, online videos, or other library websites. To complete this task, Library Peer Mentors must review a certain number of websites within each period. Since orientation can never fully cover everything the library has to offer, practicing quality control enables Library Peer Mentors to continuously learn while examining these tools. For example, they might discover new search strategies or unknown library services or tools while reviewing library tutorials.

Database exploration requires students to explore an assigned database and answer the following:

- Have you used this database before? If so, when? How often?
- Who is the intended audience for this database? Which students/faculty members would you recommend this database to? Why?
- If teaching this database:
  - In which classes or subject area would this database be appropriate to demonstrate (English, Agriculture, Physics, etc.)?
  - What sample searches might you use to demonstrate this database? Why are these useful searches? (provide keywords, Boolean logic, special symbols, etc.)
  - What is frustrating about this database? Is it hard to navigate? Hard to locate full text? What would you want to make sure you explain well to classes so they don't get stuck?

Responses to these questions not only are sent to all Library Peer Mentors and the Coordinator, but also must be distributed to the information desk listserv in order to complete the task. In this way, all information desk workers can refresh their database knowledge.

Library Peer Mentors must also interview a library employee outside the Reference and Instruction Department to broaden their horizons and learn more about other library services and areas. Interviews can be with full-time or part-time staff or student employees not employed in Reference and Instruction, and Library Peer Mentors must fill out a worksheet and e-mail it to their fellow Library Peer Mentors and the Coordinator in order to earn credit for this task. The worksheet guides the conversation and ensures that Library Peer Mentors are gleaning some useful information, but this task is also meant to encourage the Library Peer Mentor and library staff member to build a collegial relationship and learn from each other. These interviews must be done in person and help expand the knowledge of Library Peer Mentors beyond reference and instruction. The Library Peer Mentors have mentioned how helpful this task is in learning about the library beyond our department.

Lastly, Library Peer Mentors must straighten an assigned area of the reference stacks and locate an interesting book. They must then fill out a worksheet about the reference item, which includes instructions to locate a similar reference material online in our eBook collection. Library Peer Mentors analyze the two sources and the completed worksheet is e-mailed to fellow Mentors and the Coordinator. Often these e-mails are quite engaging as Library Peer Mentors attach interesting information, such as the origins of fellow Mentors' names or images of cute animals taken from the chosen books.

The self-guided training tasks, in addition to helping the library, keep the Library Peer Mentors busy on the information desk between reference questions and during their project hours when there are no other projects and no classes to teach. Often this happens at times when librarians are overwhelmed by classes or meetings. However, this is not just busy work. The self-guided work ensures that Library Peer Mentors are continuously learning about and engaging with the library while helping us maintain resources and refresh our own knowledge.

While all the Library Peer Mentor training helps to inform their work on the desk, it is also particularly helpful in the classroom, where Mentors need to draw on a wide breadth of knowledge about the library. For Mentors, classes are not just groups of students to educate, but also audiences of their peers. Mentors need to be knowledgeable, flexible, and unflappable in front of each class. Having an expansive knowledge of the library, including our tools, our website, and our people, helps them to answer the myriad questions they field in any given class.

IMPLEMENTATION OF THE PROGRAM

Schedule

Library Peer Mentor schedules need to be full and yet flexible. While Library Peer Mentors officially report to me as the Coordinator for Outreach and Peer Learning, all librarians in the Reference and Instruction Department work with them constantly, whether on the information desk, in the office, or in the classroom. The Library Peer Mentor Program is engineered to benefit the entire Reference and Instruction Department, and, as such, Library Peer Mentors are constantly collaborating with different librarians. While I do have to occasionally remind Reference and Instruction that Library Peer Mentors are available for projects large and small, this system tends to work well. It enables each librarian to build collegial relationships with the Library Peer Mentors and gives Library Peer Mentors a well-rounded experience and makes them feel integral to the success of the department.

The typical Library Peer Mentor works 17–20 hours a week with roughly half designated as information desk hours and half designated as project hours. Since we have no regularly scheduled for-credit classes, consistent teaching hours cannot be scheduled. However, if we need teaching assistance, the classroom always takes precedence. For example, if a Library Peer Mentor is scheduled for desk or project hours but a librarian needs assistance in a class, the Library Peer Mentor is relieved from the other duties to help with the session. Library Peer Mentors can also pick up a few extra hours by helping with classes outside their regular work hours, when available.

Project hours are directed by departmental and librarian needs. Of note is the work that Library Peer Mentors do to support assessment initiatives as well as librarians' research projects. Library Peer Mentors' project hours are instrumental in gathering data for assessment of instruction. By collecting and organizing academic course offerings and major requirements, Library Peer Mentors helped us map the curricula of USU departments. We used this curriculum-mapping information to target specific classes for possible library instruction integration. Library Peer Mentors also organized 10 years of library instruction data into a useable format for our Assessment in Action project. While we had recorded which classes incorporated library instruction for the past decade, Library Peer Mentors helped us track course numbers and semesters in a uniform way that allowed us to analyze what impact library instruction has on course grades. Mentors have also worked on many research projects in the library. Under the direction of the primary investigators, Library Peer Mentors have transcribed audio from focus groups and interviews, organized excel files for data gathering, and assisted in citation audits of student papers. These opportunities allow students to examine the impact of the instruction we do in the library, as well as gain professional and academic experience that they can later leverage in résumés and graduate school applications.

In the Classroom

At USU, we used a course-integrated approach. We integrate most heavily in general education composition courses, though library instruction sessions are incorporated in almost all departments across the campus. Our instruction role in the disciplines continues to expand as we participate in curriculum mapping and large-scale assessment in order to better target courses across campus. Peer Mentors are involved in every stage of the instructional process from planning to assessment. Most often, Peer Mentors in the classroom are scheduled a week before by librarian request. A library instructor will consider her class schedule for the upcoming week, and if she needs assistance in the classroom, she sends a request for Library Peer Mentor help.

Most often, Library Peer Mentors serve as teaching assistants in classes, and Peer Mentor classroom assistance normally falls on "research days." These are days when classes visit the library primarily to strategize and search for sources to complete a specific class assignment. Research days are usually proceeded by more formal library demos, whether this takes place in a previous library session, at the beginning of class, or in a library video students watched online for homework. Library Peer Mentor work on these days is very similar to reference interviews on the information desk, though often there is a greater volume of more in-depth research questions in the classroom. Library Peer Mentors are also encouraged to initiate conversations with the students rather than waiting for students to ask for help. Students might need help on the front end of research, such as brainstorming or refining topics and exploring different keywords, or they might simply need help finding the full text of an article, locating a book on the shelves, or borrowing an item through interlibrary services. In the classroom, Library Peer Mentor assistance can double the reach of the library, providing more students with one-on-one help at their point of need.

In addition to research days, Library Peer Mentors also take on lead roles in the classroom—co-teaching alongside librarians or fellow Library Peer Mentors. A prime example of this is an upper-division psychology class that was recently co-taught by our psychology librarian and a Library Peer Mentor who majors in psychology and had recently completed the course. This course has included integrated library instruction in the past, but the librarian and the Library Peer Mentor worked jointly on the lesson plan, drawing on their experience as library instructor and student to revamp the lesson and make it more relevant to students. Both the librarian and the Library Peer Mentor led sections of the lesson.

Library Peer Mentors also lead their own sessions, including the orientation session we present to incoming freshmen and a library lab taught regularly in conjunction with the University's study skills course. The orientation sessions are taught to incoming freshmen about a week before official classes begin. Around 2,000 freshmen attend these sessions as part of a for-credit orientation/first-year experience class. The lesson plan for this class is developed by the Reference and Instruction Department and incorporates feedback from Library Peer Mentors. Formal trainings are held for all library instructors of these sessions, including Library Peer Mentors. In the orientations, Mentors lead an interactive presentation designed to give incoming students general library information and incorporating student feedback via Poll Everywhere. The study skills library labs take place periodically throughout every semester and, though fewer students attend these labs, are run similarly to the orientation sessions. Depending on scheduling, Library Peer Mentors or librarians teach lab lesson plans that were created by the department. Trainings are less formal, usually only requiring a refresher after the first sessions is taught. In the labs, Mentors lead students through a mock scenario and help them access and evaluate information to resolve a dilemma.

Library Peer Mentors help behind the scenes by gathering materials for classes, brainstorming sample searches, refining handouts, and working on lesson plans. Library Peer Mentors often do the simple but necessary work of printing and collating handouts for classes. This especially comes in handy when we hit our busy teaching time in the first-year English composition classes. One of our lessons for this class involves multiple sources for group work and specific worksheets for each source. Library Peer Mentors prep all handouts for the lessons so that librarians can just grab a file folder full of materials right before class.

Library Peer Mentors also often help us brainstorm and create material for classes. When needed, they choose sample sources that both appeal to undergraduates and fit criteria required by the lesson. They update or rework handouts for classes. Sometimes librarians will sit down with a Library Peer Mentor to run a lesson plan past them or brainstorm engaging sample searches for demonstration. Library Peer Mentors have even attended departmental library instruction retreats and offered input on how information literacy sessions could be more meaningful to students, or pinpointed areas where students tend to become stuck. In the past, we've experimented with forms for Library Peer Mentor feedback on classes in which they assist. Since Library Peer Mentors vacillate between the role of the student and the role of the teacher, their feedback and unique viewpoints are extremely valuable.

EVALUATION OF THE PROGRAM

Evaluation of the Library Peer Mentor Program has been sporadic at best. While we have done a great job assessing our instruction program (often with the help of Library Peer Mentors), we have not adequately measured how the Library Peer Mentors have impacted our teaching or the entire library. In the past, we have been so grateful for and impressed by the Library Peer Mentors that we have done no programmatic assessment.

After all, the Library Peer Mentors help us prep for classes, improve our lessons and the library's website, and help the library reach more students. Their very presence makes us feel more productive, so we have fallen into the trap of assuming these good feelings are all the evaluation of Library Peer Mentors we need. After one semester of good performance, Library Peer Mentors are given a small raise, but the criteria and standards by which to judge "good performance" have never been codified.

Of course, we have had some efforts to evaluate Library Peer Mentor performance. In particular, new Library Peer Mentors have to fill out orientation quizzes, and together, the Coordinator and the Library Peer Mentor evaluate their performance. Though we need a better mechanism to catch when and where Library Peer Mentors struggle, quizzes have been created and assigned if Library Peer Mentors have problems grappling with certain questions. These quizzes are usually very specific and focus on such challenges as searching for print journals or creating permanent, proxy-enabled URLs to library resources. Occasionally Library Peer Mentors are asked to redo quizzes if their responses are lacking.

Library Peer Mentors are also evaluated on teaching and reference interviews. Classroom observation feedback has not been standardized, but both fellow Library Peer Mentors and the Coordinator observe and offer feedback. Library Peer Mentors might be observed while practicing a class presentation or while leading a live class session. It would be easy to streamline this process and create a worksheet or feedback form to standardize teaching observations. Feedback on reference interviews has been more systematically implemented, with part of almost every meeting reserved for running reference scenarios. Every week, Library Peer Mentors must bring to our meeting a tough reference question they encountered on the information desk or the classroom; they use the questions to role-play with their fellow Library Peer Mentors and the Coordinator. After the mock reference interview, we all share feedback and discuss what went well and what could have gone better.

Library Peer Mentors have also participated in exit interviews to help improve the program, though, again, these have been sporadic. After the first semester of implementing self-guided work, two graduating Library Peer Mentors were interviewed before they left. Their feedback helped us improve this system while encouraging its continuation.

IMPLICATIONS AND LESSONS LEARNED

One of the most important things we have learned from the Library Peer Mentor Program is to listen. These students are bright and hardworking, but their biggest asset is simply that they are students. They keep us in touch with their peers. They can advise on anything from which sample sources might engage their fellow students to how we should approach online tutorials or lesson plans.

We've also learned that it's important to have a dedicated librarian in charge of the program with Library Peer Mentor supervisory duties written into the job description to foster consistency and build a trajectory for the program. Running a successful Library Peer Mentor Program, even if it is a small one, takes time. In order for Library Peer Mentors to be truly helpful to our department, they must be well trained and busy doing work that matters. While Library Peer Mentors work on projects from many different librarians, as the Coordinator, I make sure these projects get distributed among the Library Peer Mentors and I fill in downtime by maintaining self-guided work designed to expand their knowledge of the library.

Library Peer Mentors also need to see the "big picture." When I took over the Library Peer Mentor Program, students expressed a desire to know why they were assigned certain projects and how their work contributes to the library. Library Peer Mentors wanted to know why they were building a giant excel file or prepping thousands of multicolored Post-It notes. They want and need context to understand more fully what our department does and their own contribution to that mission. Explaining outcomes of projects to Library Peer Mentors lets them see the larger goals of the library and empowers them to become a full partner in achieving those goals.

NEXT STEPS

Library Peer Mentors have become an indispensable part of the Reference and Instruction Department at USU, helping us better serve students and extend the library's reach. They have been involved in every step of library instruction at USU, from planning to teaching to assessing our program. Our next steps principally center on the evaluation of the program. Currently, there is no thoughtful programmatic assessment of the Library Peer Mentors. We need to have both a more systematic way to evaluate individual Library Peer Mentors and also a system for measuring the specific benefits of Library Peer Mentors to the library. Though the latter is difficult to quantify, we have made some steps toward this in our departmental annual report where we keep track of some Library Peer Mentor–assisted classes and projects. However, projects, tours, events, and classes that Library Peer Mentors are involved in should be more carefully documented. We also need to catch Library Peer Mentors when they are struggling. This could be done by implementing weekly or monthly quizzes or by simply asking librarians to evaluate Library Peer Mentors after working together in classes or on the information desk. Better assessment of the Library Peer Mentor Program will help us demonstrate the immense benefits and justify the continuation of the program in the future. Though funding has fortunately never been an issue, permanence of the program cannot be assumed as budgets tighten and new administrators take the reins.

Since the program began in 2004, it has evolved and yet remained largely the same. While we now have an official Coordinator for the program and a more rigorous training schedule, Library Peer Mentors continue to fulfill their original goal of extending the reach of the library and engaging students.

REFERENCES

Association of College and Research Libraries. (2000). *Information literacy competency standards for higher education.* Retrieved from http://www.ala.org/acrl/standards/informationliteracycompetency

Association of College and Research Libraries. (2016, January 11). *Framework for information literacy for higher education.* Retrieved from http://www.ala.org/acrl/standards/ilframework

Fister, B. (2013). *Decode academy.* Retrieved from http://homepages.gac.edu/~fister/loex13.pdf

Holliday, W., & Nordgren, C. (2005). Extending the reach of librarians: Library peer mentor program at Utah State University. *College & Research Libraries News, 66*(4), 282–284. Retrieved from http://crln.acrl.org/

Ross, C. S. (2002). *Conducting the reference interview: A how-to manual for librarians.* New York: Neal-Schuman Publishers.

Utah State University. (2014, January 9). *Strategic plan.* Retrieved from https://library.usu.edu/portrait/strategic_plan.php

Zollinger, C., & Huff, S. (2013, May). *Build your own lean mean training machine.* Presented at the Utah Library Association, Provo, UT.

APPENDIX 4–1: SAMPLE QUIZ

KNOWN ITEM SEARCHING

These are all *real* requests that I have received from patrons via e-mail. Please respond to the requests as if you are answering an e-mail from a library patron. Your response should be in the form of an e-mail. Include whether the library owns the material and, if so, in what format. Please also include directions for the patron on the easiest way to access the papers (whether or not we own them). Can you provide a link? Attach a PDF file? Should the patron request it from the BARN (Borrower's Automated Retrieval Network)? Let the patron know what they can do to get these papers.

For your first time through, do *not* consult with librarians. After you have tried to work through all four questions on your own, you are allowed to ask librarians for help, but you should still do the work. Do *not* let a librarian take over! Do *not* consult with other Library Peer Mentors.

1. I was wondering if you could help me find a seminal article in spatial ability that I cannot seem to locate through EBSCO or Google Scholar. There is no hurry on it but at some time I do need to read it to develop a grant. The article is referenced below.

   Miller, C. L. (1996). A historical review of applied and theoretical spatial visualization publications in engineering graphics. *Engineering Design Graphics Journal, 60*, 12–31.
2. I can't download the "Polyester-degrading thermophilic actinomycetes isolated from different environment in Taiwan" PDF: http://link.springer.com/article/10.1007/s10532–006–9089-z. Can you send it to me?
3. Can you find the refereed journal article cited below? I am using it in my research. Thank you!

   "Anaerobic treatment of high-strength cheese-whey wastewaters in laboratory and pilot UASB-reactors" *Bioresource Technology* Volume 60, Issue 1, April 1997, Page 59.
4. Could you please help me download two papers?
   - "3D printed microfluidic devices with integrated versatile and reusable electrodes"
   - "Configurable 3D-Printed millifluidic and microfluidic 'lab on a chip' reactionware devices."

5

The Mason Undergraduate Peer Research Coach Program at the University of Nevada, Las Vegas Libraries

Erin Rinto, John Watts, and Rosan Mitola

This chapter describes the Mason Undergraduate Peer Research Coach Program at the University of Nevada, Las Vegas (UNLV) Libraries. Specially, we discuss how we developed, implemented, and assessed a successful peer-assisted learning program in which Peer Coaches co-teach information literacy instruction sessions for English 102 (ENG 102), the research-based writing course at UNLV. Highlights of the chapter include our robust six-week training program, which is focused on helping Peer Coaches develop soft skills related to teaching, and our two-pronged programmatic assessment, which allows us to see the perceived value of the Peer Coaches by the students enrolled in ENG 102, as well as the impact of peer-assisted learning on the development of the Peer Coaches' personal, academic, and professional skills.

INSTITUTIONAL CONTEXT

The University of Nevada, Las Vegas (UNLV) is a large metropolitan research university located just a few miles east of the Las Vegas Strip. One of only two four-year public research universities in the state of Nevada, UNLV had a fall 2015 total student enrollment of 28,600, with the undergraduate population consisting of 23,801 students. Our student population is characterized by two important demographics: over 84 percent of students (24,000) are Nevada residents, and many undergraduates choose to live off campus and commute. Additionally, over 55 percent (15,868) of students are from a minority background: in 2012, the U.S. Department of Education designated UNLV as a Minority-Serving Institution, and in 2015, U.S. News and World Report ranked UNLV as tied for second most ethnically diverse campus in the country (UNLV Office of Diversity Initiatives, n.d.; U.S. News and World Report, n.d.).

A major initiative at UNLV is to become, by 2025, a "top tier public university in research, education, and community impact" (University of Nevada, Las Vegas, n.d.). Our campus leadership has identified pathways to meet this goal, one of which is student achievement. This initiative aims to improve student retention, progression, and completion, with objectives centered on improving our six-year graduation rate and increasing freshman-sophomore retention, in addition to enhanced student learning and engagement.

The UNLV Libraries are committed to supporting the university in many of these top tier pathways, but our role as a campus partner in student learning means that we are especially dedicated to student achievement: the Libraries' strategic plan states that we will "embed library instruction and other library instructional interventions throughout general education courses," and "expand co-curricular programs to graduates and undergraduates in support of academic achievement, life skills, and lifelong learning." Our department, Educational Initiatives, is at the forefront of this work: we coordinate and embed information literacy instruction in first-year courses, plan and implement co-curricular outreach activities, provide faculty development workshops, conduct assessments of student learning, and generally support student success in and out of the classroom.

One departmental initiative that supports many of these goals is the Mason Undergraduate Peer Research Coach Program, in which trained Peer Coaches assist in the delivery of information literacy instruction to English composition courses. This peer-assisted learning program has allowed us to enhance our delivery of one-shot instruction sessions, thus benefiting first-year students, as well as develop transferable life skills in our Peer Coaches. This has resulted in a wonderfully enriching and mutually beneficial experience in which instruction librarians and Peer Coaches work together to support student achievement and uphold our institutional mission.

BACKGROUND OF THE PROGRAM

A pilot of the Mason Undergraduate Peer Research Coach Program began in 2006. The success of this initial rollout led to an endowment from local donors, Flora and Stuart Mason, to fund the program. Over the years, a number of organizational changes within the library led to the Peer Coaches serving in various capacities, including providing traditional desk reference, assisting in roving reference, providing tours of the library, and participating in assigned research projects. In 2013, UNLV Libraries hired an Outreach Librarian, who joined the Educational Initiatives Department and began to supervise the Peer Coaches. It was during this transition that the department reenvisioned the role of the Peer Coaches to focus on co-teaching and campus outreach.

The overarching goal of the Mason Undergraduate Peer Research Coach Program is to create an environment for college students to achieve academic success and personal growth and to excel in their chosen degree program. As such, the program differs from traditional student employment at the library in several ways. Students are hired in their first year at UNLV to work throughout their undergraduate career as Peer Coaches. They are specifically recruited to serve in this role and do not have responsibilities in other areas of the library, such as stacks management or circulation. Peer Coaches are mentored by librarians and trained in academic research, and they hone and apply these skills by assisting their peers.

Peer Coaches also go through a more rigorous application process than other student employees; in addition to an online application requiring information about academic, volunteer, and work experiences from high school, applicants also complete several short-answer questions regarding their interest in the Peer Coach Program and how it would contribute to their success as a student at UNLV. A unique facet of the application process is that current Peer Coaches are involved in the evaluation of applications. Working with their supervisor, Peer Coaches apply a rubric to each application; the high-scoring candidates are invited for a series of interviews. Finalists for the position give a 10-minute presentation on a topic of their choosing to Peer Coaches and librarians.

Since the revitalized program began in 2013, one new cohort of Peer Coaches has been hired; we currently have four senior Peer Coaches and three sophomores. Under the new program, the Peer Coaches serve as library ambassadors and contribute to the UNLV Libraries' co-curricular outreach programs. The Peer Coaches are the face of the library at campus events, including New Student Orientation. The hallmark, however, of the revitalized Peer Coach program is the role the Peer Coaches take as co-instructors of English composition information literacy instruction sessions.

As previously stated, the Educational Initiatives Department coordinates the information literacy instruction component of various required general education courses, including English 102 (ENG 102), a research-based writing course that most UNLV students complete within their first three semesters. ENG 102 is a high-enrollment course, with approximately 65–80 sections every semester. The final assignment of ENG 102 is an 8–10 page researched argument essay, so information literacy instruction is an integral aspect of the course. Every section of ENG 102 comes to the library for a 75-minute research workshop, and the Educational Initiatives team developed a shared lesson plan that we use across all ENG 102 library sessions. Outcomes of the session include evaluating sources, developing keywords, and searching for information sources using the library's discovery tool, Summon (or, at UNLV, "Quick Search"). ENG 102 is therefore a very time-intensive program for our department—we see all sections in a three- or four-week period, and the lesson plan includes many opportunities for active learning as well as time for individuals to work and ask questions. These factors—the large number of sessions, a shared lesson plan, and the need to facilitate group work as well as conduct individual consultations—led to the decision to include the Peer Coaches in ENG 102 library instruction sessions.

In 2014, the Outreach Librarian and two Teaching and Learning Librarians, one of whom coordinates the library instruction component of ENG 102, formed a facilitation team for implementing peer-assisted learning and developed learning outcomes for the co-teaching aspect of the Mason Undergraduate Peer Research Coach Program. We wanted these outcomes to be twofold—to benefit the ENG 102 library instruction program and to benefit the Peer Coaches themselves in the form of transferable life skills:

1. Peer Coaches will become proficient in the concepts of topic development, source evaluation, and keyword searching in order to contribute to ENG 102 library workshops through peer-assisted learning.
2. Peer Coaches will practice the skills of facilitation, oral communication, problem solving, and one-on-one consultations in order to develop career readiness.

Our aim was to have the Peer Coaches assist with ENG 102 instruction in several capacities—facilitating group activities, demonstrating the use of our discovery system (Quick Search), and assisting students in individual consultations about their topics and search progress.

TRAINING AND PREPARATION OF PEER COACHES

Over the summer of 2014, the facilitation team developed a six-week training program to effectively prepare the Peer Coaches for co-teaching in the classroom. We based our

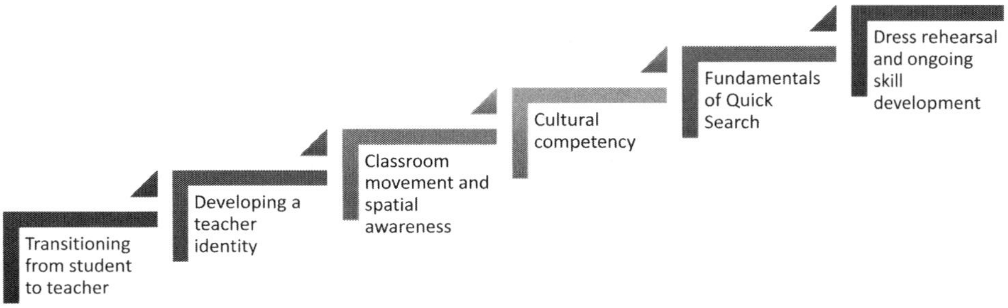

Figure 5.1 The six-week training program for the Mason Undergraduate Peer Research Coach Program.

training program on ideas from a variety of disciplines, including education, counseling, and theater. We wanted to create a well-rounded program that trained aspects of the "whole student"; our philosophy from the outset was to develop a program that focused on foundational and transferable skills—confidence in public speaking, physical movement and spatial awareness, developing a sense of teacher identity, cultural competencies, and personal goal-setting—and develop library research skills at the culmination of these other modules. It was important for Peer Coaches to become comfortable in the classroom before they mastered the discovery tool itself—their success in teaching Quick Search would depend on their ability to speak, move, and engage with their peers.

Peer Coaches are trained to co-teach in their sophomore year, after they have already completed their own coursework in ENG 102. Our training program consists of five modules, which are delivered over six weeks and build upon each other: (1) teacher identity, (2) classroom movement and spatial awareness, (3) cultural competency, (4) fundamentals of Quick Search, and (5) practice and dress rehearsal (see Figure 5.1). Each module includes prework, activities, and a reflective assessment. As facilitators, we actively participate in all training activities and discussions—we want to make sure the Peer Coaches feel comfortable, and we also want to build a sense of partnership and community with them.

Module 1: Teacher Identity

This module focuses on helping the Peer Coaches understand their role in the library instruction program and developing their own identities as teachers, creating a sense of presence and authority in the classroom even though they themselves are still college students (Palmer, 1998, p. 13).

We begin by introducing the Peer Coaches to the purpose of the peer instruction program and why they are an important aspect of the educational mission of the Libraries (Keenan, 2014). We introduce our two learning outcomes and discuss why their role in ENG 102 benefits both themselves and the ENG 102 students. We also discuss the purpose of peer learning and ask the Peer Coaches to reflect on how they feel about working in the classroom and what they want to learn from the experience. In past trainings, Peer Coaches indicated that they felt both nervous and excited to become co-teachers and that they wanted to learn skills like how to interact and engage with other students. The Peer Coaches also were excited about developing themselves as leaders and honing their research skills for their own courses.

The second part of this module centers on developing a teacher identity. Using a flip chart, Peer Coaches identify positive and negative qualities of teachers they have had in the past and discuss qualities they would like to adopt and avoid in their own work as co-teachers. The purpose of this activity is to help the Peer Coaches make connections between their own experiences as students and the new information they will encounter in the training program, an idea based in the educational theory of constructivism, which argues that learners create new knowledge based on existing knowledge and experiences (Gagnon, Collay, & Schmuck, 2006).

We then ask Peer Coaches to draw how they see themselves as a teacher, or the kind of teacher they would like to be. We discuss what they drew and why—for example, one Peer Coach drew a treasure map, because he felt it was his job as a peer mentor to help lead students in the right direction in order to be successful on their assignment. As described in the counseling literature, drawing the self in a particular context (i.e., as a teacher) can be a helpful strategy for stepping out of oneself and looking at feelings and thoughts without self-judgment. The act of expressing oneself without words can also be a helpful way of reflecting in an honest and meaningful way (Muri, 2007).

The final activity in Module 1 is a discussion of "Every Kid Needs a Champion," a TED Talk by Rita Pierson (2013). The outcome for this video is to help the Peer Coaches realize that they can impact students even in a brief one-shot session and that it's okay to make mistakes—not everyone is perfect but it's important to have an open mind.

Module 2: Classroom Movement and Spatial Awareness

The goal of this module is to help the Peer Coaches become comfortable in classroom spaces in their new role as teachers. Additionally, we want Peer Coaches to become aware of the power of nonverbal communication and how this can be used to effectively communicate and engage with other students. Several activities are used to demonstrate how movement and gesturing can be used to a teacher's advantage.

First we complete a classroom mapping activity: all three library instruction classrooms are mapped out on flip charts. Each Peer Coach is given stickers and asked to place the sticker on each map based on where they would stand if they were observing the class, where they would stand if they were co-teaching, and where they would stand if they were teaching by themselves. We then review patterns in the placement of stickers and discuss the best places to stand in the classroom for different purposes. Peer Coaches also physically explore the three classrooms and test the places that they identified with their stickers. The Peer Coaches are usually surprised at how it feels to stand at the front of the room, and in past trainings have noted peculiarities of the different spaces, such as "This room is long—I'll really have to project," or "I'll probably stand opposite of the librarian so we can play off each other." When asked about the training experience, Peer Coaches indicated that this exercise was invaluable to them—they had never before thought about the physical classroom spaces, and this helped them more clearly picture themselves as teachers.

The second series of activities in Module 2 focuses on gesturing and body awareness, as nonverbal communication is an important part of teaching and public speaking. These skills are complex and difficult—and nearly impossible to teach in one sitting—but our goal is to give Peer Coaches an awareness of their own bodies in motion and how the body can be a vessel of communication, both intentionally and unintentionally.

First, the Peer Coaches and facilitators watch a video from Outspoken.co (2014) about effectively utilizing public speaking gestures. The video highlights four types of gestures: descriptive, emphatic, suggestive, and prompting. After viewing the video, Peer Coaches put what they watched into practice in an activity titled "Hickory Dickory Dock," which we developed to highlight the power of body language in teaching. This technique comes from an acting exercise developed by Sanford Misner and was initially intended to help actors learn to express emotion without thinking about the use of meaningful words (Silverberg, 2000). In our use of the activity, the words to the short nursery rhyme "Hickory Dickory Dock" are projected on the wall. Each Peer Coach is given a message that they needed to convey to the rest of the group (i.e., asking the group if we have any questions), but they are only allowed to use the text from the nursery rhyme and their own body language to convey the message (in this case, the student might raise their own hand).

Finally, Peer Coaches complete a fill-in-the blank "elevator speech" on a library service of their choosing (Oakleaf & Albert, 2015). They have a few days to develop their speeches, and then present to the rest of the group, incorporating at least two types of gestures in an intentional way throughout the elevator speech. Peer Coaches and facilitators give feedback to each other, noting two things they liked and one area for improvement. See Appendix 5–1.

Module 3: Cultural Competency

In this module, we want Peer Coaches to consider the diversity of our student body and to approach their teaching with an aim toward inclusion and respect. To accomplish our goal, we collaborated with the Coordinator for Multicultural Student Programs in UNLV's Department of Student Engagement and Diversity to deliver a customized workshop. In the workshop, we define different kinds of identities (sex, gender, race, nationality, etc.) and discuss our understanding of these identities and how they relate to instruction. We also participate in an activity in which everyone draws their idea of an alien and presents to the rest of the group. We discuss how we could draw an alien when we've never seen one, which leads to a conversation about assumptions and bias and the importance of being inclusive and nonjudgmental. At the end of the workshop, everyone sets an individual goal to incorporate one inclusive practice into one's work in the classroom.

Module 4: Fundamentals of Quick Search

The last two modules of our training program are directly related to the Peer Coach's responsibilities in the ENG 102 classroom. During ENG 102 library sessions, the Peer Coaches are responsible for instructing the class on how to use Quick Search, our library's discovery tool, to find book and articles. We therefore need to make sure they understand how Quick Search functions and how to explain it to a class of first-year students.

At the beginning of this module, the facilitators demonstrate the use of Quick Search as we would in a normal ENG 102 session, pausing for the Peer Coaches to ask questions and clarifying our rationale for using various limiters or filters. After the demonstration, each Peer Coach completes a series of worksheets that guides them through various search strategies in Quick Search in order to locate a scholarly article for a given research topic.

When the group reconvenes, the Peer Coaches and facilitators discuss what they learned about Quick Search from completing the worksheets. What was easy? What was difficult? We want the Peer Coaches to develop an awareness of how Quick Search functions, so we divide them into teams of two or three and have them answer the following questions about Quick Search:

- Explain Quick Search. What is it?
- How is Quick Search different from other library databases?

- What is Quick Search good at?
- What is frustrating about Quick Search?
- Compare Quick Search to something else in your daily life. Why is it like that?

Peer Coaches report out their team responses and swap ideas for how they could explain Quick Search to other students. Some excellent analogies have emerged from these discussions: one Peer Coach compared Quick Search to a Las Vegas buffet—there is a little bit of everything (books, magazines, articles, on all different topics), whereas a subject-specific database is like a restaurant that only serves one kind of cuisine. Another compared it to online shopping: you can use the filters to narrow down to the exact item you want—when shopping, it may be a strapless blue dress, while in research, it may be a scholarly article from the last two years. Hearing how the Peer Coaches understand and describe Quick Search was truly eye-opening for us. We were especially struck by their ability to explain what Quick Search was and how it functioned without the use of any library jargon.

Next, we follow up this exercise with a series of search drills—we give the Peer Coaches various topics and task them to find a book or an article on the topic. The first to find the item and use Quick Search's cite and e-mail feature to send it to one of the facilitators wins a prize.

Module 5: Practice and Dress Rehearsal

In this final module, the Peer Coaches put together all of the things they learned during training. The culmination of this module is a live dress rehearsal for the Peer Coaches, other library student assistants, and the Educational Initiatives Department, in which each Peer Coach takes a turn explaining and demonstrating Quick Search and facilitating a brief "individual search time" for the larger group, who role-play as ENG 102 students.

To prepare the Peer Coaches for the final dress rehearsal, we film each Peer Coach doing their Quick Search demonstration. We give individual feedback, and the Peer Coaches are able to watch themselves teach and identify their own areas for improvement.

At the end of the dress rehearsal, the invited guests submit an index card with feedback for each Peer Coach. We aggregate the feedback and meet with the Peer Coaches individually to reinforce what went well and what areas in which they could improve. At the conclusion of this module, Peer Coaches are ready to start actively participating as co-teachers in ENG 102 library instruction sessions.

IMPLEMENTATION OF THE PROGRAM

The daily experience of our peer-assisted learning program is linked to the ebb and flow of ENG 102 library instruction sessions. Therefore, after Peer Coaches are trained, they are usually engaged in instructional activities from the beginning of October through early November, and again from the beginning of March through early April. During this time, ENG 102 instruction is the primary work duty for the Peer Coaches. Peer Coaches sign themselves up to assist with ENG 102 sessions, and the Outreach Librarian, as the Peer Coach supervisor, oversees their schedule to make sure all ENG 102 courses are covered and that Peer Coaches have a balanced teaching load.

During the ENG 102 class, the Peer Coaches serve in several capacities. The class opens with an evaluating sources exercise in which students work in groups to answer questions about an article they are given to read. During this activity, Peer Coaches circulate and help facilitate the group work, asking students prompting questions to keep them engaged and helping them understand the task and how it relates to their annotated bibliography assignment. Peer Coaches also demonstrate the use of Quick Search to the class, and answer individual student research questions, if they can—Peer Coaches are instructed to bring in the librarian whenever a question becomes too difficult for them.

In addition to their work in the classroom, Peer Coaches are also expected to participate in weekly reflection activities relating to their teaching experiences, attend a weekly one-on-one meeting with their supervisor, and participate in a weekly Peer Coach department meeting. Though many of their regular duties are suspended while they are teaching, Peer Coaches work 20 hours per week, so there are additional projects they engage in based on department need and their weekly teaching load.

One aspect of our program implementation that can be a little confusing at times is the number of people involved. While the Peer Coaches report directly to the Outreach Librarian, they are trained for co-teaching by their supervisor and two other Teaching and Learning Librarians. The three of us work together very closely in order to keep a consistent message so the Peer Coaches do not receive conflicting information or feedback, but we are not the only librarians the Peer Coaches work with. Since the entire Educational Initiatives Department is involved in ENG 102 instruction, there are five additional librarians the Peer Coaches may be assigned to co-teach with, who are not involved in their training or mentoring. The program is well supported at all levels, including our Dean and Department Head, but the number of people involved does mean that we, as facilitators, had to get buy-in from our department and make sure everyone understood the role of the Peer Coaches in our ENG 102 instruction program. Some elements that were crucial to this were: having all teaching librarians adhere to the same lesson plan (we wanted our Peer Coaches to have consistency so they knew what they were expected to do in each class), a shared understanding of how to give feedback to the Peer Coaches (we funnel this through the facilitators so that we can make sure feedback is constructive and clear), and a commitment to having the Peer Coaches demonstrate Quick Search and generally be partners in the classroom. While all members of the department were happy to have the Peer Coaches' help, it did take a few semesters to pin down our shared expectations and clearly communicate this to all members of the department.

EVALUATION OF THE PROGRAM

Our peer-assisted learning program is evaluated in two ways, in order to reflect our two program outcomes: our primary assessment method consists of critical self-reflection, which allows us to examine the benefits of co-teaching on the Peer Coaches themselves; every semester, we also conduct a quantitative analysis that compares the kinds of questions ENG 102 students ask the Peer Coaches during instruction sessions as opposed to the questions they ask teaching librarians, which is one way we can assess the impact of peer-assisted learning on the ENG 102 instruction program.

Critical Self-Reflection

Due to the experiential nature of peer-assisted learning, it is very difficult to capture meaningful assessment data. It can be very challenging to get students to think deeply about their experiences, a lesson that we learned the hard way. In our first semester conducting the program, we introduced a very simple reflection, in which each time the Peer Coaches co-taught, they would answer two questions about the library session: "What part of the lesson went well?" and "What will you do differently next time you are in the classroom?" These prompts did not result in true reflections—the repetitive nature of the prompts meant that the answers themselves were very repetitive. Peer Coaches liked when the class was engaged, students asked them questions, and they felt useful; most of what they would do differently had to do with a need for more communication between Peer Coaches and librarians about expectations and roles—an issue we were able to address and correct. But the Peer Coaches were not reflecting on their own learning, how they had grown, how their expectations changed, or any of the transferable life skills we wanted our program to instill in them. We knew we had to change our assessment method if we wanted to foster critical self-reflection.

Two of the facilitators attended the 2015 Library Orientation Exchange (LOEX) Conference, in which Anne-Marie Deitering gave a plenary address on just this issue—how to foster reflection in our students (Deitering, 2015). Deitering's discussion gave way to an exploration of reflective learning, and we created a new series of reflection questions based on best practices from the literature (Brookfield, 1995; James & Brookfield, 2014; Schön, 1983). Our goal was to eliminate questions that had students label an experience as "good" or "bad" and instead helped them describe an experience and their feelings about it in a more holistic way. The questions we asked were sometimes related to co-teaching, but sometimes more about their experiences overall, and were meant to engage the Peer Coaches with connecting their classroom experiences to their own education, work, and personal lives—thus enabling them to learn more about themselves, which was the outcome we wanted to assess. For a list of all reflection prompts used during training and co-teaching, see Appendix 5–2.

We asked the Peer Coaches reflective questions throughout their training as well as the weeks they were actively co-teaching. At the end of the fall 2015 semester, we used ATLAS.ti to code the answers to each question in order to uncover patterns. In doing so, we discovered that our Peer Coach reflections could be categorized in three areas: reflections about the development of teaching skills (knowledge and tactile competencies), reflections about the development of attitudes and beliefs (personal development and self-exploration), and reflections about the meaning of authority in the classroom. For a sample of Peer Coach reflections for each theme, see Appendix 5–3.

These reflections demonstrate that students are thinking more critically about their training and instructional experiences, and trying to make connections to their daily lives. We were pleased with these assessment results, but there were still many cases where students just reported on an interaction without reflecting—we will need to continue to evaluate our reflection prompts in order to help our Peer Coaches think more deeply about their experiences in future semesters.

Question Tracking

In order to address our second outcome (that peer-assisted learning would benefit the ENG 102 students), we examined the types of questions ENG 102 students ask librarians versus Peer Coaches. We hoped this would tell us if ENG 102 students perceived the Peer Coaches as useful resources and, if so, to what extent. At the end of each library instruction session, librarians and Peer Coaches recorded the questions ENG 102 students asked them during the session. We developed a modified READ scale to classify the types of questions asked into four categories (Gerlich & Berard, 2010):

1. transactional questions (how to login to the computer, how to print, how to get a library card);
2. activity-based questions (how to complete the class activity);
3. tool-based questions (how to cite, how to e-mail, how to use Quick Search);
4. research assistance (how to narrow a topic, how to choose keywords).

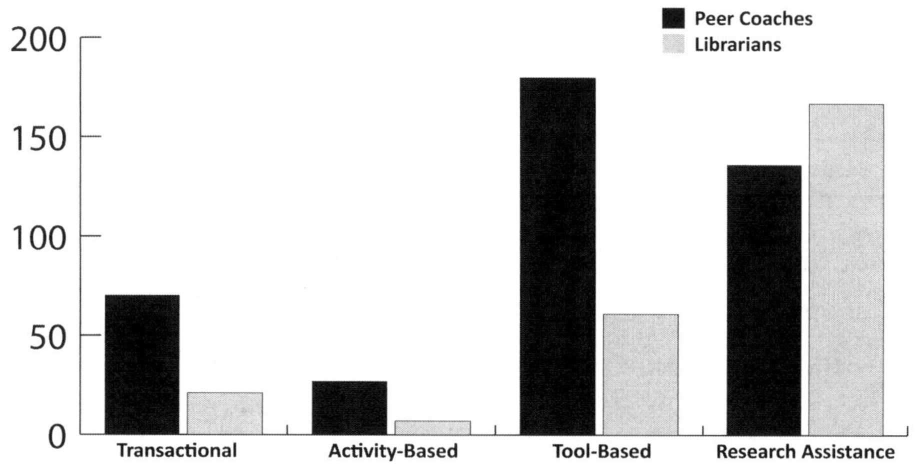

Figure 5.2 Types of questions ENG 102 students asked Peer Coaches and librarians.

Results from this assessment show that Peer Coaches are asked many more level 1 and level 2 questions than librarians; Peer Coaches almost exclusively are asked activity-based questions (see Figure 5.2). Since librarians are rarely asked activity-based questions, we hypothesize that classroom activities become more clear and meaningful when a Peer Coach is there to answer questions—students just do not seem comfortable asking the librarian if they do not understand the purpose of an exercise. We also were pleased to see that the Peer Coaches are asked so many questions about Quick Search as well as research-assistance level questions. This not only shows that students in the classroom value the Peer Coaches as research experts who can help them, but also shows that it frees up the librarian to answer many more in-depth research questions. While Peer Coaches are assisting with level 1, 2, and 3 questions, the librarian can work with students who need more extensive help. Between them, Peer Coaches and teaching librarians are providing a great deal of assistance to students in the classroom; for us, this means the program is well worth the time it takes to train the Peer Coaches.

IMPLICATIONS AND LESSONS LEARNED

One major implication of our peer-assisted learning program is the impact it has had on student learning. As stated earlier, ENG 102 students are experiencing more individual attention and have more opportunities to ask questions and receive feedback. Since this course is so crucial to the general education curriculum at UNLV—it's the first time many students experience college-level research-based writing—it is imperative that we provide consistent and high-quality instruction when we have the students face-to-face in a library session. The Peer Coaches enable us to do just that. On the flip side, the Peer Coaches themselves are also positively impacted by our program in the form of the transferable skills they gain through their training and experiences as co-teachers. As evidenced in their responses to our reflection questions, Peer Coaches are improving their communication and public speaking skills, becoming more self-confident, and learning professionalism—all skills they will need as they move on from UNLV and enter into graduate school or their careers. Additionally, they are becoming more proficient researchers, which can positively impact their academic success in other courses they take.

Our peer-assisted learning program has also influenced other library services and our own pedagogical practice as teaching librarians. For example, our outreach capabilities are now enhanced; since Peer Coaches have become more adept public speakers and presenters, we can assign them larger roles at orientations and campus events, which enables librarians to work on other activities, such as planning and assessment. Additionally, the presence of Peer Coaches in the classroom means we can deliver more involved lesson plans—activities that require a great deal of explanation and facilitation are more easily taught with the assistance of Peer Coaches.

Finally, seeing how the Peer Coaches understand and explain library resources was extremely influential in terms of how we think about our own instruction—our use of jargon (even by accident), how students conceptualize research, and what kind of workflows they utilize. For example, we didn't realize how important it was that we get students in the habit of e-mailing themselves permalinks to articles through Quick Search until one Peer Coach said that in her freshman year, she used to post article links to her Facebook wall for safekeeping and then couldn't reopen them later. We also became hyperaware of our use of words like "database" and "keywords"—these aren't terms the Peer Coaches ever use when they teach, because they don't mean anything significant to them. Rather, the Peer Coaches taught us how to better connect with students by using more familiar concepts and language when we teach.

Over the last few years, we have learned several lessons from our program. On the one hand, we feel that it is a very successful program that works well in many ways. Having a team of facilitators has been really helpful, as it allows us to split up the work, and it also gives the Peer Coaches different points of view and various pedagogical perspectives. In a similar vein, having small cohorts of Peer Coaches (three or four at a time) makes the training feel very manageable and allows us to really establish deep connections with the Peer Coaches. We treat them as partners in their own training—we ask for advice about what they want to learn more about, and we participate in all activities alongside them—so they feel ownership over the program, which contributes to their buy-in and sense of self-confidence.

There are, however, still things we need to change or improve upon. Some issues we are currently grappling with are the need to think about the sustainability of the program as more Peer Coaches are hired—every year or two, there will be a new cohort who needs trained plus current Peer Coaches to oversee. Managing these two tracks while keeping all Peer Coaches engaged may be difficult, and it is something we need to intentionally build into the training program. We also have some concerns about Peer Coach burnout—after three or four years of intensive instruction, they may lose interest or feel like the sessions are boring or repetitive (indeed, this feeling was voiced by one Peer Coach at the end of the semester). We therefore will need to work on strategies to keep things fresh. And while our assessment has improved, we still need to keep experimenting with our question prompts to see if we can tap into even more critical self-reflection in the future.

That said, if we could offer advice to any institutions interested in starting their own peer-assisted learning program, it would be to intentionally build the assessment component into the design of the program and not leave it until the end. Having an assessment plan from the outset not only helps establish buy-in from stakeholders and colleagues, but also helps direct the program through evidenced-based decision making. Even though we learned early on that we wanted to change our assessment model, we stuck with our original plan for the first year in order to establish a baseline and thoroughly vet our pilot program. After that, we felt really clear about the direction we wanted to go in and adjusted our assessment methods accordingly. Additionally, we would encourage other institutions to think outside the box when it comes to designing a training program: we utilized ideas from counseling, theater, and education, and the training that resulted was engaging, well-rounded, and fun. Peer Coaches were kept "on their toes" and were able to explore the concept of teaching from many different angles. We believe that there is more to teacher development than content knowledge, and our training program reflects this notion.

NEXT STEPS

We are excited about the future of the Mason Undergraduate Peer Research Coach Program. We are on track to continually have two cohorts of Peer Coaches, two years apart, so we are looking forward to adapting our training program to include more student-led activities that the seasoned Peer Coaches can deliver to those in training. We are also exploring the idea of placing more training content online so that face-to-face meetings can be even more active and discussion-based.

We are also in the process of putting together a survey that we will distribute to all of our Peer Coaches to clearly assess their perceptions of transferability of skills gained from their co-teaching experiences. We are very interested in learning more about this, since development of student academic and life skills is not only part of the UNLV Libraries' strategic plan, but also a core learning outcome of the Peer Coach program.

In conclusion, the two years we spent developing our peer-assisted learning program have been an invaluable learning experience that not only has positively impacted student learning at UNLV, but also has been extremely rewarding to our own practice as librarians. While building, implementing, and assessing a peer-assisted learning program is an admittedly time-consuming endeavor, we have found the benefits to outweigh the challenges many times over. The Mason Undergraduate Peer Research Coaches have become an integral component of our English composition information literacy instruction program, and we are excited to see how this partnership continues to develop in the future.

REFERENCES

Brookfield, S. (1995). *Becoming a critically reflective teacher*. San Francisco: Jossey-Bass.

Deitering, A. (2014, February 26). *What? So what? Now what?* [Web blog post]. Retrieved from http://info-fetishist.org/2014/02/26/what-so-what-now-what/

Deitering, A. (2015, May 1). *LOEX 2015* [Web blog post]. Retrieved from http://info-fetishist.org/2015/05/01/loex2015/

Gagnon, G.W., Collay, M., & Schmuck, R.A. (2006). *Constructivist learning design: Key questions for teaching to standards*. Thousand Oaks: Corwin Press.

Gerlich, B.K., & Berard, G.L. (2010). Testing the viability of the READ scale (Reference Effort Assessment Data)©: Qualitative statistics for academic reference services. *College and Research Libraries, 71*(2), 116–137. doi:10.5860/0710116

James, A., & Brookfield, S. (2014). *Engaging imagination: Helping students become creative and reflective thinkers*. San Francisco: Jossey-Bass.

Keenan, C. (2014). *Mapping student-led peer learning in the UK*. Retrieved from https://www.heacademy.ac.uk/sites/default/files/resources/peer_led_learning_keenan_nov_14-final.pdf

Muri, S.A. (2007). Beyond the face: Art therapy and self-portraiture. *The Arts in Psychotherapy, 34*(4), 331–339. doi:10.1016/j.aip.2007.05.002

Oakleaf, M., & Albert, A. (2015, March). *Library value communication: Conceptualizing impact, centering on stakeholders, crafting messages, and conveying the story.* Conference workshop presented at the Association of College & Research Libraries 2015 Conference, Portland, OR.

Outspoken.co. (2014, January 1). *The four public speaking gestures and how to use them* [Video file]. Retrieved from https://www.youtube.com/watch?v=1VCaJ4dSHak

Palmer, P. J. (1998). *The courage to teach: Exploring the inner landscape of a teacher's life.* San Francisco: Jossey-Bass.

Pierson, R. (2013, May). *Rita Pierson: Every kid needs a champion* [Video file]. Retrieved from https://www.ted.com/talks/rita_pierson_every_kid_needs_a_champion?language=en

Schön, D. A. (1983). *The reflective practitioner: How professionals think in action.* New York: Basic Books.

Silverberg, L. (2000). *The Sanford Meisner approach: Workbook four: Playing the part.* Hanover, NH: Smith & Kraus.

University of Nevada, Las Vegas. (n.d.). "UNLV's top tier mission." Retrieved from https://www.unlv.edu/toptier/vision

University of Nevada, Las Vegas, Office of Diversity Initiatives. (n.d.)."Minority-Serving Institution (MSI)." Retrieved from https://www.unlv.edu/diversityinitiatives/msi

U.S. News and World Report. (n.d.). "Campus ethnic diversity." Retrieved from http://colleges.usnews.rankingsandreviews.com/best-colleges/rankings/national-universities/campus-ethnic-diversity

APPENDIX 5–1: ELEVATOR SPEECH TEMPLATE

1. The library offers ____
   ____.
2. ____
   __________. (Additional information about service mentioned in #1 or another service that the audience may find useful.)
3. I really like or have benefited from this service because ______________________
   ____
   ______________________________.
4. ______________________________ are really helpful ______________________. (Encourage audience to use service(s).)

Notes

____

____

____

____

____

APPENDIX 5–2: REFLECTION QUESTIONS

Reflection questions used during training program:

Module 1: Teaching Identity

- How do you feel about working in the classroom? Why?
- What do you want to learn?
- How do you think this can apply to other situations?
- What do you think you're bringing to the program?
- In your own words, what would be the benefit to English 102 of peer-assisted learning?
- What difficulties do you perceive that you will have to overcome to become the teacher you would like to be?
- What part of yourself as a teacher would you most like to develop?
- What are your greatest strengths?

Module 2: Classroom Movement and Spatial Awareness

- Observe your teachers, or anyone who is leading a group/giving a presentation this week. What physicalities, gestures, or postures would you like to adopt? Which would you like to avoid?
- What is one body language or gesturing habit that you would like to work on this semester?

Module 3: Cultural Competence

- What made you curious in today's session? Why?
- Name three things that stuck in your mind from today's training. Why do you think these resonated with you?
- Did I do an effective job of communicating to others? How do I know?
- What's one strategy you could use to make yourself approachable in the classroom?

Module 4: Fundamentals of Quick Search

- At this point, how are you progressing as a peer teacher?
- How can you use your strengths to improve?

Module 5: Dress Rehearsal

- **What?** What have you learned about teaching and being a leader in the classroom over the last six weeks?
- **So what?** Why is this important to your work as a peer instructor?
- **Now what?** What will you try to apply from this training moving forward? (Deitering, 2014).

Reflection questions used during co-teaching (one question per week, over a four-week teaching period):

- If you could do it over again, what would you do differently?
- How did the students' responses to you make you feel?
- How would you do this differently if you were in charge?
- Who determines what's best for the students in the classroom? Why does that matter?

REFERENCE

Deitering, A. (2014, February 26). *What? So what? Now what?* [Web blog post]. Retrieved from http://info-fetishist.org/2014/02/26/what-so-what-now-what/

APPENDIX 5–3: SAMPLE PEER COACH REFLECTIONS CLASSIFIED BY THEME

Theme	*Peer Coach Reflections*
Authority	Of course, the professor sets guidelines to the student's topic; however, the librarian and peer coaches really help determine what is best for the students. Students often need help figuring out how to create a well-developed topic, and librarians and peer coaches help significantly with that process. The most important thing I've learned this semester about my students is that I only know when a student needs help when I ask questions and interact with them. Most of the time, my students would ask me something if it's a technical question or something I can clarify, but usually when I'm in the classroom I have to interact with students to gain more of these types of questions or ones that are in-depth. At various times, small interactions with students can lead to cooperative research that benefits both the teacher and the student.
Development of attitudes	To be honest, at the beginning of the training, I was a little nervous about teaching to people my own age. But with all these trainings we've received I feel more at ease. I think I can go into the classrooms and make a difference! Since there are many students all at once, it's easy to just mentally ignore and give up on a student. I want to be able to care and value each student the same.
Development of skills	The most important thing I've learned about my teaching this past semester is that I engage the students more when I use the physical environment to my advantage (i.e., walking and pointing on the screen during my demos, walking around and not staying behind the podium). This is important to know because it allows me to connect more with the students. The most important thing I've learned about my teaching in the past semester is that keeping everything I demonstrate as simple as it needs to be is very beneficial to help students understand what it is I am teaching about and it makes them more attentive of what is being taught. I want to learn more about how I can improve my skills, socially and professionally, by working with the students and the faculty.

Part II

PEER-ASSISTED LEARNING IN CO-CURRICULAR OUTREACH

6

Library House Outreach Program at Harvard College

Anna Esty, Alexis Gomez, Ramona Islam,
Vegas Longlois, and Reed Lowrie

The Library House Outreach Program at Harvard College, begun as a pilot in 2015, focuses on undergraduate students (Peer Research Fellows) reaching out to their peers in residential communities (Houses). The Fellows lower the bar to access, alleviating some of the confusion and intimidation associated with library research. Through them, the library seeks to expose more students to Harvard's extensive collections and research expertise while bolstering academic integrity initiatives and supporting all aspects of student life. This chapter describes the program in general, sharing particulars on the recently assessed pilot phase, during which two Houses each had one Fellow, each of whom was matched with a Mentor Librarian. Once Fellows are hired, they undergo a five-week training period, after which they continue to meet weekly with their Mentor Librarians. The Fellows conduct in-person and electronic outreach to their respective Houses and are generally available for research questions and consults. The pilot assessment included pretraining and posttraining tests, statistics on Fellow-led events and research questions, statistics on e-mail newsletters, and a House residents survey. The Fellows benefit from the program through gains in their own research skills, and in turn, Mentor Librarians learn more about the student experience, particularly regarding research and the library.

INSTITUTIONAL CONTEXT

Harvard College is the undergraduate degree-granting school of Harvard University, with a mission to "educate the citizens and citizen leaders for our society" through "commitment to the transformative power of a liberal arts and sciences education" (Harvard College, n.d.). There are approximately 6,700 college students at Harvard, from every U.S. state and over 160 countries. In addition to their geographic and cultural diversity, students come from different economic backgrounds and they arrive at Harvard with varying levels of preparation and experience with libraries.

During their first year at Harvard, students live in dormitories in and around Harvard Yard, the oldest part of the campus. After first year, they are assigned to one of 12 "Houses," where they will spend their final three academic years. The Houses are largely self-sufficient units, with dining halls, common spaces, libraries, and other amenities. They are overseen by a senior faculty member and a large administrative staff made up of faculty, graduate student subject-area tutors, and staff. Each House contains approximately 350–500 students, and the Houses are grouped in neighborhoods. The College's mission statement enshrines the importance placed on this residential arrangement: "Through a diverse living environment, where students live with people who are studying different topics, who come from different walks of life and have evolving identities, intellectual transformation is deepened and conditions for social transformation are created" (Harvard College, n.d.). Much of an undergraduate's identity at Harvard revolves around their House; when two Harvard alumni meet for the first time, inevitably, one will ask what House the other lived in.

Mirroring the university as a whole, the library system at Harvard is also largely decentralized. There are 73 libraries in the system, ranging from small rooms housing modest collections to Widener Library, the largest academic library in the world. The digital library environment is similarly diffuse: each school has its own library website, tailored to the needs of its students. There is, of course, a shared catalog and shared access to (most) publications and databases. Nevertheless the library remains a rich and complex ecosystem requiring a high level of knowledge and patience to navigate.

All first-year students are required to take one term of Expository Writing, a small (15-student) intensive writing course, with an end-of-term research paper assignment. Over 90 percent of sections involve a librarian in some form, usually in the classic "one-shot" instruction session. This is usually the first opportunity librarians have to reach students, as there is no required library orientation for first-year students. After Expository Writing, a student's level of exposure to the library generally depends on the department where the student concentrates (majors). The degree of engagement with subject librarians varies among departments; a lack of consistency across the curriculum leads to varying levels of research skills and knowledge among the undergraduates. This challenge was one of the driving forces behind the launch of the Library House Outreach Program in 2015.

BACKGROUND OF THE PROGRAM

In 2009, a few years prior to the Library House Outreach Program, librarians submitted a proposal to the Harvard Library administration for reaching students at the intersection of their academic and personal lives. Unfortunately, budget cuts due to the financial crisis prevented this proposal from going forward until the start of the multiyear House Renewal initiative in 2012, which sought to renovate physical spaces and reexamine the services each House offered. Houses already employed a range of staff members, including, but not limited to, preprofessional advisors, writing and fellowships tutors, concentration advisors, and Resident Deans to assist students with academic crises and the like. The House Renewal project offered a perfect opportunity for librarians to enter the scene; in May 2013, a committee of librarians convened to develop the Library House Outreach Program, a model for embedding students knowledgeable about library research and services in the Houses. Over the course of the summer, the committee divided into smaller groups to: (1) produce a literature review of what models of peer outreach other universities employed and (2) conduct an environmental scan to determine the current research needs of Harvard undergraduates and examine established services for students in the Houses.

The literature review (Barber, 2009; Barnes & Peyton, 2007; Bodemer, 2014; Foster & Gibbons, 2007; Riehle & Witt, 2009; Rudin, 2008; Strothmann & Antell, 2010) revealed several themes: librarians entering student spaces, marketing library services in student spaces, employing students as assistants to librarians within library buildings, adding students as research tutors in existing tutoring services, and embedding peer assistants in students' residential spaces.

The environmental scan confirmed several points borne out in the literature and what librarians had long assumed from interactions with students at Reference Desks and in the classroom: First, undergraduates find the libraries (and librarians) intimidating; second, they lead heavily scheduled lives and often do their work at the last minute; third, most undergraduates do research and write their papers or complete projects after 10 p.m., when librarians are not available for assistance. In addition, students view other people as the most important part of the research process and often turn first to friends, family, or other trusted acquaintances—not librarians—for help (Gilroy, 2007). The scan also revealed that undergraduates welcome additional academic support in the Houses (Harvard College Institutional Research, 2012).

After completing the literature review and environmental scan, the committee crafted and presented to library administration a proposal for a House outreach pilot that would serve residents through informal introductions to the libraries, academic and extracurricular research assistance, best practices for research in alignment with academic integrity, and outreach to sophomores choosing their concentrations. The proposal also recognized House outreach as an opportunity for librarians to learn more about undergraduates' research needs. The team recommended following the peer instruction model by training students already living in each House (one student per House) to act as liaisons to the library. These students would hold the official position of Peer Research Fellows and would be compensated for their time in this role (the Fellows are paid at an hourly rate for five hours of work per week during the academic year). Each Fellow would be trained by a librarian dedicated to their House who would act as their Mentor. The proposal submitted to the library administration in fall 2013 outlined plans not only for the program as a whole but also for the pilot phase (to take place in spring 2015 through fall 2015), which involved placing Fellows in two Houses. If the pilot proved successful, the program could eventually scale up to all 12 Houses. The proposal also included details on funding, staff time commitment, and plans for program assessment. Buy-in for the program came through the library administration's approval of the pilot proposal. Staff buy-in happened more informally, through announcements about the program and inclusion of colleagues in additional training sessions.

After the proposal was approved in summer 2014, the committee began preparation for the launch of the pilot program in spring 2015. Two members volunteered to serve as Mentor Librarians and drafted the training curriculum with input from committee members. Other members of the committee focused on building support for the program through meetings with senior faculty and administrators in the Houses, the Honor Council, the Office of Student Life, the Advising Programs Office, the Bureau of Study Counsel, and other related departments on campus that had been identified as valuable partners. In order to determine what type of library assistance would be most useful to undergraduates, the Library House Outreach Program committee conducted focus groups with circulation student employees. The committee also interviewed and hired a student who was recommended as a possible candidate for one of the Fellow positions, due to her previous work in another area of the library. Prior to the pilot's launch, this student served as the Assistant Coordinator for the Library House Outreach Program and helped develop program materials, including test-driving and collaboratively revising the training curriculum.

The committee selected two Houses, Adams and Currier, for the pilot, and Mentor Librarians arranged meetings with stakeholders in each of them to ensure a smooth launch. They selected Currier because the Assistant Coordinator, a junior, lived there, and they wanted to hire her as the first Peer Fellow. They selected Adams due to its central location, as well as the receptiveness of the House Administrators there, who helped advertise the Fellow position over the Adams's e-mail listserv. Out of the applicants interviewed, the committee decided to hire a senior to benefit from her broader experience, even though that meant she would graduate halfway into the one-year pilot. Happily, one of the remaining applicants accepted an invitation to serve as the senior's successor. She was hired and trained in time to have her shadow and work alongside the senior for a few weeks before taking over the Adams House position in September 2015.

The committee always intended that if the pilot proved successful, the program would continue. Because it did succeed, the committee has been pleased to employ all Fellows, whether hired in their sophomore, junior, or senior years, through graduation (unless they choose otherwise). The hiring of successors overlaps with graduating Fellows by one semester to accommodate the training period and allow time for new Fellows to shadow their more experienced peers. Interested candidates are invited to submit a resume and cover letter, and meet with House Outreach Team members for an interview. The main qualification for Fellows is interest in the library and passion for helping peers.

TRAINING AND PREPARATION OF PEER RESEARCH FELLOWS

Training for Fellows follows the same curriculum introduced in the pilot phase. When Fellows are hired, they report to the Curricular Design and Research Librarian, who acts as their official supervisor and guides the program. They are also paired with a Mentor Librarian, with whom they work throughout training and program implementation. The Library House Outreach Program provides 25 hours of training over five weeks to prepare new Fellows to forge connections between Harvard undergraduates and the Harvard College Library. The training curriculum is designed to help the Fellows become proficient at conducting basic library research while simultaneously introducing them to expert librarians to whom they may refer more sophisticated inquiries. The training also incorporates self-reflection and peer discussion about the role of research in students' academic and personal lives. It challenges the Fellows to think about how they might assess their own and others' research needs.

A typical training week entails five hours per Fellow and three hours per Mentor Librarian and usually takes place at the beginning of the semester. It generally proceeds as follows: Fellows meet individually with their Mentors for two hours at the beginning of each week to receive instruction. During this time, Mentors present learning activities from the training curriculum. Then, the Fellow uses two training hours to work on independent learning activities and read assigned articles. In the last hour of training each week, all Fellows and Mentors meet as a group to discuss any questions that may have arisen while completing the assignments and to expand upon the skills learned. This way, the Fellows have the opportunity to learn from one another as well as from librarians. The Mentors assess the trainees' work and engage with them in reflective dialogue, asking questions and providing demonstration and scaffolding as necessary. This kind of personal attention builds a trusting relationship between the Fellows and their Mentors; it also opens the door toward creating a community of practice among Fellows and the larger library community.

The training curriculum was developed to close gaps identified through the internal environmental scan and incorporates information literacy learning goals derived from the Association of College and Research Libraries *Framework* and relevant library literature (Association of College and Research Libraries, 2014; Bruce, 1997; Head, 2012, 2013; Head & Eisenberg, 2009; Head, Van Hoeck, Eschler, & Fullerton, 2013; Jisc, 2014). Framed by pre- and posttraining tests (see Appendix 6–1) that allow librarians to gauge its effectiveness, the training curriculum comprises a set of lesson plans and assignment prompts. These materials are stored on an internal website, along with best practices guidelines informed by the collective wisdom of Harvard colleagues in the Library, the Bureau of Study Counsel, the Honor Council, and other offices. Following is a summary of the training schedule.

Week 1: Learning the Basics

The goal of the first week is to orient Fellows to the Library House Outreach Program, introduce general concepts, and prepare them for the training to come. Mentors welcome their Fellows and introduce them to other librarians and staff members, provide them with a training syllabus, and teach them basic skills and information about the library (e.g., item request functions in the library catalog, locations of different libraries on campus). In the process, Fellows become acquainted with Lamont and Widener Libraries (two of the libraries most closely associated with undergraduate life), practice operating scanners and microfilm readers, and learn how to locate library research contacts and subject liaisons so they can refer questions appropriately. Fostering thoughtful referrals is a hallmark of the program. While Fellows are encouraged to assist their peers in conducting preliminary research, Mentors recommend they turn to librarians for in-depth guidance. Peer Fellows practice referring questions in training through the use of referral scenarios. They are also asked to book a research consultation with a librarian whose expertise is relevant to their coursework.

Additionally, during this first week, Fellows complete a drawing exercise, adapted from a Retrospective Interview Protocol (Foster, 2013), to take stock of how they typically engage in library research and make explicit many of their tacit research habits and assumptions. In accordance with the protocol, Mentors ask Fellows to document the steps they took to complete a recent research project. Drawings vary, but typically, Fellows sketch stick figures to represent individuals involved, write down the names of favorite databases, scribble an image of a book or an article, and insert arrows between discrete tasks. Finally, on their own time, Fellows are asked to identify and photograph two library study spaces of their choosing, which encourages them to explore new library spaces.

Week 2: Understanding What Librarians Do

During the second week, training emphasizes the value of librarians to the scholarly enterprise. The goal is for Fellows to inform their peers about librarians' expertise and services and to utilize the approaches they find most helpful. Fellows experience the receiving end of services such as document delivery, Ask a Librarian, and research guides. They also consult with their chosen research librarian to seek resources related to their own coursework; emulating that interaction, they subsequently engage in a role-playing exercise to practice conducting a reference interview. The exercise involves a deliberate obfuscation of the patron's real need; for example, the patron may state "I am researching the World Cup" but the Fellow will need to dig a bit deeper in order to discover that the patron is actually looking for information around why uniform changes have taken place at various times in World Cup history. Throughout the week, the Fellows consider how they might assess their peers' information needs in light of these experiences. Additionally, Fellows schedule a get-to-know-you meeting with graduate students who serve as writing tutors in the Houses, read about information literacy (see Appendix 6–2 for assigned articles), and learn how to log statistics for queries they receive from their peers.

Week 3: Finding and Evaluating Resources

The third week of training prepares the Fellows to find and thoughtfully use a range of sources and formats. In one exercise, they reverse-engineer a scholarly argument by finding the sources cited, evaluating them, and considering how they function. An essay by Patel (2010) serves as the case study, wherein they judge whether he has used particular sources to: (a) underscore "claims, opinions, or interpretations"; (b) communicate "facts, information, or data"; (c) outline "general concepts"; or (d) supply "comparable instances or versions" of subject matter (Harvey, 2008). In another task, the Fellows receive a hypothetical research question and, coached by their Mentors, practice generating reference source suggestions. After they have finished brainstorming, they examine a selection of those reference books to encounter firsthand the quality and variety of information provided by this genre. In addition to learning about reference and scholarly sources, Mentors introduce Fellows to nontraditional information formats, including media and archival materials. This entails touring relevant libraries on campus.

Week 4: Developing Outreach Strategies

In the fourth week of training, Fellows create an outreach plan for their work in the Houses. They talk with members of the House community, such as administrators and tutors, to learn how they can join existing support networks. During the pilot phase, the Fellows used these conversations to generate a strategy to meet students where they are. After the pilot phase, the Fellows also build their strategy on the work of previous Fellows. For example, the first Fellow decided to reach her House through weekly study breaks and e-mail newsletters, occasional workshops, partnerships with tutors and other members of the House community, and personal research assistance (described in the program implementation section). Once training is complete, the Fellows start to put these plans in place. Ideally, the same services are offered across Houses, although the implementation may differ.

Meanwhile, alongside their Mentors, Fellows develop their searching acumen. With a hypothetical research question in mind, Fellows practice selecting appropriate research databases (including the library catalog), experiment with Library of Congress Subject Headings, keywords, and thesaurus terms, and construct queries with Boolean operators and wildcards. They also take a quiz on locating items listed in a bibliography. Ultimately, the Fellows conceptualize how best to teach one of the strategies they have learned and begin developing a screencast for their peers on a topic of their choosing. Previous screencast topics have included "Boolean Phrases," "Biobibliographies," and "Library of Congress Subject Headings."

Week 5: Ethical and Legal Issues

In the last week of training, Fellows delve into economic, legal, and social issues surrounding the use of information. They read about library patrons' privacy rights in the *Privacy Tool Kit* (American Library Association, 2014), tour the Harvard University Archives to get a sense of its role in preserving institutional history, learn about fair use from a librarian versed in copyright law, and visit the Honor Council to discuss how they can best support academic integrity initiatives on campus. This latter visit helps them identify typical stumbling blocks for students and anticipate issues that may arise. To bolster this experience, Fellows meet with their Mentors to examine a selection of citation manuals and contemplate disciplinary approaches to source documentation. Finally, Fellows finish creating the learning objects they began crafting in week four (see http://tinyurl.com/PRF-Tutorials for examples).

Ongoing Training

In addition to this core training, opportunities for additional learning continue throughout the program. During summer 2015, the Fellows toured eight Harvard libraries to gain a deeper understanding of their services and of how to advise students who might visit them. The tours also facilitated opportunities for supplemental education, such as a tutorial on PubMed. Additionally, Mentor Librarians have arranged guest lectures by a librarian specializing in newspaper research and an associate director of the Derek Bok Center for Teaching and Learning on campus, who held two sessions on micro-teaching techniques (http://bokcenter.harvard.edu/what-microteaching) to improve Fellow-led workshops. As the program expands, the training will scale up accordingly (see the Next Steps section).

IMPLEMENTATION OF THE PROGRAM

After the conclusion of the five-week training, Fellows begin to work in their Houses with the continued assistance and supervision of their Mentor Librarians. The Fellows use four basic outreach efforts designed to bring library awareness and research skills to the undergraduate community: weekly study breaks, informational workshops, newsletters, and personal research assistance.

Study Breaks

Study breaks are held by many organizations at Harvard. They are a way to share information about a cause or group by setting up food and information tables in high-traffic areas in the Houses (such as dining halls). Study breaks are commonly held near meal hours in order to reach the most students, depending on the availability of the coordinating students. The Fellows' breaks offer candy and a half-sheet handout (see Appendix 6–3), outlining specific research tips and tools relating to rotating weekly themes, such as in-person services (e.g., making appointments with research librarians), search strategies (e.g., using Boolean operators), and tips to maintain academic integrity (e.g., organizing notes in a way that reduces the chance of plagiarism).

Students can visit the table, grab a candy and a handout, and leave if they are pressed for time, or they can discuss the week's topic in more detail. Some students come consistently every week for handouts without staying to talk, but others will occasionally sit down and walk through topics step-by-step with the Fellow. This is also an opportunity for Fellows to answer questions their peers might have about the Library House Outreach Program.

Workshops

Along with the weekly study breaks, the Fellows hold two workshops per semester to provide more detailed instruction about library resources. The first of these workshops typically addresses in-depth exploration of one aspect of the research process, for instance, how to determine the area of focus for a project by using scholarly resources. The second workshop is held toward the end of the semester and gives students tools and knowledge to do quality research quickly without resorting to academic dishonesty due to time constraints. The workshops are run in special seminar rooms in each House.

Newsletters

Weekly House-specific newsletters, developed by the Fellows and edited by the Mentors, are sent out over House-wide e-mail lists. The newsletters are updated each week and comprise six sections:

1. An introductory outline;
2. "Study Space of the Week," providing a photo and description of a library study location;
3. "Did you know. . .?," introducing library services that students may not have known existed (e.g., access to special collections);
4. "Quick Tips," providing concrete search tips (e.g., how to use subject headings);
5. "Book Recommendation of the Week," with rotating book recommendations submitted by students in the Fellows' own Houses (via survey);
6. "Upcoming Events."

The newsletter's purpose is to reach out to all students, even if they cannot attend or are not interested in coming to the study breaks. Indeed, students have thanked our Fellows for the useful newsletters even if they have never attended a study break or workshop. The newsletters are House-specific in an attempt to foster a direct connection between the Fellow and their House's community.

Research Assistance

The final element of the program is one-on-one research assistance in each House. The Fellows in each House are available by e-mail to answer students' research questions and point them toward the right library resources or to schedule an in-person consultation. Answers to e-mailed questions are guaranteed within 24 business hours, with either a full answer or an interim response while the Fellow works with their Mentor to provide the student with the right information. The introduction section of the newsletters provides Fellows' e-mail addresses, as do pages on House websites describing the Peer Research Fellow program. Fellows can also share their e-mail address during study breaks if students have questions but do not have time in that moment. If questions are beyond the Fellows' training level, they refer the student to other librarians, typically to subject specialists, who will be able to provide the required assistance. The Fellows reach out to their Mentors for assistance in the referral process if necessary.

EVALUATION OF THE PROGRAM

In concert with the College's mission to emphasize effectiveness over efficiency in House learning communities (Lambert, 2013), the program's service philosophy follows a "white glove treatment" model, that is, placing high importance on interactions with individuals and striving to provide personalized assistance. Thus, program assessments focus more on how well individuals are served by the program rather than how many individuals are served.

The Mentors and Fellows developed assessments for the program in general that they also used specifically during fall 2015 to assess the pilot phase of the program. The pilot assessment of the program's effectiveness was intended to help determine whether or not to enter the next program phase of scaling up to more Houses. The most illuminating elements of the assessment included pretraining and posttraining tests, statistics on Fellow-led events and research questions, statistics on e-mail newsletters, and a House residents survey.

Pre- and Posttraining Tests

The Fellows take a test on library services knowledge prior to and after their training in order to test the training's effectiveness in these areas. The questions (see Appendix 6–1) cover Harvard-specific services and locations, as well as some general library- and research-related skills and concepts. During the pilot phase, the training test revealed that the Fellows made learning gains in the following areas: how to obtain library materials via methods such as interlibrary loan, how to use a microfilm reader, how to recognize differences between various call number systems, how to use Library of Congress Subject Headings, how to use special collections, and knowledge about specific locations and services within the library, such as the Multimedia Lab. The Fellows moved from being unsure about or unaware of these things to having experience with them and being comfortable explaining them to others. This significant change in comfort level indicated that the training was effective. Since the Fellows were students who likely already knew more about library services than their peers, the Mentors surmised that the information covered in the training curriculum would likely be particularly useful to the Fellows' peers, and thus, the program is addressing an area of need for undergraduates.

Query and Event Statistics

The Fellows keep statistics on all of their peer interactions through a tool from Springshare called LibAnalytics. They have one form for their general peer interactions, whether electronic or in person, and another form for events. These forms are used to record numerical data on how many students attend events and make use of Fellows' services. The Fellows also use them to report qualitative data, including questions asked and answers given, plus any referrals made to librarians. The Fellows and Mentors review these questions and answers on a regular basis to see what types of research tasks students seek help for and to assess how well the Fellows assist their peers.

During the pilot assessment, the majority of queries were about finding sources on a particular topic or finding sources of a particular type (e.g., newspaper articles, scholarly articles, data sets). Tracking referrals revealed when and why Fellows directed students to librarians for further assistance. For example, out of 25 queries handled in 2015, seven of them resulted in a librarian referral. Although the number of research queries during the pilot was low, the substance of the questions asked and the depth of support provided by the Fellows point to the effectiveness and importance of their work.

E-mail Newsletters

The Fellows send e-mail newsletters to their peers over House listservs. Newsletters are archived for student access for one academic year on the Fellow website and are permanently archived in the program's MailChimp account for future reference. During the spring 2015 semester, the frequency of these newsletters varied, but in fall 2015, the Fellows started e-mailing the newsletters on a regular, weekly basis. The Fellows explored a few options for delivering the newsletters before settling on MailChimp, which allows users to gather statistics on the number of e-mails opened and links clicked. Because of the delay in choosing MailChimp, data are only available for a six-week period in the late fall of 2015. During that time, the newsletters were opened by 21 percent of students in one House and 22 percent of students in the other, though less than 1 percent of students clicked through the newsletter links in either House. Further data collection across a greater period of time is needed before making a conclusive assessment of newsletter usage. Encouragingly, some students have recommended books to be featured in the newsletters, and Fellows report that students often stop them in the halls to tell them how helpful the newsletters have been.

House Residents Survey

The Fellows conducted a survey of their House peers' use of their services in fall 2015 as another measure of the effectiveness of the program. The survey had a low response rate, and the majority of responses came from people who were unaware of the program. However, the students who made use of Fellow services rated the Fellows highly, and half of them made use of Fellow services multiple times. While the positive interactions with Fellows are encouraging, the lack of awareness of the program as a whole speaks to the need to advertise more effectively. Since the program has only been present in two Houses as part of the pilot phase, advertising across the entire undergraduate population was not possible. As the program expands, formal advertising should increase.

Assessment Summary

Students made the most use of regular Fellow services, such as the weekly study breaks and newsletters, but largely did not attend the one-off events, with the exception of Write Night, a study session offered by Fellows and House writing tutors during reading period. It is difficult to convince students to take time out of their busy schedules to participate in Fellow workshops, though when food is present, attendance goes up. The Fellows' flexibility works well with the different types of support that students appreciate: some students like to take study break handouts on a regular basis; some like to go over resources in-person; others prefer to read newsletters or e-mail questions. Besides the formal assessment methods discussed, the Fellows have also received informal feedback about the helpfulness of their services. While only a small number of students have been served so far, the Fellows filled an important need for the peers they did reach. After reviewing the pilot assessment, Library Administrators decided to continue the program and scale it up to serve more Houses, with the understanding that new initiatives take time to be recognized and for word of mouth to spread. As the program continues, the presence of the Fellows should become a recognized part of student life in the Houses.

IMPLICATIONS AND LESSONS LEARNED

Supportive Community

The greatest impact of the Library House Outreach Program emerges in the relationship between the Fellows and the Mentor Librarians. Through regular contact during training sessions, weekly meetings, and e-mails, the Fellows and Mentors build a supportive learning community. Aside from weekly meetings, Fellows regularly send drafts of handouts or newsletters to their Mentors for feedback. Thus, the Fellows have the opportunity to receive in-depth guidance on any difficult questions they have received, while the Mentors receive valuable perspectives on library services and the undergraduate experience—information they can share with colleagues to inform related programming. Because typical student–librarian interactions have largely been somewhat formal and discontinuous, the opportunity for students and librarians to work together on an individual, ongoing basis has been highly rewarding.

Student Benefits

The program training directly benefits the Fellows themselves in a number of ways. First, through the training, the Fellows' own research skills and ability to complete research assignments for classes improved appreciably. Throughout their training and tenure, the Fellows learn several skills through the program not necessarily taught in traditional academic classes: how to design websites, create newsletters, make lesson plans, build screencasts, lead workshops, conduct reference interviews, interact with peers in a customer service setting, create marketing materials, and so on. The Fellows reap a long-term benefit from these experiences, which they can carry forward post-graduation into new jobs.

Student Input and Advertising

The benefits of the Library House Outreach Program ripple outward. Fellows often provide input on the projects of librarians beyond the program, including advice about whether undergraduates would be interested in a given event topic, ideas for best times to hold an event, and suggestions on how to market the event to undergraduates. In addition, the ability of the Fellows to send out advertisements over their House lists strengthens the library's capacity to reach undergraduates.

Student Investment

Mentors find that inviting the Fellows to help determine how the program should run is a better option than a more prescriptive approach. The Fellows are personally invested in the program and have as much impact in shaping it as the Mentors. Between the spring and fall semesters of 2015, for instance, the Fellows played a key role in altering and reinventing the structure of the program. Originally, the program relied on weekly office hours (an open time for students to come and ask their Fellow questions) as the main form of outreach. However, the office hours were not drawing as many students as initially hoped for, likely because students were not aware how Fellows could assist them. To remedy this, the Fellows suggested replacing office hours with study breaks, focusing on discrete themes of relevance to undergraduates. This format drew a greater number of students each week and supplied students with information they may not have known to ask for, but which they recognized as useful once provided. The Fellows also worked to improve the quality and formatting of their weekly newsletters and provided guiding feedback and original ideas to shape the program website. Their observations and understanding of their fellow students have been essential to the program's success.

Unique Features

Libraries considering a similar program should take advantage of the unique features of their institution. Harvard is based on a residential House system that seeks to provide both community and academic support to undergraduate students, so it made sense to take advantage of these strengths. Many other academic and social support programs already had presences in the Houses; thus, the Fellows fit into a familiar model of service. However, for other institutions, especially smaller ones, it may make more sense to try a peer-outreach program based in a student center or another area of campus where students already receive academic or other types of support.

Partnerships

The Library House Outreach Program committee spoke to successful programs on campus that already used a peer advising model, such as the House-based Resource Efficiency Program, the Advising Programs Office, and the Bureau of Study Counsel, in order to hear their advice on what works and also to acquire partners moving forward. Partnership is also important within the library itself. Giving colleagues exposure to students in the program through additional training will add their valuable expertise and also clarify that students extend librarians' reach rather than substitute for librarians.

NEXT STEPS

Following the pilot assessment, the Mentors and Fellows judged that the Fellows handled the level of work in their individual Houses very well and could easily expand their outreach to the other two Houses in a three-House neighborhood. With the employment of four Fellows guided by four Mentor Librarians, the program could expand to all 12 Houses with a continued focus on individual interactions and personalized service but at a more manageable level and a lower cost than originally envisioned under the one Fellow to one House model. As the program expands, the Mentor–Fellow training will continue, along with weekly meetings of the Mentor Librarians to coordinate work among the different neighborhoods.

The program continues to evolve, as the Mentors and Fellows gather event ideas from other libraries and from students themselves. The User Research Center at Harvard Library held a brainstorming session in spring 2016 for undergraduate House residents about what they would expect from the Library House Outreach Program, to see if there are additional ways to meet their needs or better market the program. Fellow-led workshops may be reconsidered, as these have had low attendance. As new Fellows join the program, they will continue to help shape it through their unique perspectives and experiences. The Library House Outreach Program should flourish alongside Harvard's House Renewal initiative to provide a meaningful and sustainable bridge between the Library and students' residential lives.

REFERENCES

American Library Association. (2014). *Privacy tool kit.* Retrieved from http://www.ala.org/advocacy/privacyconfidentiality/toolkitsprivacy/privacy

Association of College and Research Libraries (2014). *Revised draft framework for information literacy for higher education.* Retrieved from http://acrl.ala.org/ilstandards/wp-content/uploads/2014/02/Framework-for-IL-for-HE-Draft-2.pdf

Barber, G. (2009). SOS—Supporting other students: The role of student library ambassadors at Southampton Solent University. *SCONUL Focus, 45*, 15–19.

Barnes, N., & Peyton, G. (2007). Reaching out to the net generation on campus: Promoting the MSU Libraries in the residence halls. *Public Services Quarterly, 2*(4), 47–68. doi: 10.1300/J295v02n04_03

Bodemer, B. B. (2014). They can and they should: Undergraduates providing peer reference and instruction. *College & Research Libraries, 75*(2),162–178. doi: 10.5860/crl12-411

Bruce, C. (1997). *The seven faces of information literacy*. Adelaide: Auslib Press.

Foster, N. F. (2013). *Studying students: A second look*. Chicago: Association of College and Research Libraries.

Foster, N. F., & Gibbons, S. L. (2007). *Studying students: The undergraduate research project at the University of Rochester*. Chicago: Association of College & Research Libraries.

Gilroy, S. (2007). *Project Information Literacy: The Harvard context*. Unpublished summary, Harvard College Library, Cambridge, MA.

Harvard College. (n.d.) *Mission, vision, and history*. Retrieved from https://college.harvard.edu/about/history

Harvard College Institutional Research. (2012). *Results of the 2012 senior survey*. Harvard University, Cambridge, MA.

Harvey, G. (2008). *Writing with sources: A guide for students* (2nd ed.). Indianapolis, IN: Hackett Publishing Company.

Head, A. J. (2012). *Learning curve: How college graduates solve information problems once they join the workplace*. Retrieved from http://projectinfolit.org/images/pdfs/pil_fall2012_workplacestudy_fullreport_revised.pdf

Head, A. J. (2013). *Learning the ropes: How freshmen conduct course research once they enter college*. Retrieved from http://projectinfolit.org/images/pdfs/pil_2013_freshmenstudy_fullreport.pdf

Head, A. J., & Eisenberg, M. B. (2009). *Finding context: What today's college students say about conducting research in the digital age*. Retrieved from http://projectinfolit.org/images/pdfs/pil_progressreport_2_2009.pdf

Head, A. J., Van Hoeck, M., Eschler, J., & Fullerton, S. (2013). What information competencies matter in today's workplace? *Library and Information Research, 37*(114), 74–104. Retrieved from http://www.lirgjournal.org.uk/lir/ojs/index.php/lir/index

Jisc. (2014). Developing digital literacies (InfoNet kit). Retrieved from https://www.jisc.ac.uk/guides/developing-digital-literacieshttp://www.jiscinfonet.ac.uk/infokits/digital-literacies

Lambert, C. (2013, November–December). Learning, and life, in the houses: The singular character of the college's residences, now in renewal. *Harvard Magazine*, n.p. Retrieved from http://harvardmagazine.com/2013/11/learning-and-life-in-the-houses

Patel, R. (2010). *The value of nothing: How to reshape market society and redefine democracy*. New York: Picador.

Riehle, C. F., & Witt, M. (2009). Librarians in the hall: Instructional outreach in campus residences. *College & Undergraduate Libraries, 16*(2), 107–121. doi:10.1080/10691310902958616

Rudin, P. (2008). No fixed address: The evolution of outreach library services on university campuses. *Reference Librarian, 49*(1), 55–75. doi:10.1080/02763870802103761

Strothmann, M., & Antell, K. (2010). The live-in librarian: Developing library outreach to university residence halls. *Reference & User Services Quarterly 50*(1), 48–58. Retrieved from https://journals.ala.org/rusq/index

APPENDIX 6–1: PRE- AND POST- TRAINING TESTS

Included below is an excerpt from the test administered to Fellows at the beginning of and the end of their five-week training period. In addition, the test also included questions about Harvard-specific services and locations.

For the following skills and strategies involved in locating and obtaining a source, please indicate whether you:

- aren't sure or don't know how to do it;
- have done it;
- know how to do it;
- are comfortable explaining that skill to a peer.

Please check all the bubbles that apply. It is conceivable that it might make sense to even check all four of the bubbles for a single skill, so please be as accurate and honest as possible!

	Not Sure/ Don't Know	***Have Done***	***Know How***	***Comfortable Explaining***
Use citation management tools such as RefWorks or Zotero				
Request items via Interlibrary Loan				
Use Harvard's "Ask a Librarian" service				
Use a microform/microfilm reader				
Use online research guides to find relevant sources				
Assess the quality of and appropriately use sources in a research project				
Track down a source from a citation				

If you would like to ask questions about the above skills or elaborate on any of your answers, please enter those here:

Are you familiar with the following:

	Not Familiar	***Somewhat Familiar***	***Familiar***	***Comfortable Explaining***
Plagiarism issues				
Copyright issues				

If you would like to ask questions about the above skills or elaborate on any of your answers, please enter those here:

APPENDIX 6–2: INFORMATION LITERACY READINGS

Alvarez, B., & Dimmock, N. (2013). Faculty expectations of student research. In Foster, N. F. (Ed.), *Studying students: A second look* (pp. 1–6). Chicago: Association of College and Research Libraries.

Asher, A. D., & Duke, L. M. (2012). Searching for answers: Student research behavior at Illinois Wesleyan University. In Duke, L. M., & Asher, A.D. (Eds.), *College libraries and student culture: What we now know* (pp. 71–85). Chicago: American Library Association.

Burns, V., & Harper, K. (2013). Asking students about their research. In Foster, N. F. (Ed.), *Studying students: A second look* (pp. 7–15). Chicago: Association of College and Research Libraries.

Head, A. J. (2012). *Learning curve: How college graduates solve information problems once they join the workplace.* Retrieved from http://projectinfolit.org/images/pdfs/pil_fall2012_workplacestudy_fullreport_revised.pdf

Head, A. J. (2016). *Staying smart: How today's graduates continue to learn once they complete college.* Retrieved from http://projectinfolit.org/images/pdfs/2016_lifelonglearning_full%20report.pdf

Head, A. J., Van Hoeck, M., Eschler, J., & Fullerton, S. (2013). What information competencies matter in today's workplace? *Library and Information Research, 37*(114), 74, 91, 95. Retrieved from http://www.lirgjournal.org.uk/lir/ojs/index.php/lir/index

APPENDIX 6–3: STUDY BREAK HANDOUTS

This is an example of a handout students might receive at a study break. Other handout topics include how to get free textbooks through the library, Boolean operators, how to contact research librarians, citation management tools, and so on.

Search Strategies of the Week: Subject headings and using the library to decide on a concentration!

<table>
<tr>
<td>

Subject Headings are an incredibly useful trick to streamline the research process. They are a series of keywords, like tags, that are assigned to each source and make that source searchable by those terms.

For example, if I was interested in studying shellshock, I might be tempted to type "shellshock" into a basic keyword search. But what if shellshock doesn't show up in the title? Or anywhere else in the citation information? I won't see those sources in the search results? And what if shellshock is only one of many terms (e.g. combat fatigue, war neuroses, and cowardice) that have been used to describe the same disorder? I can use the Library of Congress Subject Heading (which happens to be "War Neuroses") in an advanced search box in order to pull up all sources about the topic that I'm truly interested in!

But how to find that subject heading? You can either find an applicable source via a keyword search and look at the subject heading used in its citation information or you can look up the appropriate term through these nifty online PDFs of the Library of Congress Subject Headings. If you look up shellshock, it will show you that "War Neuroses" is the actual term you want. Use this trick to quickly get results that are actually applicable to your project!

</td>
<td>

Attention Sophomores!
Did you know that there are ways to use the library to help you decide on which concentration to pursue?

1) Talk with the library liaison for the departments you are interested in.
2) Check out the research guides for various subjects/classes/departments to see what the field is all about.
3) Browse through current periodicals in Lamont and Cabot libraries or check out a book in the *Very Short Introduction* series to see what's being studied currently and what still needs researching!
4) Glance through the collection of Hoopes prize-winning student essays on display in Lamont right next to the new books section.
5) Search HOLLIS+ for books about career paths in any given field. Examples of recommended search terms are:
—anthropology and "vocational guidance"
—social sciences and "vocational guidance"

Visit projects.iq.harvard.edu/prf to access the online, hyperlinked version of this handout!

</td>
</tr>
</table>

7

Library Living Learning Connection at Indiana University of Pennsylvania Libraries

Theresa McDevitt and Malaika M. Turner

Throughout college and university campuses, academic libraries and residence life offices share the goal of supporting students' academic success by creating and promoting the use of educationally rich environments where students can prosper. This overlap in mission can lead to productive collaborations that promote library use. For the past five years, Indiana University of Pennsylvania (IUP) Libraries worked with the IUP Campus Housing office to recruit and educate residence hall Peer Educators to assist with library outreach and instruction. This program embeds library instruction sessions in the annual orientation for new residence life Peer Educators, which prepares these Peer Educators to create and deliver library-related bulletin boards and educational programming within the residence halls. Our program also involves feedback sessions with members of the Residence Hall Association and the development of monthly and yearly awards for residence hall library-themed bulletin boards. This chapter will discuss the development, goals, and impact of the program and provide advice on how it can be mirrored at other institutions.

INSTITUTIONAL CONTEXT

Indiana University of Pennsylvania (IUP) is a comprehensive, doctoral/research university and is among the largest of the 14 universities in the Pennsylvania State System of Higher Education. It is accredited by the Middle States Commission on Higher Education and in fall 2014 had approximately 14,369 undergraduate and graduate students coming from 44 states and 61 countries (Indiana University of Pennsylvania, 2016).

IUP recently completed a new strategic plan, which centers on the preparation of all students for "success in work and life, in addition to academic success" (Division of Academic Affairs, Indiana University of Pennsylvania, 2016b). IUP tracks student success in a variety of ways, including assessing Expected Undergraduate Learning Outcomes. All academic and support programs are required to develop measures to assess these student learning outcomes and implement action plans for program improvement. Some of these outcomes specifically address information literacy skill development (Division of

Academic Affairs, Indiana University of Pennsylvania, 2016a). IUP Libraries are therefore very invested in connecting resources, spaces, and services to the university's effort to support student success and the achievement of Expected Undergraduate Learning Outcomes.

The Libraries' mission includes offering "support for teaching, research, and the personal enrichment of members of the IUP community," which includes information literacy skill development through "library orientation activities, formal and informal bibliographic instruction" so as to "enable students to meet current academic requirements and to become informed and productive members of society" (Libraries Administration, Indiana University of Pennsylvania, 2016). The library instruction and outreach program operates year-round, from summer orientation sessions through finals preparation activities offered at the end of the semester. To make the most of limited time, staff, and funding, our outreach program makes every effort to partner with campus offices to reach students, support the development of the Expected Undergraduate Learning Outcomes, and spread the word about how our libraries can help students. One of our most valued partners is the Office of Housing, Residential Living, and Dining, our Campus Housing.

Campus Housing provides accommodations, dining, educational programming, and other support programs for the 27 percent of students who live on campus. The majority of residential students are in their first year due to a student residency requirement that mandates all students live on campus during their first two semesters unless they qualify to have the requirement waived. All students who live on campus enjoy the benefits of a recently completed residence hall reconstruction project, which resulted in eight new residential buildings featuring learning support spaces for programs and activities that facilitate IUP's living learning initiatives. Many of the residential communities are themed to academic colleges and supported by clusters for specific subject disciplines.

Just as working with campus partners is central to IUP Libraries' outreach initiatives, partnerships and collaboration are central to the goals of Campus Housing and its living learning programs (Office of Housing, Residential Living, and Dining, Indiana University of Pennsylvania, 2016). Campus Housing works closely with campus partners, including teaching faculty who might offer discipline-related extracurricular programing in the residence halls, representatives from Career Services, International Education, the Writing Center, and of course, the Libraries.

Personnel from the Libraries and Campus Housing recognize the overlap in our missions and share an interest in collaborating with campus partners when possible to achieve our goals. Administrative directives relating to the importance of divisions moving outside of "silos" and a push for increased efforts to include students in educational support initiatives have also encouraged us to work together. A beneficial collaboration between the two offices has developed, which is most clearly evidenced in our Library Living Learning Program, in which librarians work with Campus Housing Peer Educators to inform students in the residence halls of library support for academic success.

BACKGROUND OF THE PROGRAM

Campus Housing has a long history of working with student leaders to create optimum living and learning environments for IUP students. They recognize the unique contributions that Peer Educators make to the learning of other students, and the positive social and educational impact of serving as a peer educator on the students who offer this service, especially in terms of the acquisition of an expanded knowledge base and the development of leadership skills. The Peer Educators employed by Campus Housing work as Community Assistants and Academic Success Mentors.

Community Assistants live in the residence halls and facilitate the personal and academic growth and development of residential students. They have a variety of duties, including assisting in the enforcement of hall regulations, building a sense of community, and supporting student retention. They are also charged with developing and holding educational and social programming. Academic Success Mentors differ from the Community Assistants in that they often do not live in the residence halls and their sole focus is on academic initiatives and providing academic assistance to at-risk students. This is done through the provision of workshops (monthly academic resource programs), one-on-one consultations, passive programming (such as library-related educational bulletin boards or displays), and working with other offices to improve services to students. There are approximately 60–90 Community Assistants and 10–15 Academic Success Mentors in a given year, depending upon the number of students living in the halls that year.

In 2010, IUP Libraries outreach personnel began an intentional collaboration with Campus Housing professional employees to increase the awareness of students living in the residence halls (many of which were first-year students) of the benefits of library use. Almost immediately, library personnel became aware of the educational roles of Campus Housing Peer Educators and their unique ability to assist the Libraries in better connecting residential students to library services, resources, and spaces. This led to the development of the Library Living Learning Program.

In the beginning, the lack of a full understanding of how our different divisions operated, the extent to which our missions overlapped, and what opportunities might be available for efficient, effective, and inexpensive partnering limited collaborative activities. Increased understanding of the mission and day-to-day operations of both divisions developed over time. This was fostered by inclusion of library personnel on campus housing committees (e.g., the Advisory Board for Living Learning Excellence), and shared assessment projects (e.g., the Assessment in Action Project, Middle States Review Committees). These interactions increased understanding and built personal relationships and trust between permanent employees and Peer Educators from both divisions. The program developed more each year in a series of gradual, small steps. It is still evolving. As part of this evolution, the library moved from passively supplying residence halls with general library promotional materials to more active initiatives, such as embedding a library instruction session in the annual Campus Housing peer educator orientation. The transition to more interactive approaches was facilitated by an Assessment in Action grant, which was jointly awarded to Campus Housing and the IUP Libraries (American College and Research Libraries, 2013). This project investigated how we could collaboratively create meaningful experiences for residents in IUP's living learning communities to: (a) increase usage of the physical libraries, (b) create a physical and virtual library presence in residence halls, and (c) build the information literacy skills of students living in the residence halls through residential-based programming.

By the end of the Assessment in Action grant period, we had developed a solid program consisting of annual training for Peer Educators, peer educator support for library-themed educational bulletin boards and programs, and annual focus groups with Peer Educators.

We have also developed an award for library-related educational displays in the residence halls to recognize and reward the efforts of Campus Housing Peer Educators.

Objectives of the Library Living Learning Program

Professional staff objectives include the following:

- Library employees increase their understanding of Campus Housing and the broader Division of Student Affairs' mission, methods, and practices.
- Campus Housing employees increase their understanding of the Libraries' mission, methods, and practices.

Student learning outcomes include the following:

- Peer Educators increase their knowledge of library offerings and deepen their learning as they create library-related programs and bulletin boards for the residence halls.
- Residence hall students build information literacy skills and knowledge of library support for student success through peer-generated residential-based educational programming.

Library outreach objectives include the following:

- Creating a physical and virtual library presence in residence halls to support student success
- Increasing usage of the physical libraries and our services
- Forging closer connections with students to gather information to use in planning library spaces, programs, and services to better support student success
- Enlisting Campus Housing Peer Educators to pilot outreach collaborations that could be used again with other campus partners

Funding and Staffing

Peer Educators are hired and supervised by Campus Housing personnel, so there are no library personnel costs associated with this program. The only cost is the time of the librarians who act as liaisons to the program and those minimal expenditures related to materials purchased for educational programs and library giveaways, or to fund the library bulletin board awards.

Peer Educators are recruited via e-mail announcements to students as well as faculty, staff, and administrators who might recommend students for the program. Interviews are conducted by Campus Housing professional staff. Successful candidates are offered positions to be Community Assistants or Academic Success Mentors, depending upon their characteristics, qualifications, and the personnel needs of the residence halls.

TRAINING AND PREPARATION OF PEER EDUCATORS

All Campus Housing Peer Educators must undergo further training before they can begin their work. Community Assistants must complete Community Assistant seminar training, and Academic Success Mentors must complete a one-credit course, "The Role of the Peer Educator," which is taught by a faculty member from Department of Developmental Studies and developed in coordination with Campus Housing. All training supplements the general August orientation that all new and continuing Peer Educators complete.

All Campus Housing Peer Educators who will be working in a given year must participate in a two-week orientation and training program held in August prior to the opening of the residence halls. It is facilitated by Campus Housing professionals and veteran Peer Educators and is designed to build community and leadership skills, and develop a basic knowledge of the services and resources available on campus to support students' academic success. Many campus academic and social support units provide sessions during the training, including the Office of International Education, Advising and Testing, the Developmental Studies Office, Financial Aid, and the Career and Professional Development Center. As a key stakeholder among campus partners, the Libraries also deliver a one-hour instruction session as part of peer educator orientation.

The library-specific training session is provided by the outreach librarian and generally takes place in the library. The session is designed to share basic information about library services, resources, and spaces that support student success to Community Assistants and Academic Success Mentors who work directly with the students so they will (1) be aware of how libraries support students, (2) have a familiar face to contact when they encounter students who can benefit from librarian help or library services, and (3) stimulate the creation of library-themed bulletin boards and educational programs for the residence halls in the upcoming year.

The types of training session offered to Peer Educators have varied over the years. The library can only take advantage of the opportunities offered so the session must be developed each year to mesh with the themes and design of the overall Campus Housing orientation. For example, in 2012, the request was for something challenging and active, so the library session consisted of a library discovery orientation similar to the one described in McDevitt and Stilwell (2011), in which students choose a library space or service, investigate it, and then introduce it to their peers in a library tour.

In 2014, the library was only offered a table at a "Student Success Expo." The expo replaced a previous format that offered individual sessions from various academic service providers on campus. On this occasion, the library set up a table that included handouts on various library services and resources, free pens and highlighters, and a notebook of suggested topics for library-related displays or educational programs that Peer Educators could easily adapt for use as part of their educational programming work.

In 2015, the training took the form of an Amazing Race scavenger hunt. Fashioned after the *Amazing Race* television program, in this game students worked in teams to correctly answer 10 randomly assigned questions about library places, resources, and services. The first group of students to complete the challenge was declared the winners of the game and awarded library T-shirts. Pictures of all winners were tweeted to the library twitter account (McDevitt & Fuller, 2015).

In addition to the formal training sessions offered, librarians also provide less-structured training through occasional visits to Community Assistant and Academic Success Mentor weekly meetings. On these infrequent occasions (only once or twice a semester at most), librarians drop by for short visits to ask for participation in upcoming library educational programs or events or remind Peer Educators of what the library could do for students at that point in the semester. Librarians also meet individually with Peer Educators to develop library-themed bulletin boards and provide residence hall programs.

Our training session has been different almost every year and is developed in light of best practices and feedback from the students, and in response to themes, trends, and advice provided by Campus Housing professional staff and Peer Educators. Library educational games have yielded the most enthusiastic response from the participants. In addition, articles from the library literature about outreach to students in the residence halls have been beneficial in planning library-specific training sessions and programming for students in the residence halls (Cummings, 2007; Strothmann & Antell, 2010).

IMPLEMENTATION OF THE PROGRAM

Management and supervision of Peer Educators are handled by Campus Housing professional employees and graduate assistants. Librarians are available to provide support and help develop and deliver educational programs when needed, but provide no direct supervision.

Community Assistants live in the residence halls and have responsibilities for promoting the development of community, safety, and security, in addition to more incidental educational support. They are required to create at least one informational wall display a month. Academic Success Mentors may or may not live in the halls, and their role is exclusively to provide academic mentoring to academically high-risk students who may, or may not, live in the residence halls. They are expected to provide educational programming of some kind, though the number and type are not specified. In spite of these differences in their roles, there are many commonalities in the work of Community Assistants and Academic Success Mentors.

Both groups of Peer Educators are required to attend weekly staff meetings with their supervisors, which sometimes include other Community Assistants and Academic Success Mentors. Such staff meetings are excellent opportunities for librarians to meet with Peer Educators, remind them of how the Libraries can help students, tell them about library special events or services, and offer to provide specific assistance. Residence Directors may require weekly one-on-one meetings to gauge the peers' progress in outreach and interaction activities with students.

Both groups have advertised office hours and must otherwise be available to their residents and track their interaction with residents in some form. Community Assistants keep a weekly journal and Academic Success Mentors record statistics on the type and quality of interactions with mentees.

Peer Educators are also required to create educational bulletin boards and/or programs educational in nature. Programs can be active or passive. Active programs are structured events with a goal/objective, bound by place and time, and facilitated by a staff member or invited presenter. Passive programming has little structure, minimal planning, and interaction. These are informational in nature and are typically designed to raise awareness. They include decoration of bulletin boards, wall panels, or doors with educational information. Another example of a passive program is distributing information to students in the lobby as they enter a building. Some communities require an outside presenter be involved. Often active programs are developed collaboratively between Peer Educators.

Resident Directors review programs for quality and content. In order for a program to be approved, peers have to make concerted efforts to create and market a program. If passive programs are of dubious quality, changes are requested and must be addressed before credit is awarded. Active programs require Peer Educators to submit a post-programming survey.

Community Assistants and Academic Success Mentors who create displays are also eligible to submit educational bulletin boards and programs related to the library bulletin board award contest. This content is designed to encourage Peer Educators to choose the library as the theme of their displays and programs. Awards are given out monthly and yearly. To enter, applicants e-mail images of library-related bulletin boards they created in the residence halls to the outreach librarian. In the e-mail, they are asked to include a short narrative on where and when the bulletin board was available, what they hoped students would learn from viewing the displays, and what, if anything, they felt they learned from creating the display.

EVALUATION OF THE PROGRAM

Evaluation of the program has included surveys given after peer educator orientation training sessions; about 75–100 Peer Educators attend the library training sessions held each year in August. We have always gathered informal feedback at the conclusion of the session. Recently, however, we have been moving to more formal methods of assessment, including post-training surveys and the collection of student reflections from those who submitted entries for the residence hall library bulletin board award.

Surveys given after the 2015 library orientation training, the Amazing Race game, suggested the training was effective. Students reported after playing the game that they felt more comfortable using the Libraries, had learned things that they felt would be helpful to share with residence hall students, and felt library staff were helpful and willing to answer questions. Some student comments included "Great, helpful, fun way of getting to know the library," "It was cool," "I loved how interactive the game was," and "It kept my attention." In addition, there was some constructive feedback, including "I think it's important to try and somehow incorporate a method for retaining the information as some of it got swept away in the excitement of the competition." The feedback helped us tweak the game for use with other groups including a first-year orientation session with IUP's Honor's College students. Also, in fall 2015, on two occasions residence hall Peer Educators asked librarians to offer the game for students in their halls. This suggests that they felt it was a valuable and enjoyable learning experience.

Annual focus groups with the Residence Hall Association (the governing body of the Campus Housing, which includes some Community Assistant and Academic Success Mentors) provided valuable information on how the Library Living Learning Program could be improved and how librarians might better connect with and inform residence hall students. The first year we held focus groups at the beginning of the fall semester. At that session, the Peer Educators requested additional formal library orientations, so we structured some of their meetings around formal library tours and discussions in the library.

More recently, we have met with the Residence Hall Association at the end of the semester during National Library Week as a way of gathering additional insight, but also to show our appreciation for the Peer Educators' assistance in directing students to the library and developing bulletin boards and programs relating to library services, resources, and programs. Such sessions have yielded useful feedback. Suggestions offered during such sessions included a request that we create notebooks with basic library information resources and ideas for possible library-related bulletin board topics and programs and make them available in residence hall resource rooms. On another occasion, this group helped us choose the type of library-themed giveaways we should offer to students who attend library programming. Finally, one of the best ideas that came out of the Residence Hall Association meetings was the idea to offer a library residence hall bulletin board award.

The library bulletin board award has increased the Libraries' ability to track the number of library-related bulletin boards in the residence halls and increased peer educator interest in doing such passive programs. It also is a way for the Libraries to recognize the quality of the Peer Educators' work and show our appreciation.

This was the first year of the award and we are happy with the results. We received 12 submissions, which we believe represents an increased number of displays in the residence halls. They were very creative and dealt with a variety of topics, including the citation station submission that shared the basics of two bibliographic citation styles and two interactive displays that not only provided basic information about how the library can help but also invited students in the halls to share their favorite library tips and books.

Feedback from Peer Educators on what they felt they had learned, if anything, was also sought as part of the submission process. Peer Educators most often reported that they felt they had learned something more about the library in preparing the display. For example, a peer educator who developed a display on reference assistance was happy to report that she didn't know about the library's Bring Your Assignment service prior to preparing the display and that she would use it in the future. Another peer educator who created a display on bibliographic citation styles reported making the display helped her learn about bibliographic styles that she had not known about before.

IMPLICATIONS AND LESSONS LEARNED

At a time of shrinking budgets and increasing need for both efficiency and effectiveness in programming, colleges and universities are encouraging the development of cross-campus partnerships to achieve goals. Partnering with students to improve their learning and career potential is also very common. Our Library Living Learning Program is an example of both.

A library peer educator program run exclusively by the library would, in order to be successful, necessitate advance planning, dedicated professional employees to supervise the program, and careful selection, training, and supervision. Working with the residence hall program (or any other program that already uses peer educators to provide academic support to students) offers efficiency and economy not possible in a library-only endeavor. One impact of our collaboration with Campus Housing has been the recognition of the efficiency of such partnerships. IUP Libraries now has increased interest in seeking these collaborations with other interested campus partners.

Another impact of the collaboration between IUP Libraries and Campus Housing has been the opportunity for librarians, residence hall professionals, and Peer Educators to explore the mission and objectives of our units and discover how they overlap. This has allowed us to learn from each other's successful practices. For example, librarians learned how to conduct assessment relating to co-curricular learning that can demonstrate library value. We also learned ways to engage students by working with Peer Educators and professional staff.

We have discovered that extending an invitation to Peer Educators to join in planning for training and outreach activities is an essential step to any successful effort to engage and inform students. Peer Educators bring insights informed by their experience as successful students, unique skill sets (particularly in connection with new media), and discipline-specific expertise. Advice and opinions of Peer Educators have allowed us to improve upon the activities we offer at general new student orientation sessions. Some of these activities have later been adopted by teaching faculty for class use or extra credit opportunities.

As a result of developing library-themed bulletin board displays and educational programs, Peer Educators indicate that they have learned more about libraries and that they believe they will use this information in the future. In addition, offering a larger number of library displays and educational programs in the residence halls means that students who live there have a greater opportunity to learn about library offerings and take advantage of them.

We would urge other libraries to reach out to campus housing or any campus office that employs peer educators to provide academic support to students to attempt to build similar partnerships. While helping the students they serve, peer educators can increase their knowledge of library resources, spaces, and services, which can help them be successful as well. Equally valuable is that when libraries connect with peer educators and include their insights into planning for library programs and services, it can help libraries remain relevant. Potential benefits are significant for professional employees, peer educators, and other students.

NEXT STEPS

We expect that in the future our program will continue to develop, but will still include existing essential elements, such as the library peer educator orientation session, holding meetings with the Residence Hall Association, and offering awards for excellent work. The annual training is something that has been very successful and will be continued as long as we are invited to provide it. It takes little investment in staff time and money and creates a connection between librarians and peer educators, in addition to increasing peer educators' knowledge of the library. Receiving approval from our institutional review board to more formally assess the outcomes of this training is one goal for the coming year. We are also planning to attempt to hold additional formal meetings between librarians and Peer Educators over the course of the year.

The library bulletin board award is a new addition to our program, but it has been fairly successful. We will work to increase awareness of the award and hopefully increase submissions for the next year. In the future, we will also ask Peer Educators to submit their bulletin boards images as a PowerPoint slide so we can put them on the digital signage in the residence halls across the campus and in the library. We also plan to more formally assess the learning outcomes associated with the creation of the displays and the impact of viewing them.

We recognize that we should do more to measure the educational impact of the Library Living Learning Program as a whole, both on the Peer Educators that we have direct contacts with and on the students they serve. Planning in this area will take place in collaboration with Campus Housing staff, who share our interest in achieving learning and measuring it.

Regardless of the future steps that our program will take, it is clearly one that is in keeping with trends of higher education, which encourage collaboration across divisions and the development of increased opportunities for Peer Educators to join in efforts to support student success. Effective and efficient and requiring little expenditure in staff time and money, it allows both the Libraries and Campus Housing to achieve our goals as we learn from the successful practices of each division. Perhaps most importantly, it brings us in closer contact with Peer Educators, and through them undergraduate students at large, boosting our ability to serve them and support student learning outcomes.

REFERENCES

American College and Research Libraries. (2013). *Assessment in Action: Academic libraries and student success.* Retrieved from http://www.ala.org/acrl/AiA.ACRL

Cummings, L. U. (2007). Bursting out of the box: Outreach to the millennial generation through student services programs. *Reference Services Review, 35*(2), 285–295. doi:10.1108/00907320710749191

Division of Academic Affairs, Indiana University of Pennsylvania. (2016a). *EUSLOs and measures.* Retrieved from http://www.iup.edu/academicaffairs/student-learning-outcomes-assessment/euslos-and-measures/

Division of Academic Affairs, Indiana University of Pennsylvania. (2016b). *IUP strategic plan, 2015–2020.* Retrieved from http://www.iup.edu/templates_old/page.aspx?id=184074

Indiana University of Pennsylvania. (2016). *IUP at a glance.* Retrieved from http://www.iup.edu/about/iup/

Libraries Administration, Indiana University of Pennsylvania. (2016). *Mission of the IUP Libraries.* Retrieved from http://www.iup.edu/library/administration/

Office of Housing, Residential Living, and Dining, Indiana University of Pennsylvania. (2016). *Living learning.* Retrieved from http://www.iup.edu/livinglearning/

McDevitt, T. (2013). Everyone likes a challenge: Getting students' attention with interactive games and authentic assignments. *Pennsylvania Libraries: Research and Practice, 1*(2), 149. doi:10.5195/palrap.2013.25

McDevitt, T., & Fuller, B. (2015, fall). Races make amazing library orientations. *Western Pennsylvania/West Virginia ACRL Fall Newsletter*, 5. Retrieved from http://www.wpwvcacrl.org/newsletter.html

McDevitt, T., & Stilwell, R. (2011). Library's best beach ball. In T. McDevitt (Ed.), *Let the games begin: Engaging students with field-tested interactive information literacy instruction* (pp. 23–24). New York: Neal-Schuman.

Strothmann, M., & Antell, K. (2010). The live-in librarian: Developing library outreach to university residence halls. *Reference & User Services Quarterly, 50*(1), 48–58. Retrieved from https://journals.ala.org/rusq/index

8

Peer Research Coaches at the University of Texas at San Antonio Libraries

Tyler A. Dunn, Jan H. Kemp, and Ellen V. Blumberg

The Peer Research Coaches Program at the University of Texas at San Antonio (UTSA) Libraries places a strong emphasis on student outreach. Since 2011, the Libraries have received funding from local sources to implement a student employment program with the goal of contributing to the success of fellow students who are demographically at risk for not completing a bachelor's degree. Peer Coaches themselves may also be demographically at risk, but this status is not a requirement for selection as a Peer Coach. The program recruits outgoing, friendly students with strong academic backgrounds and employs them as Peer Coaches. An experiential training program prepares them to provide peer-to-peer services including outreach, reference, and instruction. The program is evaluated by several methods, including tracking the academic persistence of Peer Coaches. The chapter includes lessons learned and ideas for future development of this and other peer-assisted learning programs.

INSTITUTIONAL CONTEXT

The University of Texas at San Antonio (UTSA) was founded in 1969 as the city's first public university and now includes three campuses, the Main Campus, Downtown Campus, and HemisFair Campus. The third largest of nine academic universities and six health institutions in the University of Texas system, UTSA enrolls 30,000 students, including 4,000 graduate students (UTSA Office of Institutional Research, 2015). From 2000 to 2010, UTSA was one of the fastest-growing universities in Texas with a growth rate of 39 percent over the previous decade. Degree offerings include 63 bachelor programs, 51 master programs, and 24 doctoral programs.

UTSA has been designated as a Hispanic Serving Institution, and Hispanic students make up just over 50 percent of the student body. The school also enrolls high numbers of first-generation college students, and in 2014, 47 percent were first generation and nearly that many students were economically disadvantaged or eligible for Federal Pell Grants (UTSA Office of Institutional Research, 2014). The Peer Research Coaches Program serves these student groups by employing a diverse cohort of Peer Coaches who help them feel welcome in the library and support their academic success through co-curricular outreach.

UTSA Libraries

The UTSA Libraries includes the John Peace Library and the Applied Engineering and Technology Library on the Main Campus, the Downtown Campus Library, and a Special Collections division at the HemisFair Campus. The Libraries hold 2.4 million print and electronic volumes and provide access to more than 350 databases. In FY 2014, total library expenditures were 12.1 million. The Libraries are staffed by 111 full-time employees and approximately 24 student assistants.

The Libraries' public services staff members, including the Peer Coaches, compose the Blue Crew service team. Blue Crew staff members provide information and services at multiple in-person locations across the libraries. The library is incredibly busy: in FY 2015, librarians answered up to 1,000 chat questions per week, totaling 27,000 chat questions annually. Library staff, including Peer Coaches, also answered over 20,000 in-person questions.

Institutional Objectives

The Peer Research Coaches Program directly supports UTSA's 2016 strategic plan goal to increase student retention and graduation rates by supporting the Libraries' outreach efforts to fellow students and providing a friendly peer presence at outreach activities, at Information Desks, and on social media. In its mission statement, the university describes itself as an institution of "access and excellence," implying a commitment to helping students succeed academically. The Peer Coaches know firsthand the challenges their peers experience when using the library; since the program's inception, this student perspective has helped the Libraries better support academic success.

The program also supports the Libraries' current strategic plan, particularly its first two outcomes: Outcome 1: "Students and faculty get what they need, when they need it"; and Outcome 2: "Users can find, evaluate, and use information effectively" (UTSA Libraries, n.d.a). The Peer Coaches increase students' awareness of library resources and services through outreach and student engagement efforts, and the reference and instruction services they provide enable users to find, evaluate, and use information.

BACKGROUND OF THE PROGRAM

The Peer Research Coaches Program was the result of collaboration between the Libraries' part-time development officer and library administrators. The development officer was aware that local foundations were interested in supporting UTSA student success by funding student employment programs. The Peer Research Coaches Program was created as a means of offering campus employment to first-generation or other students demographically at risk for not completing a bachelor's degree while also providing peer-to-peer academic support for all UTSA students. Being at risk is a preferred qualification for the peer coach position, but it is not a requirement.

In spring 2011, after being presented with a grant proposal for the Peer Research Coaches Program, a local foundation established an endowment to support the program. The endowment generates funds to provide stipends, enabling the Libraries to pay the Peer Coaches at a higher hourly rate to compensate these students for their additional training and advanced, high-profile job duties. In early 2012, again through the efforts of the development officer, a second local foundation agreed to support the program with a one-year grant that funded several additional peer coach positions. After receiving annual reports on the program and thank-you letters from the Peer Coaches, the second foundation has subsequently renewed the annual grant at the same level of funding each year since 2012. Each year, the endowment and grant funding support four to six Peer Coaches who work approximately 15 hours per week.

Program Goals

The goal of the program is to improve student retention and graduation in two ways: (1) by providing Peer Coaches with financial support in the form of campus employment and (2) by supporting other students with peer-to-peer outreach and library assistance via the Peer Coaches. At UTSA, first-year students have lower retention rates than upper-division students. The Peer Coaches engage with these students at new student orientation and other outreach events to inform them about the library services that will help them succeed academically.

Peer Coach Selection Process

The program seeks to recruit students who are from historically underrepresented backgrounds or who are first-generation college students, providing them with paid campus employment and thereby encouraging their progress to graduation. Research consistently shows that students who have on-campus jobs are more academically successful and more likely to complete a degree (Pike, Kuh, & Massa-McKinley, 2009).

The job advertisements for Peer Coach positions invite applications from undergraduate students at the sophomore through senior level who are outgoing, who enjoy meeting people and helping other students, and who have demonstrated strong academic performance. Because the Peer Coaches receive extensive training, we prefer students who are sophomores or juniors, hoping they will stay with the Libraries for several semesters. The selection process is fairly rigorous. In addition to applying through UTSA's online portal for student positions on campus, candidates must submit a résumé. Based on the application and résumé, selected candidates are invited to complete an additional essay application that addresses their experience and comfort using the library, as well as interest and ability in working with others. The top candidates are then invited for a face-to-face interview. The face-to-face portion of the selection process is crucial, as this gives us an opportunity to get a sense of each candidate's personality, enthusiasm, and interest in the position. Due to the nature of the job duties and the high expectations for communications skills, the pay rate for Peer Coach positions is $1 per hour more than most other library student positions.

TRAINING AND PREPARATION OF PEER COACHES

Due to the position requirements, most Peer Coaches begin the job already prepared with basic knowledge of campus, good interpersonal and communication skills, and some experience using the library. Their supervisor, the Student Engagement Librarian, is responsible for building on this foundation by training the Peer Coaches. The training philosophy for the program is that the Peer Coaches receive the same training in customer service, general library services, and basic reference as the entry-level, full-time Library Services Assistant staff positions. Beyond this, they receive ongoing training to further develop their knowledge and skills, along with regular feedback from their supervisor. This level of training is appropriate, given their duties and the relative longevity of the Peer Coaches in their positions.

Initial training takes the form of instruction (small group and one-on-one) with a focus on active learning. Instruction is supplemented by a combination of guided and independent practice activities, as well as online learning for certain topics. Most outreach activities involve a high level of patron interaction, and early on in their training, the Peer Coaches receive customer service and reference interview training.

Outreach Training

Training for outreach duties is provided by the supervisor, the Student Engagement Librarian. The Peer Coaches represent the Libraries by staffing library tours, welcome tables, campus information fairs, and finals de-stress activities—as well as a range of other library outreach programs. These activities require that Peer Coaches are friendly and approachable, and have basic knowledge about the library. Initial training for outreach therefore begins with the Libraries' customer service module, Service with a Smile, which was developed in cooperation with the University's Human Resources training specialists. Peer Coaches learn the SMILE principles (Start with a smile, Make their day, Invest yourself, Leave no stone unturned, and End with a thank-you). To reinforce these concepts, the supervisor works alongside the Peer Coaches at several events to model and reinforce the friendly, informative behaviors expected.

Welcome Tables and Other Student Engagement Events

When a Peer Coach staffs a welcome table along with a librarian, the librarians report that students consistently approach and speak with the Peer Coach rather than the librarian. Given this, in addition to customer service skills, it is important that the Peer Coaches also have the training to answer basic questions accurately and to refer questions appropriately. Since the Peer Coaches often staff outreach events along with librarians and full-time staff members, they can also refer any complex questions to the librarian and learn by listening to the librarian's answers. The training appears to work well. Recently, an experienced subject librarian sat beside a Peer Coach at a campus welcome event outside the library, and the librarian noted that throughout the two hours, the Peer Coach was repeatedly approached first by students. Moreover, the Peer Coach answered every question correctly! And although the Peer Coaches' level of library-related knowledge does not approach that of the librarians, the Peer Coaches sometimes know the answers to campus questions that librarians do not.

Summer Orientation Tour and Video Hosting

Throughout the summer, the Peer Coaches have a key role in hosting the library orientation tour and showing a video that provides an introduction to library services. Peer Coaches receive training in giving a standard library tour during the first few weeks of their employment. As a result, learning to give the first-year student orientation tour, which is much shorter than a standard library tour, builds upon previously acquired skills. Training includes reviewing the tour script and practicing giving the tour with their supervisor. The supervisor also trains the Peer Coaches to show the video and prepares them to respond to typical questions posed during the question-and-answer session following the video. Typical questions from incoming first-year students at orientation include "how much does it cost to print?" and "how late is the library open?"

Social Media

The Peer Coaches also perform outreach via social media to provide a student perspective on library services. For these duties, they receive instruction, guidance, and mentoring from the staff person who manages the Libraries' social media presence. There is no formal training since the duties are quite variable, but Peer Coaches have opportunities to use their creativity and develop collaborative skills on the job.

User Experience Training

When the Peer Coaches are asked to assist with user experience projects, the training is typically brief and is specific to each project. As one example, when the Peer Coaches assisted with user testing to determine the findability of streaming video in our discovery system, they were given a short script with directions on recruiting patrons to participate, introducing the test, and guiding users through the testing session. This training was provided by the subject librarian who was the user experience project lead, and it was reinforced by the Peer Coach supervisor. The supervisor checked in with each Peer Coach on their first day of user testing to ensure they were following the procedure and to give them a chance to ask questions.

Reference Training

Because the focus of this chapter is outreach rather than reference, reference training will not be covered in detail. The training is based on the *Guidelines for Behavioral Performance of Reference and Information Service Providers* found on the Reference and User Services Association website (2004). In a nutshell, reference training includes tutorials and face-to-face training by the supervisor on topics including using the library discovery system to find materials, the reference interview, hands-on search strategy assignments, comparison of the results when a search is conducted in different databases or search engines, use of Research Guides, and more.

Ongoing Training

The supervisor holds monthly group meetings with the Peer Coaches, and the hour-long meetings usually include a training component, for example, an overview of basic resources in the field of Education. Peer Coaches also attend the monthly Reference and Public Services meetings when their schedules allow. At these meetings, staff members discuss current issues in information and reference services, learn about new databases and other content, hear updates about library projects, and discuss policies and procedures. The meetings provide an opportunity for the Peer Coaches to observe how professional meetings are conducted and to see the roles of both the meeting facilitator and participants. They witness staff members debating issues and making decisions. The Peer Coaches are also invited to contribute their own observations and suggestions, particularly since they spend more time roving the library building than most other staff.

Participation in meetings strengthens the Peer Coaches' understanding of library priorities and goals and provides an opportunity for other library staff members to hear student perspectives and voices on a regular basis. This is something that had not occurred prior to the implementation of the Peer Research Coaches Program. The Peer Coaches are also invited to attend webinars, presentations by subject librarians, campus-wide staff trainings, and other library-wide or public services training. Participation in the staff development activities helps develop the Peer Coaches' general library knowledge and enables them to see the fast pace of change in the information landscape—and the necessity of continuous learning for those who are knowledge workers.

IMPLEMENTATION OF THE PROGRAM

The job advertisement for Peer Coach positions states that they "serve as ambassadors for the Libraries in a variety of ways." The operative word here is "variety." Due to changing library needs, the Peer Coach duties (along with the duties of other library staff members) have evolved continually since the program began. The duties are outlined and assigned by the supervisor. Tasks vary depending on library events and initiatives; however, the job descriptions have always included a blend of outreach, reference, and instruction duties.

Outreach

Facebook Team

The Peer Coaches have participated in the Libraries' social media presence since the beginning of the program. Initially, one Peer Coach was assigned to work with the Libraries' Facebook team, which is responsible for brainstorming ideas, posting, and planning Facebook-related engagement activities. An early Facebook outreach activity in which Peer Coaches participated was a contest asking students to find a small stuffed UTSA mascot hidden at different spots throughout the library to introduce students to services and study spaces. Since then, the Peer Coaches have written posts, contributed photos, and generally provided a student outlook and voice. The Facebook team has usually included one or two Peer Coaches who have a particular interest in social media. The Peer Coaches are typically assigned topics, and then they write their own posts.

Peer Coaches Instagram Account—Rowdytips

The Peer Coaches manage and post to a library Instagram account called "Rowdytips." It is devoted to their perspective as student information experts on campus. As such, the Peer Coaches have the freedom to post whatever they think would interest and would be useful to their peers. Posts have included updates on library spaces and services, information about the services that subject librarians offer students, interesting doodles found on the library's group study room whiteboards, services provided by other student support programs located within the library (Writing Center, tutoring), events or unique places on campus or in San Antonio, or experiences from their personal travels. The frequency of posting varies depending on the time available for this task. Other duties sometimes take priority, so posting may be done on a weekly or monthly basis.

Student Engagement Events

Current student engagement goals include the following:

- Raise awareness of the Blue Crew brand so students know they can "Ask us anything." The Blue Crew is the name given to the Libraries' public services staff to market library services at the public desks and on chat. Staff members, including the Peer Coaches, wear blue shirts or sweaters when working in the public areas of the library.
- Support the university-wide initiative to create new traditions for our relatively young university.
- Raise awareness of library services and spaces that support academic success.
- Host programs that connect students to the intellectual life on campus.

At engagement events, the Peer Coaches provide a friendly point of contact as they greet students and families, talk about library services, answer questions, encourage students to play games, and give away prizes and library-branded swag. Their opinions are also solicited when choosing snacks and giveaways for events.

Examples of recurring events are National Library Week celebrations, welcome tables at the beginning of each semester, Halloween and Valentine's Day celebrations, and de-stress activities held during finals week. The Peer Coaches also represent the library at campus-wide events such as information fairs, Roadrunner Days welcome tables, joint finals de-stress events held at the recreation center and the university student center, and a student housing scavenger hunt to introduce new dorm residents to university services.

As members of the Blue Crew, the Peer Coaches helped staff the Blue Crew Clue Game activity in which patrons try to win prizes by identifying library services and spaces. One especially successful event was "We [Heart] Your Questions," a Valentine's Day event where the Peer Coaches staffed a table at the library entrance. Students wrote their questions on hundreds of blue sticky notes, which were taped on the window wall at the library entrance. Questions ranged from light-hearted and humorous to philosophical, and answers to questions pertaining to the library or the campus were posted alongside the questions on the wall. The result was a fun event for students that advertised the Blue Crew and our services. Most importantly, it let students know that their questions are important to us.

Recently the Peer Coaches staffed a Halloween film event featuring streaming classic horror films shown in an open area near the DVD shelves. The Peer Coaches handed out Halloween candy along with information on how to access the Libraries' streaming video resources.

Outreach to Student Success Partners

Outreach activities also include presentations to the campus-wide peer-led tutoring program called Supplemental Instruction. The Peer Coaches make presentations about library services during the training for the Supplemental Instruction student leaders, encouraging them to recommend the Blue Crew service to the students in their groups. Peer Coaches have also visited individual Supplemental Instruction study sessions to encourage students to use the Blue Crew service via chat or in person when they have questions or need help with research.

New Student Orientation

In summer 2013, for the first time, the Peer Coaches were given a major role in the first-year student orientation effort. Full-time staff members previously led orientation tours, but it became clear that incoming students would be receptive to hearing about the Libraries' services and resources from their peers. To accommodate the extra workload, a sixth coach was hired to provide tours and host a short video about the library.

The video stars two Peer Coaches who demonstrate how to use 11 of our most popular library services (https://www.youtube.com/watch?v=mh6NKTxQYR8). In their role as orientation hosts, the Peer Coaches welcome new students to the library, introduce the video, hold a question-and-answer session, and lead a brief tour of the main floor spaces and services. A new orientation video created for the summer 2016 features two Peer Coaches as actors and is hosted by a Peer Coach (https://www.youtube.com/watch?v=4jzYZKtcfN4&feature=youtu.be).

Tours

The Peer Coaches also give library tours to visiting school groups and prospective students. Occasionally, a high school group will come to the library to find sources for a research paper assignment, and the Peer Coaches provide invaluable assistance at these times, because school groups can be quite large. Peer Coaches have been praised by visiting high school teachers for the assistance provided to their classes.

Marketing and Video Participation

Marketing is another facet of library outreach, and along with other staff members, the Peer Coaches are the face of the library. Their images have often been used for posters to raise awareness of library services and in brochures and annual reports. The Peer Coaches have also helped brainstorm ideas for marketing materials, providing the student perspective. For example, they searched the web for ideas for a series of meme posters highlighting library services. The Peer Coaches also appeared in videos for instructional modules created by the Libraries' Learning Technology department. It has been valuable to have the Peer Coaches available to lend a student-friendly, approachable tone to the materials.

User Experience

The Peer Coaches have worked behind the scenes with the User Experience Librarian and other staff on a number of usability projects related to the website and access to electronic resources. For example, they helped test three language databases being considered for purchase and helped conduct usability testing to improve the findability of our streaming video resources.

For studies on the use of the library space, Peer Coaches participated in a series of observations to determine if the number of recycling and trash bins was appropriate by keeping logs of the fullness levels throughout the day. In summer 2015, the Peer Coaches participated in focus groups in which they and other students provided feedback about the need for additional quiet and collaborative study spaces in the main library. In addition, an ongoing duty of the Peer Coaches is to rove and gather data about noise levels and how library spaces are used, reporting problems as necessary.

Reference

In the past few years, the Peer Coaches have provided peer-to-peer assistance at all of the Libraries' John Peace and Downtown Campus service points at one time or another. At the main Information Desk, they provide basic information and reference service. They also staff a new information outpost on a previously unstaffed floor, helping students find materials in the stacks and monitoring noise and group study room usage. The new service desk was mentioned favorably by a student government representative as soon as it was instituted.

EVALUATION OF THE PROGRAM

Based on the goals of the program, we identified the following areas for evaluation.

Peer Coach Retention and Graduation Rates

Since the program's inception in fall 2011, 21 students have been hired as Peer Coaches, and to date only two have left school without finishing their degree programs. In both cases, a change in family circumstances caused them to leave school before graduating. All other Peer Coaches have either graduated or continue to make academic progress, and Peer Coaches frequently mention in their end-of-semester reflections that having a job located on campus is an immense help to them. Further, they mention that the interpersonal and research skills they develop in their Peer Coach roles are extremely helpful to their academic success. The granting organization continues to request information about the retention and graduation of the students employed as Peer Coaches, and we provide this to the organization in our annual program report.

Peer Coach Evaluations

At the end of every semester, the supervisor prepares a written performance evaluation for each Peer Coach. The evaluation ratings and comments include feedback from other library staff members who have worked with the Peer Coach. During the evaluation session, areas of strength as well as areas needing improvement are discussed. To date, all of the Peer Coaches have successfully met program expectations and have continued in their positions until graduation. A copy of the performance evaluation form, which is used for all student positions within the library, is located in Appendix 8–1.

Peer Coaches' Self-Reflection

At the end of each semester, the Peer Coaches are asked to provide a self-reflection statement, responding to the following prompts:

- This semester as a Peer Coach I learned. . .
- Being a Peer Coach helps me succeed at UTSA because. . .
- The Peer Coaches contribute to UTSA campus life by. . .
- One example of how I was able to help a student this semester is (include the information need and how I helped meet that need) . . .
- The Peer Research Coaches Program could be improved by. . .

Examples of responses are as follows:

- "This semester as a Peer Coach I learned. . . how to speak in front of larger crowds. This summer I was able to help with orientations, and it was both fun and a learning experience."
- "Being a Peer Coach this semester helped me succeed at UTSA because I was able to apply my reference, directional, and professional training to my day-to-day activities and class work. During this semester, I was assigned several research papers and presentations, and I knew where to start looking for reliable information."
- "One example of how I was able to help a student this semester. . . . There is a blind patron who is always at the library. One day I was at the Information Desk and she asked for help to open a PDF document from a database and print it. The challenge wasn't in how to open the PDF document, but in knowing how to deal with every type of patron. I needed patience, empathy, and respect. With these three skills that the Library has helped me perfect, I was able to successfully meet the expectations of the patron."
- "The Peer Coaches contributed to UTSA campus life this semester by. . . helping students with their research and promoting an overall presence on campus. We also tried to correct small and big problems alike to make campus life a welcoming and warm environment for everyone."

Comments such as these tell us that the Peer Coaches recognize and appreciate the research and communication skills they are developing. The job of Peer Coaches requires that these students work with their peers in a respectful and productive manner, representing the library to those they assist. In addition, they recognize their responsibility to communicate the student perspective to the library.

Methods of Providing Feedback

Peer Coaches receive timely feedback on their individual and group performance throughout the semester. Due to their varied work schedules, performance issues for the group are generally addressed by e-mail or in monthly meetings with the supervisor.

Individual performance feedback is provided privately and face-to-face as soon as possible. For example, the supervisor provided feedback to a Peer Coach following a complaint that the person chatted too long with a friend at service desk, and she also complimented a Peer Coach for the excellent service provided to a large group of visiting high school seniors who were working on research papers. Achievements are individually acknowledged as quickly as possible, and also publicly at the monthly Peer Coach meetings.

Occasionally, a Peer Coach may need ongoing coaching or even a performance improvement plan to succeed in the job. There have been instances where a Peer Coach missed work more than once without notifying the supervisor, and repeated problems have resulted in verbal counseling followed by a written warning. Since the goal is to support the Peer Coaches' academic progress and graduation, the supervisor normally supports schedule changes requested for academic purposes.

IMPLICATIONS AND LESSONS LEARNED

Peer-assisted learning has positively impacted the library in a number of ways. Having the Peer Coaches as library employees allows us to gather student input in a timely manner as we plan outreach activities. Although prior to the Peer Research Coaches Program the library met with student government representatives and student members of the library committee on a regular basis, these students were busy, and we only saw them monthly for an hour, at most. The Peer Coaches provide suggestions about types of outreach events, giveaways and incentive gifts, snack and drink options, and T-shirt designs. They participate in student focus groups, and they offer feedback and ideas to improve the library through their supervisor and the other staff members with whom they work. Librarians have seen that students who might not approach a librarian at a welcome table, a de-stress event, or the Information Desk may be more comfortable approaching and talking with a peer.

The program also works well for the Peer Coaches, as indicated by comments from their end-of-semester self-reflection responses and their strong record of retention and graduation. Peer Coaches often comment that having campus employment that fits into their academic schedules is beneficial to their academic success. In their responses, Peer Coaches also frequently report that through their jobs, they learn valuable customer service, teamwork, and information literacy skills.

Other libraries should be aware that supporting a peer-assisted learning program such as this could be an attractive opportunity for a local corporation or foundation interested in supporting student success. In our experience, the program is valuable for participants, the student body, and the library. However, training and supervising the Peer Coaches are time consuming. The Peer Research Coaches Program requires at least half of the Student Engagement Librarian's time, and when recruiting and training new Peer Coaches, that percentage is higher. When seeking outside funding, it might be reasonable to include in the total program budget the cost of staff time to oversee and train the Peer Coaches.

NEXT STEPS

The Peer Research Coaches Program has changed often since its inception, and it will continue to evolve. Based on the goals of one of our funding foundations, we may attempt to recruit more Peer Coaches who are veterans, in the future. Possible new directions for the Peer Research Coaches Program could include the following:

- Assist librarians who teach information literacy concepts to general education classes.
- Spend more hours staffing the third floor information outpost.

- Help staff our popular chat service to provide answers to basic questions about patron accounts and library services.
- Seek new approaches for Peer Coach support of the Supplemental Instruction groups for courses with an information literacy component.
- Consider increasing the number of Peer Coaches if funding can be secured.
- Consider creating a half-time graduate student position to serve as Peer Coach supervisor.

The Peer Research Coaches Program has added a student presence to outreach initiatives that was previously missing from our library. Having knowledgeable, outgoing Peer Coaches as members of the library team has informed our outreach efforts and has enabled us to offer students the opportunity to interact with a peer as they learn about and use library resources and services.

REFERENCES

Pike, G. R., Kuh, G. D., & Massa-McKinley, R. C. (2009). First-year students' employment, engagement, and academic achievement: Untangling the relationship between work and grades. *NASPA Journal, 45,* 560–582. doi: 10.2202/1949–6605.2011

Reference and User Services Association. (2004). *Guidelines for behavioral performance of reference and information service providers.* Retrieved from http://www.ala.org/rusa/

UTSA Libraries. (n.d.a). *Strategic plan.* Retrieved from http://lib.utsa.edu/about/strategic-vision/

UTSA Libraries. (n.d.b). *UTSA Libraries orientation 2015* [Video file]. Retrieved from https://www.youtube.com/watch?v=mh6NKTxQYR8

UTSA Office of Institutional Research. (2014). *Student achievements at UTSA.* Retrieved from http://www.utsa.edu/ir/achievement.html

UTSA Office of Institutional Research. (2015). Student enrollment. *The UTSA fact book.* Retrieved from http://www.utsa.edu/ir/pub/factbook/2015/StudentEnrollment.pdf

APPENDIX 8–1: PERFORMANCE EVALUATION FORM

EVALUATIONS

All student employees will be evaluated by their immediate supervisor at the conclusion of each semester.

EVALUATION FORM

Student Employee Name:______________________________
Supervisor Name: ______________________________
Evaluation Period: ______________________________
Evaluate each student employee using the following rating scale:
1—Unacceptable; 2—Requires improvement; 3—Meets requirements; 4—Exceeds requirements; 5—Exceptional; 6—Not Applicable.

Rating	*Performance Factors/Category*
1 2 3 4 5 6	*Adherence to policies*: Complies with department and university policies (confidentiality of records, safety guidelines, computer use, etc.).
1 2 3 4 5 6	*Attendance*: Reports to work on time; rarely absent, notifies supervisor in a timely manner.
1 2 3 4 5 6	*Communication/Interpersonal skills*: Communicates effectively, tactful, able to work cooperatively with others, handles conflict well.
1 2 3 4 5 6	*Customer service*: Is attentive and courteous to patrons, provides friendly service, is helpful and goes "above and beyond" to help.
1 2 3 4 5 6	*Professionalism*: Conducts self in a professional manner. Dress, grooming, and appearance are appropriate. Projects a positive image.
1 2 3 4 5 6	*Performance of core duties*: Performs the primary duties of the job within expectations.
1 2 3 4 5 6	*Quality of work*: Consistently completes work with few errors, pays attention to detail, seeks to learn and shows initiative.
1 2 3 4 5 6	*Work productivity*: Follows instructions, completes tasks promptly, uses time efficiently, requires minimal supervision.

Supervisor comments (include areas requiring improvement and suggestions for improving):

____
____
____
____

Student employee comments:

____
____
____
____

Student employee signature: ____________________ Date: __________
Supervisor signature: ____________________ Date: __________

9

Master Builders of build IT @San Diego State University Library

Jenny Wong-Welch

New strategic goals at San Diego State University (SDSU) Library led to an exploration of ways to renovate library space and services. As a result of these discussions, we created build IT @SDSU Library, a technology-rich learning environment known as a makerspace. One goal of the makerspace is to help democratize access to emerging technology such as 3D printers. Also, the makerspace's service philosophy is focused on teaching students how to utilize technology for specific projects and applications. In implementing the makerspace, librarians were able to create a peer-to-peer instructional model that utilizes student volunteers known as Master Builders to assist with teaching technology. The program has allowed the library to change its perception from a building with study space and books to an active environment where librarians and student peers can facilitate teaching and learning, as well as a place for students to gain valuable work experience and develop desirable skills for future employment.

INSTITUTIONAL CONTEXT

San Diego State University (SDSU) is a large public institution, with over 30,000 full-time students, and is one of 23 universities in the California State University (CSU) system. The mission of SDSU, where the focus is on the teaching and learning of its students, is greatly influenced by the California Master Plan for Higher Education, which created the University of California (UC) system, the CSU system, and the California Community College system. Based on the Master Plan, the UC system is designated as the state's primary academic research institution and the CSU system focuses on undergraduate education.

As the southernmost CSU, SDSU epitomizes its surrounding culture and environment. The SDSU student population is primarily undergraduate students, with a ratio of six undergraduate students to one graduate student (San Diego State University Analytical Studies & Institutional Research, 2015a). Many of these students come from the San Diego region. For instance, in fall 2015, 37.1 percent of first-time first-year students at SDSU were from San Diego County (San Diego State University Analytical Studies & Institutional Research, 2015b). Also, many of our alumni remain in San Diego, where

50 percent of the thousands of graduates produced by SDSU pursue their careers, making SDSU a primary educator of the region's workforce (San Diego State University, n.d.b). The student demographics of SDSU are influenced by the university's status as a Hispanic Serving Institution (HSI) (San Diego State University, n.d.a). In fall 2015, 27.6 percent of the enrolled undergraduate student population were Hispanic (San Diego State University Analytical Studies & Institutional Research, 2015a).

To guarantee institutional support for build IT @SDSU Library and its Master Builder Program, it was important to align with the university's strategic plan. The strategic plan contains three categories: student success, research and creative endeavors, and community and communication. While there are aspects of our program that fit into all three categories, the Master Builder Program is most closely aligned with the university's student success goal by emphasizing high-impact practices that produce transformational educational experiences and fostering an institutional culture that recognizes and rewards student achievement (San Diego State University, 2013). Also, our program aligns with the library's strategic plan to advance teaching and learning through the integration of library content and tools into the curriculum, delivery of information literacy instruction, and design of optimal learning environments for 21st-century student success (San Diego State University Library & Information Access, 2015).

BACKGROUND OF THE PROGRAM

The Master Builder Program originated from a new library space known as build IT @SDSU Library. build IT @SDSU Library started in spring 2015 with the mission to be "a mini makerspace designed to foster creativity and innovation by providing an infrastructure for student-motivated DIY learning of technology to transform ideas into awesome products" (build IT @SDSU Library, 2014). As technology has become an essential feature of everyday life, it has become ever more important for students to successfully adopt and utilize these new tools. In order to achieve this, students must be given access to technology. There are many barriers to accessing emerging technology, such as cost, time, and expertise. build IT @SDSU Library provides access to emerging technology by overcoming these barriers.

The SDSU Library has been fortunate to have a strong funding line for purchasing technology. As of December 2015, build IT @SDSU Library housed technology such as 3D printers, 3D scanners, vinyl cutters, virtual reality headsets, wearable technology, a multi-touch table, craft supplies, and hand tools. However, access through procurement is not enough. By its nature, emerging technology is novel and mysterious; this often fuels apprehension to the adoption and use of it. build IT @SDSU Library strives to demystify technology to allow students to gain the skills needed to adopt and use it. The program provides an open atmosphere where friendly technology experts, who are student volunteers and librarians, teach students how to leverage technology to build prototypes for specialized projects.

Start-up of build IT @SDSU Library and the Master Builder Program

There are four fundamental parts to build IT @SDSU Library: the technology, the space, the service, and the people. build IT @SDSU Library started when I persuaded the library administration to purchase one 3D printer and allocate a small, 120-square-foot space to pilot the build IT program. After the purchase of the equipment and allotment of space, I had to figure out how the library was going to offer a 3D printing service. I looked at other libraries to see how they were handling this new technology and found two predominant methods. One was to have patrons submit a 3D print request, either online or in person. Then library staff would operate the 3D printer to fulfill the request. The other method entailed allowing patrons to reserve time to use the 3D printer. Both of these methods require at least one dedicated library staff member. In my case, while I received the equipment and space, I did not have funding for staff. However, in the past, I had students express interest in becoming involved with 3D printing in the library. So, I decided to recruit students to volunteer their time to operate the 3D printers to help fulfill 3D print requests, staff the space, and answer questions regarding the new technology. With this staffing system, I was able to develop a new peer-assisted learning program known as the Master Builder Program, where the library would facilitate the teaching and learning of technology via peer-to-peer hands-on instruction.

When I set out to use student volunteers in build IT, I surprisingly did not receive any pushback from the university or the library. In fact, it was quite the opposite, as many stakeholders consider it a great opportunity for the students. The Master Builder Program fits a need on campus for providing more students with the opportunity for work experience, which aligns with SDSU's strategic plan initiative of "strengthen[ing] internship and mentoring programs to foster students' professional development" (San Diego State University, 2013).

Goals of the Master Builder Program

A goal of the Master Builder Program is to increase student engagement with technology. Student volunteers known as Master Builders are recruited to serve as technology advocates, who will greet any student who enters the space and provide a quick demonstration of how the technology works and how it can be used for future projects. Through these interactions, Master Builders can demystify technology to provide more students with the opportunity to utilize it for their projects.

Another goal of the Master Builder Program is to create opportunities for students to develop new skills through the teaching of technology. Today's average student is a digital native, someone who has spent their entire life surrounded by computers, video games, cellphones, and all other toys and tools of the digital age (Prensky, 2001). As digital natives, many students have experience with using technology. The innovative environment of build IT @SDSU Library naturally attracts many of these technically advanced students to become Master Builders. The Master Builder Program allows these students to work on developing various skills. Through specialized projects, each Master Builder can expand their understanding of the applications of the available technology. For example, a student with advanced 3D modeling skills can expand their skill set to include 3D printing. With the mentorship of librarians, a Master Builder can realize their potential to harness their knowledge to assist with teaching others about technology. The process of teaching creates a means for them to develop skills related to communication, problem-solving, computational thinking, design thinking, and other critical skills.

A valuable objective of the Master Builder Program is to prepare students for their future careers. The program prepares students by giving them the opportunity to develop attractive skills that many employers are looking for, such as experience with computer programming and the ability to effectively work in a team environment. With its location in the library, the Master Builder Program is accessible to students from all disciplines. The program's diversity creates a realistic work environment similar to what a student will experience once they graduate and start their career. For example, an engineering student could work with an art student to collaboratively teach a workshop on how to 3D model a structure for 3D printing.

Finally, the Master Builder Program can provide students with the opportunity to gain valuable formal work experience. In many cases, the Master Builder position is a student's first job. While it is an unpaid position, the ability to gain work experience has translated to many of the Master Builders getting another internship within their chosen career field.

Master Builder Recruitment

After determining the staffing model behind build IT @SDSU Library, I had to recruit students to become Master Builders. It is important to remember that the Master Builder position is an unpaid position. In return for a student's time and effort, I promise the opportunity to receive one-on-one instruction on how to utilize technology and the privilege of the after-hours access to build IT. My recruitment efforts start with advertising the new positions via flyers that encourage students to learn about the opportunity to get involved with technology. During the first week of each semester, I hold multiple information sessions in which I introduce students to the mission of build IT and describe the benefits of the Master Builder position.

Realizing that to have a successful service, I need to recruit as many students as possible, I set minimal requirements to becoming a Master Builder. First, a student only needs to complete an online interest form and submit their schedule availability to get started. Next, students are required to volunteer three hours every week; I also recommend that they attend a weekly Master Builder meeting. While prior experience with technology or teaching is desirable, I want to reach the largest audience so that the Master Builders' demographics accurately reflect that of the university. So any student who is willing to volunteer the required time and expresses an eagerness to learn technology is accepted into the Master Builder Program. While I prefer to recruit new Master Builders at the start of each semester, I also accept applications on a continuous basis. Because often a student's time in build IT is a low priority in relation to school and work, there is sometimes a gap in staffing. In these situations, I either work the shift or recruit a new student to fill the gap.

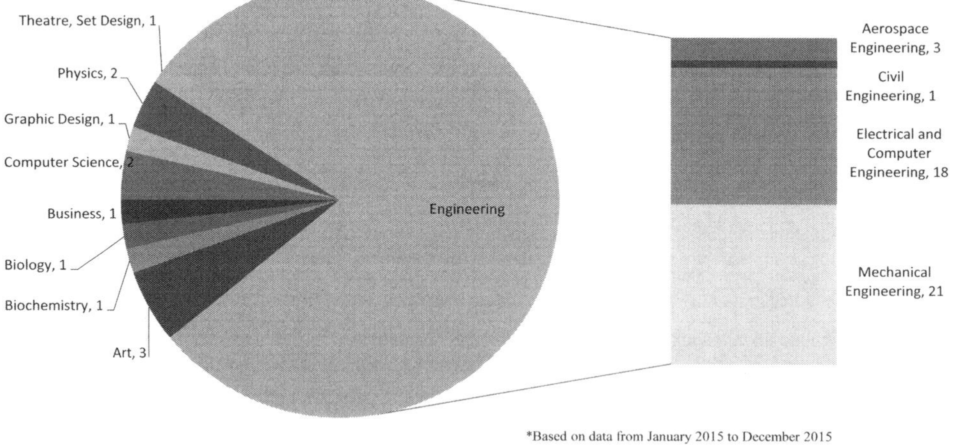

Figure 9.1 Master Builders' majors.

Over the course of two semesters, I successfully recruited 55 students to volunteer as Master Builders. Due to the nature of the program, it has primarily appealed to Engineering students, who represent 78 percent of the Master Builder student population. Other majors represented include Art, Biochemistry, Business, Graphic Design, Physics, and Theater. Aside from their majors (see Figure 9.1), Master Builders also vary in other demographics such as age, student status, residency, prior experience, and skill level. Of the Master Builders, 96 percent are undergraduate students, which reflects the university student population.

TRAINING AND PREPARATION OF MASTER BUILDERS

The Master Builders learn through a three-step process of watch, do, and teach. The student volunteers are known as Master Builders because they work to master their technology skills to build prototypes for projects. Once they have accomplished learning enough to do, they are then called upon as masters to teach other students.

Mentorship

The first step of the Master Builder training process is to watch. If a student wants to learn something, they need someone to first show them how it's done (Toren, 2014). To build a sense of community to ensure that the student volunteers stay engaged with the Master Builder Program, I serve in the essential role as mentor. My mentorship starts during their first shift, which is when their training begins. Right away, I take the time to get to know each student. The investment of time is important to help the students feel a sense of belonging. The relationship is an intricate dialogue to negotiate their current skills and what they want to learn. My work as a mentor concentrates on making them feel comfortable enough to ask me anything.

After completing the necessary paperwork and safety training, each student receives one-on-one instruction from me where I cover the process of 3D printing within build IT @SDSU Library. This session includes a discussion of how 3D printing works and important terminology. Then, working together, I steer a Master Builder through the 3D printing workflow by finding a stereolithography file that they submit as a 3D print request. After this, I guide them through prepping the file to 3D print, which entails understanding the best orientation and printer settings needed for the object to successfully be printed. Finally, I have the student 3D print their object.

Weekly Meetings

Immediately after starting the program, I realized that the nature of the schedule did not provide the Master Builders with the opportunity to get to know each other and develop a strong sense of community. So I made it a strong,recommendation that they attend a weekly meeting. Primarily these meetings allow me to uniformly share information with the students, such as details related to new schedules, updates on purchases, status of the 3D printers, and more. However, as the program developed, I was able to utilize these meetings as an instructional tool. While we still cover updates, I also have a set teaching agenda of content related to developing skills needed for their work as Master Builders.

To assist with a Master Builder's development in build IT, I created a standardized skills checklist that covers the available technology and assigns them tasks to complete to learn how to use and teach the technology. For example, their first task as a Master Builder is to design and 3D print their name tag. This task expanded over four meetings (see Figure 9.2). The first week, I lectured on the importance of copyright and Creative

Intellectual Property Rights	*3D Modeling and 3D Printing*	*Name Tag Design*
• Identify the fundamentals of authorship and how a copyright work is created and protected • Differentiate between Creative Commons licenses • Select a Creative Commons license and apply it to a work	• Construct a 3D model that articulates a personal style and name • Differentiate between 2D and 3D design elements • Demonstrate an ability to use the 3D printer	• Critically evaluate information to determine the best shape and features for a name tag • Use a range of design elements to construct a name tag design • Communicate why design decisions were made to create a name tag

Figure 9.2 Name tag assignment learning outcomes.

Commons. When starting to 3D model a name tag design, a student needs to know the intellectual property rights attached to images that they find as well as their own rights attached to what they create. The second week, I did hands-on instruction of using TinkerCAD, a 3D modeling software, to create a name tag. While some students had prior 3D modeling experience, not everyone knew where to start. The third week included a review of the 3D printing technology and its related terminology. Finally in the fourth week, I led a design discussion where we reviewed what worked and what did not work with each of their name tag designs. For example, we all learned that it is difficult to differentiate cut-out lettering compared to raised lettering. This discussion made the Master Builders contextualize what influenced their design and why they made certain decisions.

Practicing

Continuing with the Master Builder learning process, the next step is doing. With the tools of observation and a steady, constant exposure to a skill, the next step is for the Master Builder to try it on their own (Toren, 2014). The Master Builders are given many opportunities to practice their skills. These opportunities can stem from assigned projects to troubleshooting new problems. For example, in their name tag assignment, the Master Builders gain many skills through the process of doing. First, through trial and error, they are able to learn the tools of a 3D modeling software to create a name tag design. Then by 3D printing their design, they learn how to successfully use a 3D printer. Finally, by seeing the finished product, they can see how design decisions influence what their name tags look like.

Teaching

The final step in a Master Builder's learning process is the ability to teach what they have learned. Following the name tag assignment example, once the Master Builder has created their name tag, they have mastered the skills needed to accomplish the task. The Master Builders are required to wear their name tags while on shift. Often, other students will ask about their name tags and will want to make something similar. From this interaction, a Master Builder will instruct the student through the process of using a 3D modeling software to create an object that could be successfully 3D printed. The process of teaching others is another learning experience for the Master Builders. It teaches them adaptability, patience, and problem solving in totally new ways because the student will undoubtedly ask them some questions to which they don't always know the answers (Toren, 2014).

Master Builder as Trainer

Often, I have found that when a student has experience with technology, they want to share their knowledge and continue to learn from others. The Master Builders are characterized as students with a strong interest in technology with a curiosity to learn more. Through their work, a Master Builder continuously discovers uses for technology while troubleshooting new issues. For example, when a 3D printer breaks, a Master Builder with a strong background with 3D printers will take the initiative to problem solve the issue and develop an action plan to fix it. During the repair process, other Master Builders curious as to what he is doing, will gather around to observe and ask questions. The Master Builder will stop to explain his process and why he is doing something. In this case, a Master Builder is the teacher who is training everyone.

Master Builders are also leveraged to teach each other the skills checklist. Since weekly meetings are not required, and often students have class during the meeting time, some students miss out on training opportunities. Realizing that I could not train every student at once, I created a system for the Master Builders to train each other. We have a sticker incentive chart; each skill on the checklist is a column on the chart and each Master Builder's name is a row. When a Master Builder has fully accomplished mastering a new skill through completing the skills checklist, they receive a sticker in the appropriate cell. So, when another Master Builder misses a weekly meeting, they can look at the chart, find a Master Builder who has a sticker for a specific skill and ask them to teach them what was covered during the meeting.

IMPLEMENTATION OF THE PROGRAM

build IT @SDSU Library is open 10 a.m. to 6 p.m., Monday through Thursday and 10 a.m. to 4 p.m. on Friday. When I decided on these hours, I had to remember that if a student volunteer did not show for a shift, I would have to cover for them; so, build IT's hours of operation are similar to my work schedule. In order for students to truly benefit from their volunteering effort, I require them to work at least three hours per week. Some students choose to work these hours in a single day while others split the hours across multiple days. Their shifts are determined by me and are based on the each student's availability, which they submit at the start of the semester.

A Typical Day for a Master Builder

For a Master Builder, a typical day starts with clocking in; this became an important step to ensure accountability. During the first semester, my office was not located near the build IT space. Therefore, if a student did not show up for their shift without prior notification, the service would be unexpectedly closed. After struggling with this for a semester, I implemented a time clock system that would notify me when a student was present. Not only does the time clock system alleviate the problem of accountability, but it also allows the students to see quickly how much time they invested in build IT as well as have proof of volunteer work to use for community service requirements.

The types of work a Master Builder engages in fall into four main categories: technical, customer service, instructional, and self-development. The primary responsibility of a Master Builder is to ensure that 3D print requests get fulfilled, which often means that the 3D printers should be printing at all times. Based on a semi-automated request queue, a Master Builder will identify what to print next and then determine which 3D printer to use. To successfully 3D print a requested object, a Master Builder needs to understand the orientation and 3D printer settings needed to best print the object. While a Master Builder is taught the 3D printing workflow during their initial training, the ability to process a 3D print request is learned on the job through practice.

The next responsibilities involve customer service and instructional skills. To further the mission of demystifying technology, the Master Builders staff the front desk and are constantly aware of new patrons. Typically, they receive questions that can vary from directional, to interest about build IT and its services, to project-based consultation help. Patrons who enter the space fall into two categories: "newbies" and return clients. Newbies are patrons who have not heard of the space and its services. For every newbie, a Master Builder will go through a list of talking points starting with an explanation of build IT and its mission. Then the Master Builder will guide the patron through the space, pointing out the technology equipment and highlighting key examples of how to use it; this typically includes a brief instructional lesson on the 3D printers. To help jump-start a student's adoption and utilization of emerging technology, a Master Builder will also guide the student through submitting a request to 3D print an object of the student's choosing. To successfully teach newbies, the Master Builders will draw upon the information and skills they learn from completing their skills checklist.

Return client patrons are those who are familiar with build IT and have used its services before. Master Builders assist return clients in two ways. Sometimes a patron will be curious about the quality of their 3D printed object; for instance, why two printed parts do not fit or why there is extra material attached to the object. In these cases, a Master Builder will guide the patron through the 3D printer settings and recommend how to improve the finished product. These recommendations come from knowledge that a Master Builder develops as they work. A Master Builder can also be called upon to assist with a project consultation. Typically, a return client will have an idea for project and need assistance with integrating build IT's technology into their project. In these cases, I call upon the experienced Master Builders, those who have volunteered for a long time and have developed strong technology skills, to assist with consultations. Through observation and individual work with me, these experienced Master Builders learn how to conduct a consultation. First, the experienced Master Builder learns how to ask questions to identify a student's specific need. Then, using their experience, they can determine the best avenue to assist with the student's need. Finally, the experienced Master Builder guides the student through using the technology to create a solution for the need.

Lastly, while on shift, a Master Builder will work on developing their understanding of the technology offered in build IT. For the Master Builder to assist with teaching others about technology and its applications, they need to know how it works. It is important for the Master Builders to practice utilizing the technology. To assist with a Master Builder's development, I provide them with opportunities to work on new projects. For instance, to further their understanding of the mechanics of a 3D printer, I assigned a group of Master Builder to build a 3D printer. Also, students have worked on projects such as creating a custom tool clip and designing and printing name tags for library donors. While the focus is for the Master Builder to learn how to implement the technology, the process helps them prepare for the workforce. Through the learning process, they are developing key skills such as design thinking, problem solving, and computation. Also, they are mastering digital skills that are highly desirable by employers such as working with 3D modeling software or graphic design software.

Staffing

build IT and the Master Builder Program started as a self-initiated program. In the beginning, many library staff members did not have the time to dedicate to a new pilot program. So I started off alone as the sole supervisor of both programs. As the programs have grown, three library members have become involved: the Digital Technologies Librarian, the Business Librarian, and the Library IT System Administrator. Finally, as the scale of the Master Builder Program drastically increased, the library gave me funding to hire student assistants. Handpicked from the Master Builders group, I selected the most skilled student volunteers to become paid student assistants. Their roles are the same as the unpaid Master Builders, except they work longer shifts and have more responsibilities such as fixing the 3D printers. Their assistance allowed me to transition from personally staffing the space to focusing on developing the services and instruction model.

EVALUATION OF THE PROGRAM

Program Assessment

The Master Builder Program is relatively new. At this time, I have not had the opportunity to formally assess the student learning that occurs. So far, assessment has primarily focused on usage statistics. Over the course of one year, build IT and the Master Builder Program has grown drastically (see Figure 9.3). It started in a small 120-square-foot room with 18 student volunteers, who helped fulfill 397 3D print requests. It has grown to an approximately 1,700-square-foot room with 30 student volunteers, who helped fulfill 883 3D print requests.

Master Builder Feedback

At this time, assessment of the Master Builders has been very informal. By dedicating the majority of my time to build IT, I can see how each Master Builder is developing in regard to learning the technology as well as teaching others. As they work, I can provide

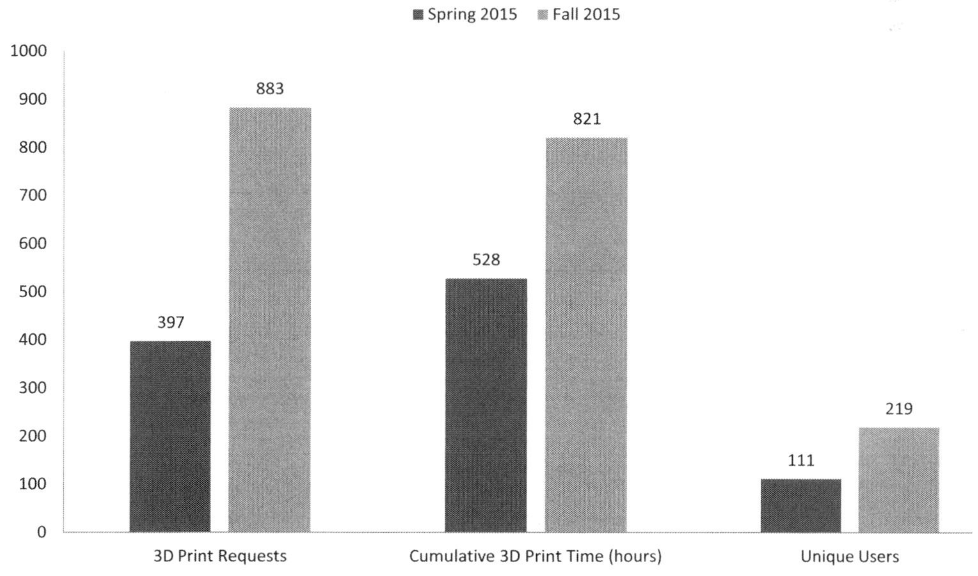

Figure 9.3 Usage of build IT.

immediate feedback based on their interactions with patrons. Often, my feedback includes simple recommendations on future concepts to consider. For instance, when a Master Builder was trying to describe to a patron how their file would be 3D printed, I recommended that the Master Builder utilize the 3D printer software to demonstrate how it would look as a finished 3D printed object. As I see them progress through the program, I give the advanced students opportunities to learn more through individual projects that involve creating a product to be used in build IT.

Master Builder Input

build IT relies heavily on the engagement and involvement of its student volunteers. Without them, the program could not exist. To build the unique environment and community needed to promote the teaching and learning of technology, the Master Builders need to be invested in the program. The easiest way to make the Master Builders become invested is to provide them with the opportunity to have a voice in what happens to build IT and the Master Builder Program. Throughout their shifts, I take the opportunity to ask them how everything is going. Sometimes, I will get responses that focus on their school or home life, but at other times, they will share what they have noticed during their shift. To make sure they feel heard, I will follow up with them on the topics that we discussed. At the end of the semester, I send out a feedback form that asks them if they have recommendations for their work schedule, what they liked about the program, and what they would like to change or improve. By reviewing their responses, I learnt that many felt their work schedule was ideal at three hours per week. Many commented that they most appreciated the people and the "laid back atmosphere" of build IT. Finally, they made recommendations for technology to be added to build IT, such as a laser cutter.

IMPLICATIONS AND LESSONS LEARNED

The Impact of Master Builders on Student Learning at SDSU

build IT with its Master Builder Program has impacted student learning at SDSU in multiple ways. The first is by simply democratizing access to technology. Before the establishment of build IT, few students had the opportunity to get their hands on cost-prohibitive emerging technology. Also, the Master Builders act as technology advocates, empowering other students to overcome their barriers of adopting new technologies. The program assists with demystifying technology for the entire student population. Finally, through the development of a peer-to-peer instruction model, the Master Builders not only learn to utilize the technology, but also develop key skills such as customer service, communication, problem solving, computational thinking, design thinking, project management, negotiation, and other critical skills for career success. Through interaction with student learners and fellow Master Builders, a Master Builder can engage with others outside their major. All of these translate to a more well-rounded student whom employers are looking to hire.

The Master Builder Program has also evolved to include more formal student learning opportunities. In partnership with the SDSU's Division of Undergraduate Studies, I have been able to offer the Master Builders the opportunity to participate in an internship where they earn academic credit for their time invested in build IT. In this context, I serve as the faculty advisor and employer to these students. As their faculty advisor, I provide them with readings and guidance on a final research project. As their employer, I supervise them to ensure that they complete their work assignments as Master Builders. So far, four students have taken the internship opportunity.

The Impact of Master Builders on Librarians and the SDSU Library

Through the creation of a peer-assisted learning program, the SDSU Library has reinvented an underutilized space into an innovative technology center with a collaborative learning environment. The Master Builder Program has demonstrated to university administrators the types of learning that the library can facilitate, such as digital literacy and design thinking. By teaching technology, librarians share their expertise through the mentorship of students to prepare them for successful careers. In return, librarians gain a deeper understanding of student life and what challenges students face in both their course work and learning technology.

NEXT STEPS

Potential Funding

The Master Builders are very aware of the limited funding available to the build IT and Master Builder Program. They know that more funding equals more opportunities, such as adding new technology and supporting more student projects. To generate funding, the library has worked to connect potential donors with the Master Builders. In these cases, I will ask a Master Builder to custom design and 3D print a name tag for a potential donor. Then the library will bring the potential donor to build IT where the Master Builder will provide a brief tour and answer any questions. Their interactions conclude with the Master Builder giving the potential donor their name tag and explaining what influenced their designs.

Future of the Master Builder Program

As build IT and the Master Builder Program continues to develop, there are areas for improvement. While I have been very successful in recruiting students to volunteer, the majority of the students are engineering majors. To improve its impact, the Master Builder Program needs to be a truer representation of the SDSU student population. So, I plan to increase recruitment efforts to target future Master Builders of different majors. Overall, the future for the Master Builder Program is promising. I hope that as the program continues, it will become increasingly self-sufficient where experienced Master Builders transition into leadership roles such as taking on the responsibilities of teaching workshops.

In summary, as a result of implementing a makerspace, the SDSU Library has created a peer-to-peer instructional model that utilizes student volunteers to teach technology skills. While the Master Builder Program was originally created to solve a staffing issue, it has become a means for any student to develop new skills. The program has allowed the library to change its perception from a building with study space and books to an active environment where librarians and student peers can facilitate teaching and learning, as well as a place for students to gain valuable work experience and develop desirable skills for future employment.

REFERENCES

build IT @SDSU Library. (2014). *About.* Retrieved from http://buildit.sdsu.edu/

Prensky, M. (2001). Digital natives, digital immigrants. *On the Horizon, 9*(5), 1–6. doi:10.1108/10748120110424816

San Diego State University. (n.d.a). *Diversity rankings and distinctions.* Retrieved from https://newscenter.sdsu.edu/lead/diversity_rankings.aspx

San Diego State University. (n.d.b). *University history.* Retrieved from https://newscenter.sdsu.edu/home/history.aspx

San Diego State University. (2013). *Building on excellence: A strategic plan for San Diego State University 2013–2018.* Retrieved from http://go.sdsu.edu/strategicplan/images/finalstrategicplanbooklet.pdf

San Diego State University Analytical Studies & Institutional Research. (2015a). *Enrollment summary fall 2015 SD campus* [Data File]. Retrieved from https://asir.sdsu.edu/Pages/enrollment.aspx

San Diego State University Analytical Studies & Institutional Research. (2015b). *Fall 2015 first-time freshmen by admission area, region & residence status* [Data File]. Retrieved from https://asir.sdsu.edu/Pages/newstd-origin-data.aspx

San Diego State University Library & Information Access. (2015). *Strategic plan.* Retrieved from http://library.sdsu.edu/about-us/strategic-plan

Toren, A. (2014, May). Master any skill with these 3 simple steps. *Entrepreneur.* Retrieved from https://www.entrepreneur.com/article/233958

Part III

PEER-ASSISTED LEARNING IN REFERENCE SERVICES

10

Peer Research Mentors at Gettysburg College

Clinton Baugess, Mallory Jallas, Meggan Smith, and Janelle Wertzberger

Research and instruction librarians at Gettysburg College developed a Peer Research Mentor (PRM) Program for undergraduate students. The program is designed to empower a group of student employees to work in partnership with experienced librarians in order to increase a PRM's own research skills and support other student researchers more effectively. The program focuses on student training, reference service, and outreach to other students. The authors share the development of the program; describe their approach to training, supervision, and assessment; and offer insight about how to operate and sustain a similar program with limited resources.

INSTITUTIONAL CONTEXT

Student employees are central to the life and operation of academic libraries. Without student labor, many libraries would be hard-pressed to quickly shelve returned materials, staff late-night library hours, keep up with incoming and outgoing interlibrary loan requests, and complete the wide variety of small tasks that are essential to library operations. Gettysburg College's Musselman Library is no different. As a four-year, residential, liberal arts college in Gettysburg, Pennsylvania, we have a full-time enrollment of 2,632 undergraduates (Office of Institutional Analysis, Gettysburg College, 2015). The library hires more student employees than any other campus office—on average, 60 student employees during the academic year.

While student employees work in all library departments, our office (Research and Instruction) has historically employed only a single student who typically worked less than six hours a week entering data or updating pages on the library website. The published literature is rich with examples of how other reference departments have hired students to work as reference assistants, training them to answer basic reference questions and referring to a professional librarian only when needed (Faix, 2014; Faix et al., 2010; Heinlen, 1976; Holliday & Nordgren, 2005; Stanfield & Palmer, 2010). For these institutions, training students to answer most reference questions has enabled librarians to spend their available work hours answering more advanced and complicated user questions through the research consultation. This model also enables librarians to provide more information literacy instruction or be more active liaisons with academic departments. However, we were not interested in shifting librarians away from the desk. Instead, we wanted to use peer-assisted learning to transform both our student employees' work and the service provided at our Research Help Desk. Our primary goal in creating the PRM Program was to empower a group of student employees to work in partnership with experienced librarians in order to increase their own research skills and to support other student researchers more effectively.

In our residential liberal arts college context, librarians from all library departments value time spent working directly with students, faculty, staff, and campus visitors. Our reference work informs a range of other library activities, including website design, cataloging, collection development, and instruction. Indeed, it is a point of pride that all Gettysburg librarians (with the exception of the dean and college archivist) work at least two hours a week at the Research Help Desk. We wanted to invite student employees into this service point and engage them with our existing service philosophy.

At the institutional level, Gettysburg College's four "strategic directions"—engagement, distinction, access, and connection—also inform the philosophy of our PRM Program. At the library, we paid particular attention to the first direction, engagement, which for Gettysburg means that we will "offer the most compelling educational experience possible, emphasizing active engagement through a variety of learning experiences inside and outside the classroom that build leadership potential in our graduates" (Gettysburg College, 2015, p. 3). Gettysburg's president has also challenged the campus to "build a culture that values academic rigor that supports students as they cultivate their intellectual and civic passions" (Riggs, 2013, pp. 4–5). In response to these priorities, library staff began to reexamine how the library supports this strategic direction through our collections, events, internships, and programs. Around the same time, the high-impact educational practices identified by George Kuh (2008) became a particular focus for our Provost. Of the eight practices that Kuh identifies as being beneficial to increasing rates of student retention and student engagement, we gave particular attention to service learning/community-based learning. This practice emphasizes opportunities that enable students to apply their classroom learning to real-world settings. We felt we could contribute to institutional goals by changing the nature of how we work with students in the library. Specifically, through our PRM Program, we wanted to structure certain student employee positions less like student jobs and more like high-impact educational experiences.

BACKGROUND OF THE PROGRAM

As a team of research and instruction librarians, we have followed the Project Information Literacy (PIL) reports since their inception in 2009 and have used them to inform our teaching practice, outreach efforts, and learning materials. PIL studies show that students benefit from librarian help but are more likely to seek assistance from peers than librarians (Head & Eisenberg, 2010), so we considered how librarians could take advantage of student peer groups. We wanted to help our first-year students with difficult transition to college and connect with the significant number of upper-level students who were not seeking help from librarians. As reference providers and information literacy instructors, we knew where students struggled in the research process and where they were and were not getting help. We were familiar with the practice of placing students at reference desks, but we wanted to go further in order to attract reluctant student researchers to our services.

After reading about a peer-assisted learning program at California Polytechnic State University in which student instructors for information literacy sessions received higher evaluation scores than librarian instructors (Bodemer, 2014), our excitement about working with student colleagues at the Research Help Desk grew. We strategized about how to capitalize on the peer-to-peer connection and knew that visibility of our student employees would be key. We wanted students in the library to see a PRM at the Research Help Desk who seemed similar to them, who knew what their assignments were like, and who could explain how to successfully conduct research in appropriate, student-friendly language.

Because peer-assisted learning is already an established part of our campus culture, we felt that students and faculty would respond positively to this model applied in the library setting. Many Gettysburg students already work as diversity peer educators, leadership mentors, orientation leaders, and course-embedded peer learning associates. We also felt that if we carefully selected PRMs from a range of disciplines and co-curricular activities, the program could capitalize on existing social relationships among students and connect the library with student researchers who may not otherwise seek help from a librarian at the desk. We intentionally chose the title "Peer Research Mentor" to associate our student employees with other peer educators in our existing campus culture.

We knew that other libraries were supporting peer-assisted learning by training students well and having them provide reference service, and we wanted these two activities to form the core of our program. However, we also knew that reference and instruction could take many other forms (such as creating online research guides, designing online tutorials, or delivering workshops), so we added a third central element to our program: an outreach project. These three pillars (training, reference, and outreach) helped us describe the PRM experience to potential applicants and drove the design of the program.

Next, we identified five major learning goals for PRMs. We wanted our PRMs to be able to:

- demonstrate a working knowledge of information resources and services available at a small, academic library;
- apply advanced search strategies and evaluative criteria in order to assist and mentor library users during the research process;
- conduct a reference interview in a variety of modes (in-person, telephone, and virtually);
- design and implement outreach programs for peers, including one-on-one research appointments, drop-in workshops, and instructional videos;
- contribute to a dynamic, supportive, PRM community. (Baugess and Mallory, 2015)

Based upon our planned goals, we drafted a job description that would be attractive to potential student applicants. The job advertisement describes a PRM as "a student who works alongside librarians to support students engaged in research, while also improving one's own research skills" (Musselman Library, 2014). In order to ensure a broad representation across class levels, we specified that the position would be open to four rising sophomores and two rising juniors in any major. We explicitly identified three important qualifications for potential applicants:

- "[a] desire to learn, improve, and master research skills in more than one academic subject area;
- [an] interest or background in education, mentoring, and/or tutoring; and
- strong communication and organization skills." (Musselman Library, 2014)

At this point in our planning process, we refined our PRM Program goals and placed them into language easily understood by students. The job advertisement articulates that PRMs will engage in the three main pillars of our program:

1. **Training**. The mentors will participate in a series of concentrated training sessions in August during the week before classes begin, as well as ongoing training throughout the year.
2. **Reference service**. Mentors will work at the library's main Research Help Desk two to four hours per week, partnered with another peer mentor and/or professional librarian.
3. **Outreach**. Mentors will design and implement an outreach program each semester. Each mentor will consult with a supervising librarian in order to customize a project that reflects the mentor's interests and skills (Musselman Library, 2014).

We used social media, campus e-mail, the student newspaper, and the library web page to advertise to students. We also asked faculty to recommend applicants. During hiring for the fall 2015 cohort, we made a special effort to attract a more diverse pool of applicants by appealing to campus offices like the Intercultural Resource Center and the Lesbian, Gay, Bisexual, Transgender, Queer, and Asexual (LGBTQA) Advocacy and Education office, as well as to various student organizations.

Based on our previous success with streamlined and accessible application requirements for library intern positions, we kept the PRM application process simple. To apply, we asked only for a letter describing their interest in the position, their education and career goals, any relevant coursework they have completed, and the names and contact information for two to three references. When reviewing applications and interviewing students, we looked for students who were eager and excited about the possibility to work with their peers in this way, who had coursework or previous jobs in which they have had to teach or mentor others, and who came from a variety of class levels, disciplines, and campus activities. After the initial round of hiring, we began including current PRMs in the interviews, too. We also routinely consider the unique qualities of the existing PRM pool and try to add fresh elements to round out the group's composition. Figure 10.1 describes PRM class levels and majors by semester.

During any given semester, the PRM cohort includes six to eight students. While the composition of the group fluctuates as students study off campus or graduate, our budget restricts us to eight students per semester. Since we began the program with no new source of funding, our library dean and department heads evaluated and consolidated existing student positions in order to reallocate funds to support this new strategic initiative. We should note that PRMs are paid a higher wage than other library student employees due to the high level of training and knowledge required. The starting wage for library student employees is $7.25/hour; PRMs earn $8.50/hour. The reallocation project made it possible for us to begin the program, but we are investigating potential donors to supplement the budget and sustain the program into the future. For now, we are able to support six to eight PRMs per semester for an average of six to eight hours per week.

TRAINING AND PREPARATION OF PRMS

We know that conducting research is challenging for students, so we predicted that our PRMs would feel even more anxious about the prospect of assisting their peers in doing research. In our initial cohort, only one of our students had worked in a library before, and

	Academic Years Represented	*Majors Represented*
Semester 1 (Fall 2014)	Sophomores (4) Juniors (2)	English French/Globalization Studies Psychology (2) Sociology Studio Art/Environmental Studies
Semester 2 (Spring 2015)	First-years (2) Sophomores (4) Juniors (2)	English (2) French/Globalization Studies Health Sciences Psychology (2) Sociology Studio Art/Environmental Studies
Semester 3 (Fall 2015)	Sophomores (4) Juniors (2) Senior (1)	English Health Sciences History/International Affairs Music Education Psychology (2) Sociology
Semester 4 (Spring 2016)	Sophomores (5) Juniors (3)	Biology English English/Women, Gender, and Sexuality Studies French/Globalization Studies Health Sciences Music Education Psychology (2)

Figure 10.1 Composition of PRMs by academic year and major, fall 2014–spring 2016.
Note. The total size of the PRM cohort averages around eight students, depending on the number of graduating students and students studying abroad. Some PRMs have double majors.

a few had experience with tutoring or teaching. None had experience with a help desk or even felt confident about the full research process.

Knowing this, we carefully developed a training design that would help PRMs feel prepared and supported from the outset of their work—this evolved into an intensive initial training we dubbed "boot camp." The boot camp curriculum provides information about our library building, how to conduct a reference interview, and best practices when working with peers. Training also includes opportunities to meet a range of library staff members such as the Library Dean, the Systems Librarian, the Director of Special Collections and Archives, and the Extended Operations Specialist who works until 11:00 p.m. These are colleagues who interact with the PRMs and to whom PRMs might refer other students. The curriculum is structured around common difficulties students face throughout the research process (Head, 2013). These challenges include starting research, defining a topic, finding articles in library databases, and evaluating sources (see Figure 10.2). By the end of the boot camp, we hope PRMs will be able to assist patrons at any point in the research process.

In order to make the training as effective as possible, we consolidate information in "chunks," avoid lecture in favor of active learning exercises, gamify pieces of content, and integrate formative assessments throughout the training. For example, we introduce

Sequence	*Content*	*Description*
Day one	**Library tour**	PRM-guided tour of the library
Day one	**Introduction to research**	Training overview, introduction to the research process model, concept mapping, finding background information with reference sources
Day one	**Research help desk basics**	Conducting the reference interview, recording reference questions, printing, technology troubleshooting
Day one	**Discovery and access: books**	Local catalog vs. WorldCat, Library of Congress classification, course reserves, interlibrary loan
Day one	**Practice—library olympics**	Games to practice skills: book relay race, "Where in the Library is it?" location-based trivia, "The hot seat" to practice reference questions related to book searches
Day two	**Discovery and access: finding articles**	Understanding database structure, identifying the best research for a question, basic and advanced search techniques
Day two	**Discovery and access: journal locator and evaluation**	Checking library holdings for serials, retrieving full-text articles, interlibrary loan, evaluating information sources (peer review, scholarly vs. popular)
Day two	**Practice: library olympics and closing ceremonies**	Games to practice skills: "Find that citation" and "Can you help me?" to practice reference interview skills
Day two	**Final reflections**	Self-reflection on own skills and possible outreach projects to discuss with supervisor

Figure 10.2 A model training curriculum for PRM boot camp.

the reference interview through a two-part role-playing activity. First, librarians model a "bad" reference interview with a PRM playing the patron role, followed by a debriefing that surfaces best practices for public service providers. Then, PRMs take turns answering questions designed to help them practice reference interview skills.

We often use games to review content, which encourages PRMs to move throughout the building and build comradery through friendly competition. This is especially effective at the end of a long training period. The book relay race, for example, requires PRMs to locate a book in our library catalog, retrieve it from the stacks, and find a clue that takes the next PRM into another area of the library. These types of games also serve as formative assessments and influence the ongoing training we deliver throughout the year.

In the fall semester, newly hired PRMs participate in a two-day version of the boot camp, which takes place the week before classes begin. The entire staff of the Research and Instruction Department is present throughout boot camp, but pairs of librarians develop and teach sections of content. Each pair keeps the program learning goals in mind when designing lessons. Now that we have delivered the boot camp several times, we rotate responsibility for different parts of the training content. As a result, our team of five research and instruction librarians shares ownership over the curriculum and update it together as needed.

The research boot camp is only one element of our training program. PRMs also receive continuous training throughout the semester through a series of biweekly meetings. These meetings help develop a sense of comradery, provide an opportunity to build upon content covered during boot camp, and introduce new concepts and skills. They also enable librarians to respond to issues and timely topics from the Research Help Desk and discuss

Librarian Led	***PRM Led***
Historical resources for research on the American Civil War	Funky technology in the library: microfilm readers and more
Interlibrary loan and off-site storage	Resources for research in music
Designing outreach projects	Searching for art images
Reading and downloading library eBooks	Academic integrity and the honor code
Using special collections and archives	Citing primary sources in Turabian

Figure 10.3 A sample of leaders and content for biweekly PRM meetings.

PRM-designed outreach projects. Initially, the meetings were librarian-led, but we now have veteran PRMs design and facilitate the meetings. In so doing, they further develop their teaching and mentoring skills. Meeting topics have included disciplinary resources, copyright issues for students using images or video, reading and downloading eBooks, open access publishing, and more (see Figure 10.3).

Other elements of our training approach are the "question of the week" and "resource of the week," which alternate weekly. These activities give PRMs a chance to puzzle out tricky reference questions without the stress of a patron waiting for an answer and to explore databases they have not yet used. Practice questions include finding statistical data, locating sources from an incomplete citation, using a reference work to identify a poem based upon its first line, and more. We also use the weekly questions to introduce PRMs to a range of specialized disciplinary indexes, digital historical primary source collections, and other less-frequently used tools. In fall 2015, we transferred these questions to Moodle, our campus learning management system (previously, we shared them via e-mail). We use the "advanced forum" feature to post the questions, so that all PRMs can respond and review other responses. In this way, PRMs see the wide range of possible strategies a person may take to arrive at the same answer or how a person's individual research experience can result in different perspectives on the same resource.

The final element of our approach to ongoing training is the "librarian buddy" system. PRMs co-staff the Research Help Desk with an experienced librarian, who may or may not be a member of the Research and Instruction Department. The PRM sits in the chair at our primary service point, and the librarian is close enough to see and hear any interactions and assist the PRM in a supportive, collaborative way. When users are not at the desk, PRMs and librarians debrief patron interactions and research questions. PRMs are encouraged to work on the weekly questions during their desk shifts so that they can discuss topics and resources with their librarian buddy. Librarians who have shifts scheduled with PRMs develop strong working relationships with them. Since any librarian working at the Research Help Desk may have a shift with a PRM, the Research and Instruction Department provides a best practices tip sheet for the librarians outside of the department.

IMPLEMENTATION OF THE PROGRAM

Our PRMs work an average of six to eight hours a week. A typical week includes two shifts at the Research Help Desk (four hours total), planning or carrying out outreach projects (about two hours), and a weekly check-in meeting with their direct librarian supervisor (30 minutes). Every other week, students attend an hour-long biweekly meeting with all PRMs and Research and Instruction Librarians.

While two Research and Instruction Librarians oversee the PRM Program, direct supervision of the PRMs is distributed across the five librarians in the Research and Instruction Department in order to balance the workload and sustain the program. This also enables PRMs to develop a close, mentoring relationship with their individual supervisor. One-on-one meetings are devoted to advising on outreach projects (which may be completed individually or in groups), debriefing reference questions, discussing areas in which PRMs would like more training, and other topics of concern to PRMs. The program thrives with support from a range of other library staff members. Staff from outside the Research and Instruction Department have been especially important to the success of the PRM outreach projects, as they have connected PRMs to key departmental faculty, assisted with technology, and provided insight about resources and issues relevant to their librarian liaison areas. Our established culture prioritizes supporting our student library interns, so working with PRMs was a natural evolution for many of our staff.

When we began the PRM Program, the least developed component was outreach, since we were unsure of the types of projects PRMs would decide to implement. We waited eagerly for the first cohort of PRMs to design, deliver, and assess their outreach projects. After three semesters, we can boast an impressive range of projects that have extended the reach of the library to new student populations on campus. Our PRMs have designed drop-in workshops on bibliographic management tools like RefWorks and Zotero. They have created a series of research workshops for first-semester international students. PRMs interested in our formal instruction program have updated and created new online research guides, designed and developed online instructional videos, and provided research consultations to students in selected courses. In many cases, PRMs have had great success working with faculty in courses they have already taken; typically, these PRMs are available during "office hours" to provide research consultations on assignments. Some PRMs have even taught brief research help lessons as part of a class or co-taught an information literacy session with a librarian. PRMs who decide to provide research consultations or instruction receive additional training from their librarian supervisor.

EVALUATION OF THE PROGRAM

From the very beginning, we planned a range of approaches to help us understand and assess the impact of our PRMs. First, we assess PRM activity at our Research Help Desk by tracking questions and answers in our Springshare LibAnswers system. We record the usual details about reference transactions (who answered it, question, answer, time, mode, and READ scale). In addition, we also track what we call a "PRM connection." A PRM connection is a patron who approaches a PRM for research assistance (at the Research Help Desk or elsewhere) because they know or at least recognize the PRM. If the PRM knows the patron from a class, residence hall, student club, or some other context, we assume a PRM connection and instruct PRMs to check this custom box in LibAnswers. PRMs do not always have a PRM connection with patrons, but they often do.

Before implementing the program, we hypothesized that PRMs would draw student patrons to the Research Help Desk who might not have come otherwise. We certainly hoped for this outcome as our reference transactions had declined 20 percent between the 2010–2011 and 2013–2014 academic years. Figure 10.4 shows the decline in reference transactions recorded during the two academic years preceding the PRM Program, as well as the initial increase in transactions experienced after PRMs started working at the desk. Although we have seen a decline in the total number of transactions during the spring

	Total Reference Questions	*Questions Answered by PRMs*	*"PRM Connection" Questions*
Fall 2012	2,196		
Spring 2013	1,487		
Fall 2013	1,933		
Spring 2014	1,230		
Fall 2014	1,997	530	94
Spring 2015	1,544	520	91
Fall 2015	2,005	463	62
Spring 2016	1,271	351	44

Figure 10.4 Reference transactions by semester: fall 2012–spring 2016.
Note. The PRM Program began in fall 2014.

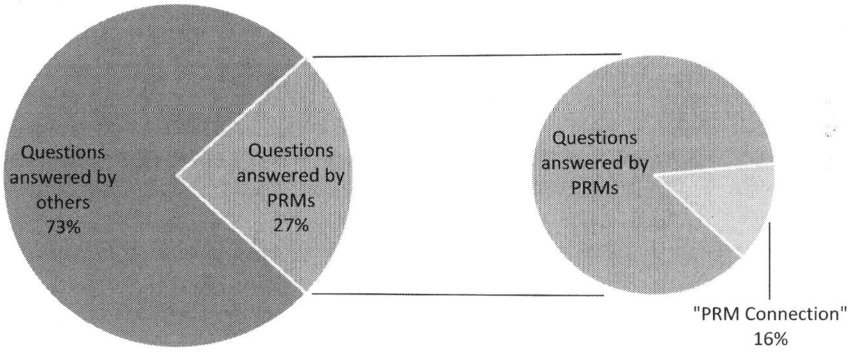

Figure 10.5 Percentage breakdown of reference transactions, 2014–2016.

2016 semester, we continue to be encouraged by the quality of the interactions between PRMs and patrons at the Research Help Desk.

Figure 10.5 shows the percentage of transactions that were handled by PRMs compared to other library staff. Over the first two years of the program, PRMs answered 27 percent of the total reference transactions, 16 percent of which were identified as a "PRM Connection."

Assessing the PRMs' research skills requires a qualitative approach. We use mid-semester and end-of-semester evaluations that ask students to reflect on their skills, their confidence in helping other students, the impact their skills have had on their own coursework, and other factors. One sophomore PRM shared the following feedback on boot camp training, which has clarified the importance of active learning exercises and games as a part of training.

> I think that August boot camp prepared me very well for working at the reference desk. . . . I learned a lot of useful tools and resources that I did not previously know about. I also liked the games interspersed in the learning. The games made learning about the library more fun, and it helped me retain information better.

The evaluations ask the PRMs to identify goals for the next semester and if there are any areas in which they would like to improve. One sophomore PRM noted that:

> My goals for next semester are to continue to familiarize myself with the library's many resources. I think there are still many online search engines that I have not used or completely

> understand. I tend to stick with a few favorite resources that I know, but it would be beneficial for me to expand my knowledge to continue to better aide [*sic*] patrons.

Another sophomore PRM noted that their involvement in the program has had the following impact:

> I think working at the desk has definitely taught me how to be a better teacher and be better at explaining things to others. One of my definite weaknesses is working with a group, and this program has definitely strengthened my skills in that area. Plus of course my research skills have been sharpened!

One of our first-year PRMs made the following remark about the program's impact on their future career:

> I think I will use the skill of finding and filtering articles and citation in my career in scientific research. Additionally, as I would like to teach, my experience at the desk has given me valuable mentoring experience and helped me learn how to teach people.

Collecting this qualitative assessment twice a semester has proved invaluable for ongoing program development.

In addition to evaluating the PRM experience through their self-reflection, we ask the PRMs to design their own assessments of their outreach projects and support them in developing ideas about how to do that. Participant feedback helps them improve design and content for future sessions. This feedback also helps PRMs develop confidence in their own skills. For example, a PRM who provided research consultations for a first-year seminar administered an end-of-the-semester survey to all 17 participants. Eighty-eight percent of respondents (15 of 17) reported that they found the consultation either very helpful or mostly helpful. Students also identified that they felt they were able to search more effectively as a result and were more likely to seek assistance at the Research Help Desk. Another PRM had presented drop-in workshops that focused on a citation management tool. The PRM created and administered a survey to participants after the session that inquired about the presentation style, level of instruction, other topics that might be of interest for a workshop, and how students found out about the workshop. The responses to these questions influenced how the PRM advertised similar sessions the following semester. While these are small assessments, they have increased the PRMs' confidence and helped to improve any issues with content or delivery.

Librarian supervisors also provide regular feedback to PRMs in their one-on-one weekly meetings. Outreach projects are debriefed throughout the project duration and at their conclusion. PRMs have a supportive and positive environment in which to discuss what worked well, what did not, and what they would change next time. Supervisors also engage PRMs in discussion about their individual learning goals for the semester.

IMPLICATIONS AND LESSONS LEARNED

PRMs have positively impacted their peers through their work at the Research Help Desk and their outreach projects, but they have also had a positive—and significant—impact on the Research and Instruction Department. PRM-developed videos, research guides, research consultations, and workshops have enabled us to expand our reference and instruction services to a wider variety of students. PRM work has also helped us strengthen collaborations with campus partners like Academic Advising and International Student Services. As we do not often have the opportunity to sustain connections with students over a span of years, the mentoring relationships we have with PRMs are especially fulfilling to librarians. PRMs have also helped librarians gain a clearer view of the student perspective. They operate as an informal student advisory group and are often the first students with whom we share ideas about new programs or changes within the library. In turn, PRMs have invited librarians into student life; one librarian is now the campus advisor to a student dance group cofounded by a PRM.

Some elements of our young program work very well. For instance, we are quite pleased with the size of our PRM cohort—a group of eight students is manageable if we share the mentoring and supervision. We also know that our tiered training program works well—providing foundational training through "boot camp" and building on that with weekly questions, biweekly meetings, and individual supervisor meetings give students a steady stream of learning and support. Just as we had hoped, our senior PRMs are mentoring newer PRMs, and all PRMs are developing their ability to mentor their peers.

We are not yet satisfied with our efforts to achieve the final learning objective: "contribute to a dynamic, supportive, peer research mentor community." The PRMs' busy course schedules keep them from spending much time with one another, with the exception of the biweekly meeting (which is a logistical challenge to schedule each semester). We have started to address this by having additional fun, informal gatherings that are not related to formal training. Now that the program is well underway, we will devote more attention to achieving this goal. We are considering reducing our hiring/training cycle to once a year. Not adding new students mid-year would reduce the training load for librarians and might help the group to become a more cohesive cohort.

We have a few issues to work on, but the program is firmly established within our library. Upon reflection, we have identified two vital factors that were essential to our early success:

- Support from the library dean. We could not have worked with colleagues outside our department to reallocate student employee positions were it not for support and leadership from the dean.
- Recognize limits and start small. By starting with a small cohort, we were able to spend time developing a well-considered, intentional training model. We also had time to identify when and how administrative work for the program needs to take place. For example, we created most of our training materials during summer and winter breaks.

NEXT STEPS

As the program matures, we continue to follow campus conversations about student engagement and high-impact practices, as well as to seek opportunities to engage students in these practices. We are already using the PRM program as a model for another library-led learning experience involving academic research and peer mentoring: our new Digital Scholarship Summer Fellowship (launched in summer 2016). We also hope the PRM Program may serve as a useful model for other parts of our campus—and for other libraries, as well.

In order to sustain what we have established, we are working with our dean and campus development office to articulate the value and impact of the program to potential donors. Ideally, we will create an endowed fund that will provide ongoing support.

Of course, we will work to maintain a strong cohort of PRMs, which will help us attract and recruit future PRMs and retain them for two to three years. We have already noticed that our PRMs seem especially active around campus and draw upon their library experience when they serve on the Honor Commission, mentor international students, or join the Queer Peer Mentor group in our LGBTQA Advocacy and Education Office. We expect that their broad engagement will continue to strengthen our program.

Our advertising materials for PRM openings describe the experience as "a student job that makes you a better student." Certainly, students benefit from the program—both the PRMs themselves and the undergraduate researchers whom they assist. The PRM Program also improves the effectiveness of the Research and Instruction Department as we are able to deepen and expand the reach and impact of our services to students. While the PRM Program continues to evolve with each new cohort, it has transformed what had previously been "just" a student job into a high-impact learning experience for students.

REFERENCES

Baugess, C., and Jallas, M. (2015). *Facilitating peer learning in the library: Crafting the perfect batch of undergraduate peer research mentors.* Denver, CO: Musselman Library, LOEX.

Bodemer, B. B. (2014). They can and they should: Undergraduates providing peer reference and instruction. *College & Research Libraries, 75*(2), 162–178. doi:10.5860/crl12–411

Faix, A. (2014). Peer reference revisited: Evolution of a peer-reference model. *Reference Services Review, 42*(2), 305–319. doi:10.1108/RSR-07–2013–0039

Faix, A. I., Bates, M. H., Hartman, L. A., Hughes, J. H., Schacher, C. N., Elliot, B. J., & Woods, A.D. (2010). Peer reference redefined: New uses for undergraduate students. *Reference Services Review, 38*(1), 90–107. doi:10.1108/00907321011020752

Gettysburg College. (2015). *Gettysburg College strategic directions: 2007–2015 report.* Retrieved from https://www.gettysburg.edu/dotAsset/fce4e2f8-ddee-4fc6–8e61-b06750f5a41d.pdf

Head, A. J. (2013, December 4). *Learning the ropes: How freshmen conduct course research once they enter college.* Retrieved from http://projectinfolit.org/images/pdfs/pil_2013_freshmenstudy_fullreport.pdf

Head, A. J., & Eisenberg, M. B. (2010, November 1). *Truth be told: How college students evaluate and use information in the digital age.* Retrieved from http://projectinfolit.org/images/pdfs/pil_fall2010_survey_fullreport1.pdf

Heinlen, W. F. (1976). Using student assistants in academic reference. *RQ, 15*(4), 323–325.

Holliday, W., & Nordgren, C. (2005). Extending the reach of librarians: Library peer mentor program at Utah State University. *College & Research Libraries News, 66*(4), 282–284. Retrieved from http://crln.acrl.org/

Kuh, G. D. (2008). *High-impact educational practices: What they are, who has access to them, and why they matter.* Washington, DC: Association of American Colleges and Universities.

Musselman Library, Gettysburg College. (2014). *Job description: Peer research mentors.* Retrieved from https://www.gettysburg.edu/library/information/general/jobs/peerresearchmentors.dot

Office of Institutional Analysis, Gettysburg College. (2015). Enrollment by semester and gender: Full-time students for degree. *Fact Book.* Gettysburg, PA: Gettysburg College.

Riggs, J. M. (2013). *September 2013 progress report on the strategic directions update: Thoughts shared with the board of trustees, February 2011.* Gettysburg College, Office of the President. Retrieved from http://www.gettysburg.edu/dotAsset/f6c1a9b5–1a26–4a0f-950c-f268e5f08416.pdf

Stanfield, A. G., & Palmer, R. L. (2010). Peer-ing into the information commons: Making the most of student assistants in new library spaces. *Reference Services Review, 38*(4), 634–646. doi:10.1108/00907321011090773

11

The Learning Commons Research Assistance Program at Indiana University Libraries

Michael Courtney and Kate Otto

This chapter discusses the Peer-Assisted Research Assistance Program that was initiated in the Indiana University Libraries Learning Commons, a technology-focused learning center with a dynamic public service model. Highly skilled upper-level undergraduate students and graduate information and library science students staff a public service desk that supports undergraduate student research needs throughout the school year. Empowering students to learn from each other in a supportive and collaborative environment has substantially impacted the public service methodologies undertaken by the Indiana University Libraries, enjoining conventional approaches to library reference and research support with an array of information literacy instruction techniques.

INSTITUTIONAL CONTEXT

Indiana University Bloomington (IUB) is the flagship campus of the eight-campus statewide Indiana University system. In the fall 2015 semester, IUB had an undergraduate enrollment of over 38,000 students, while its graduate student population comprised over 10,000 students (Indiana University, 2015a). A historically significant public research university, IUB has placed teaching and learning initiatives among its principles of excellence that serve to define the overall campus vision and shape strategic planning for future directions. Specifically, the University emphasizes "academic success and completion [initiatives in order to] enhance undergraduate student learning and success through university-wide efforts to address retention and graduation issues in a systematic, sustained fashion" as well as "innovative modes of teaching and learning that improve the educational attainments of students" (Indiana University, 2015b).

The IUB Libraries, in alignment with the overall campus mission and vision, place a considerable emphasis on information literacy integration across curricula. The Libraries' Department of Teaching and Learning contends that information literacy "involves using information critically in various contexts and for specific purposes. . . [and] includes but also extends beyond using library resources" (Indiana University Bloomington Libraries

Department of Teaching and Learning, 2015). As the Libraries have actively pursued new methods of supporting information literacy instruction across the campus at the course and curricular level, we continually identify and enact innovative approaches to undergraduate student engagement, broadening skills students have acquired in the classroom with a peer-assisted model for facilitating student research.

BACKGROUND OF THE PROGRAM

During the fall 2014 semester, the Peer-Assisted Research Assistance Program was launched in the Learning Commons, a meaningfully designed undergraduate student library space that fosters academic research success in an active, collaborative, and technology-focused environment. The Research Assistance Program operates a consultation desk in the Learning Commons service hub that supports undergraduate student research needs throughout the school year. The desk is staffed by highly skilled upper-level undergraduate students as well as graduate information and library science students. The graduate library science students serve as mentors and provide ongoing, comprehensive training to the undergraduate Research Assistants. While being offered a walk-in service, undergraduate students are also able to schedule one-on-one consultations with both undergraduate and graduate Research Assistants, seven days a week.

In addition to being the largest employer of undergraduate students on campus, the Libraries have also taken advantage of the graduate student populace (and close proximity) of the Department of Information and Library Science at IUB. The Libraries have employed many library science graduate students over the years to serve in instructional and research/reference-related capacities. Throughout this chapter, we will refer to three distinct student assistant positions within the Libraries. These are labeled and defined as follows:

- Reference Assistant: This position is staffed primarily by graduate student employees who provide in-person and virtual reference assistance at two public service points.
- Research Assistant: This position was created for undergraduate student employees to staff a Research Assistance Desk in the Libraries' Learning Commons. During the first two years of the Peer-Assisted Research Assistance Program, graduate student employees have also served in this role.
- Instruction Assistant: This role has been filled by graduate student employees who provide in-person instruction for many courses on the IUB campus. Although instructional opportunities are still offered as needed, the role of the Instruction Assistant has gradually transitioned to mentoring undergraduate Research Assistants working at the Learning Commons Research Assistance Desk.

A confluence of space and service initiatives that included renovating existing library spaces and adding new public service points in addition to a general campus climate shift over the past two years provided us with a unique opportunity to re-envision the roles of the Instruction Assistant while developing peer-assisted learning opportunities for the campus's undergraduate student population. The Libraries face a considerable challenge hiring and retaining student employees across all facets of library operational work due to a campus policy change concerning the number of hours that student employees may work coupled with declining graduate student enrollment in the Department of Information and Library Science. Not unexpectedly, we experienced a decline in the number of Instruction Assistants we could reasonably retain. This dramatically affected our ability to accommodate the high volume of one-shot instruction session requests we typically received at the time. With only three Teaching and Learning Librarians and a declining cache of graduate student Instruction Assistants, we began to evaluate the sustainability of high-volume traditional one-shot instruction. We also assessed the effectiveness of our instructional efforts and actively sought ways to make a greater impact on student learning and academic success across the undergraduate curriculum.

During this time, the Libraries also underwent significant changes in spaces and services. The Herman B Wells Library, the largest library on campus and where Teaching and Learning Librarians are physically located, began a series of much-needed renovations. The Learning Commons, a technology-focused learning space, was officially unveiled in late fall 2014. It provides students with a 24-hour, 7 days per week, dynamic space and a wide variety of individual and group study options while also presenting a rich suite of library and campus partner-provided support services. While the Learning Commons is open and actively utilized by a wide community of patrons, its largest demographic of users is the undergraduate student population. With this in mind, much of our focus on services and support within the space tends to center on the undergraduate student. Through a partnership with University Information Technology Services, the Learning Commons provides much of the necessary technical support for students, faculty, and staff. In addition, library partners, such as Writing Tutorial Services and the Office of the Vice Provost for Undergraduate Education, increase the available options for facilitating student academic life and success. We decided to maximize the opportunity the new space afforded by reimagining our public service desks—moving beyond traditional circulation and reference work and toward a peer-assisted model of facilitating student academic success out of the classroom.

Concurrent with the opening of the Learning Commons, we launched our Research Assistance Program, providing undergraduate students with the opportunity to receive research and resource guidance from their peers either by drop-in service most days of the week or by scheduled appointments. Our expectations were that peer-facilitated research consultations would provide students with the opportunity to learn from fellow students and serve as a valuable extension of our other information literacy initiatives.

We were also actively seeking ways to enjoin general reference services in the library by creating a combined training program for all public service student employees. The student employees now work across three separate public service points, including the newly created Research Assistance Desk also in the Learning Commons. This cross-training approach was envisioned to not only provide students with the broadest possible skills to perform reference and research assistance, but also enable more consistent communication between the Teaching and Learning and Reference Departments. While the Reference Department currently oversees the Reference and Circulation Desks, the Teaching and Learning Department is wholly responsible for the Research Assistance Program's desk. As this desk is in close proximity to the Learning Commons Reference Desk, we viewed it important for all of the students (Reference Assistants and Research Assistants) staffing each desk to understand their differing roles for the purpose of referral while also wishing to deliver consistent information to all library patrons. An additional benefit to this arrangement for our graduate student Instruction Assistants lies in the experience of mentoring our undergraduate Research Assistants to help facilitate more informal teaching and learning moments. We expect that the mentoring skills they develop will help improve their own instructional efforts, and in turn further our undergraduate Research Assistants' success in providing a valuable service to our undergraduate student population.

Our goals for the program are empowering undergraduate students to: discuss course content; clarify what they read and hear; analyze, question, and verify ideas; model and practice new behaviors; work on challenging problems; and, integrate newly discovered knowledge into their research. Our aim is that through peer-assisted, face-to-face interactions, undergraduate students will gain positive interdependence, individual accountability, and interpersonal skill development throughout the process.

The undergraduate Research Assistant hiring process consists of an advertised position description that is hosted on the Libraries' website and distributed widely during the first half of the summer semester (in anticipation of the start of the new academic year) and again prior to the start of the spring semester, as staffing needs dictate. In addition to general hiring criteria for student library employees, Research Assistants are hired based on demonstrated research ability (e.g., prior experience conducting research in academic coursework), recommendations, interest, and availability. While any undergraduate student may be eligible regardless of year (first year, sophomore, etc.), our focus has been on more experienced upper-level undergraduate students across a wide array of disciplines.

TRAINING AND PREPARATION OF RESEARCH ASSISTANTS

There were two distinct phases of training at the outset of the program—during the transitional period at the beginning of the program's implementation and an eventual combined effort that undertook cross-training graduate student Reference Assistants and undergraduate Research Assistants across multiple service points. In both instances, many of the methods and tools used remained the same. Initially, we began to develop reference and research skills among the graduate student Instruction Assistants who would first staff the Research Assistance Desk at the beginning of its implementation and who would then mentor and train the undergraduate Research Assistants as the program became fully established.

During the first semester of the Research Assistance Program, the Research Assistance Desk was primarily staffed by graduate student Instruction Assistants. There were two fundamental reasons for doing so: as the Learning Commons space was still in its infancy, we were attempting to gauge staffing and patron needs for such a service; further, we wanted to establish a standard for performing research consultations that could then be modeled for undergraduate Research Assistants. We anticipated that even the most adept undergraduate Research Assistants would require substantially more training than our graduate student Instruction Assistants. In consideration of the time and effort involved in fully training the undergraduate Research Assistants to be experts, we devoted the summer prior to the program launch to providing the graduate student Instruction Assistants with the skills necessary to mentor and train the undergraduate Research Assistants.

Regular meetings with the Teaching and Learning Department leading up to the launch of the research assistance service aided significantly in the transition, allowing librarians to teach particular components of the research consultation process and charging the graduate student Instruction Assistants to actively practice with their own peers while being guided and assessed in a safe and inclusive environment. We also had to cover a variety of issues that might arise beyond the primary task of providing research assistance—understanding library policies and procedures, as well as spaces, services, and locations. This was especially important to provide a consistent message and experience across multiple public service desks throughout the library. Through a series of workshops and hands-on training exercises, we fully explored the research consultation process with the graduate student Instruction Assistants (Figure 11.1).

As the consultation model we developed centers on backward design, we created a series of active learning exercises that allow Research Assistants to consider what process undergraduate students will need to go through and what knowledge/skills they'll need in order to conduct research (see Appendix 11–1). Training exercises gradually become more complex, combining the overarching idea of the research process with backward design principles (see Appendix 11–2). Our training was not limited to simple discussion prompts and written exercises, however. We spent considerable time providing active role-playing exercises, allowing students to engage in dialogue as both Research Assistant and undergraduate patron while providing opportunities for constructive criticism and continuous feedback (Figure 11.2).

In addition to training during these regular meetings, a shared online resource site was created in the campus learning management system, Canvas. The shared Canvas site provides a modular platform to access information relevant to drop-in research assistance (e.g., getting started and general desk opening procedures, answering research questions and helping students, common questions at the Research Assistance Desk, recording statistics, information and spaces and services, work schedules and substitutions, and desk closing procedures). It also provides information about scheduled research consultations (e.g., procedures for volunteering for, preparing, and wrapping up a research consultation). The site is further enhanced by offering opportunities for student assistants to contribute to content as well as interact with each other.

Training was also an ongoing initiative while the students staffed the desk. Librarians regularly made time, particularly in the first months of launching the service, to co-staff the desk with the student assistants. This proved essential in many ways, providing a positive model to follow in a behavioral and pragmatic sense. We also intentionally paired students who had previous reference experience with those student assistants who had not. We expected that the student assistants would gain valuable insight by learning from their

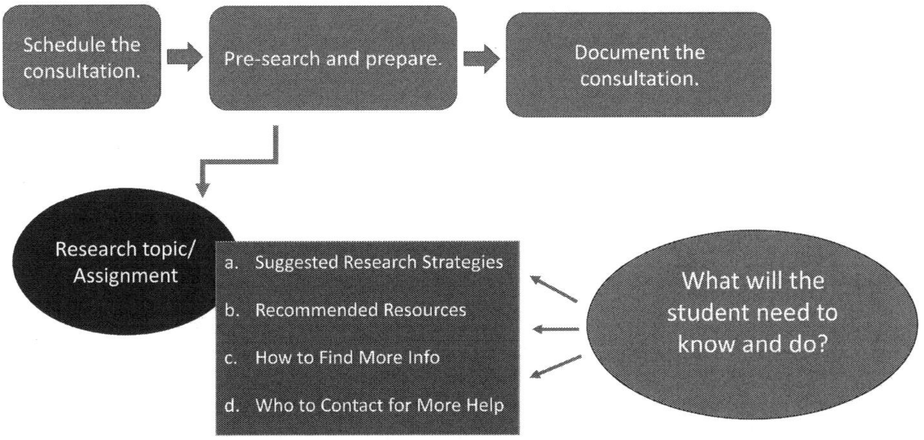

Figure 11.1 The research consultation process: Training documentation.

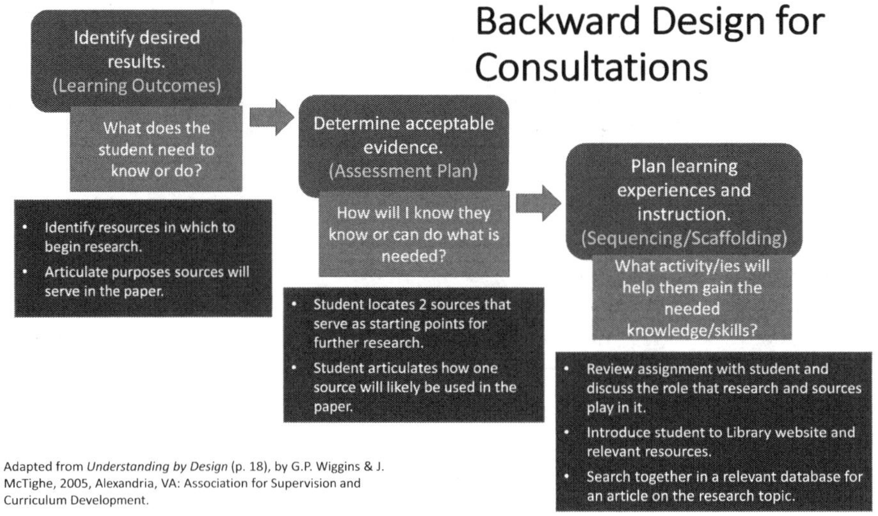

Figure 11.2 Backward design for research consultations: Training documentation.
Adapted from *Understanding by Design* (p. 18), by G.P. Wiggins & J. McTighe, 2005, Alexandria, VA: Association for Supervision and Curriculum Development.

more experienced peers for much the same reason that we established the Peer-Assisted Research Assistance Program. The inherent value in doing so cannot be understated. As the Research Assistants became more confident in their abilities, librarian presence at the desk became less of a necessity. However, it remains good practice to interact with Research Assistants as much as reasonably possible to answer questions and provide guidance when needed. Gradually, the responsibility of on-the-job training was shifted to the graduate student Instruction Assistants who provide expertise and mentorship to the undergraduate Research Assistants as they learn the process.

In year two of the program, as the role of the graduate student Instruction Assistants shifted to that of mentor and trainer for undergraduate Research Assistants, a combined training program was established between the Reference Department and the Teaching and Learning Department. Since the Research Assistants work in close proximity to Reference Assistants, it made sense to enjoin part of their training. A two-day intensive workshop for all library public service assistants was ultimately developed. In addition to the active learning exercises developed for the Research Assistants the previous year, we provided small group presentations on the library catalog, the Libraries' circulation system, the discovery and use of common library electronic resources, shared library usage policies, and a variety of other topics. We also developed a student-led library tour and orientation, tasking small groups to discover certain information about specific library locations and services. The small groups then led a series of presentations to the larger group conveying what they learned. Much of our training centers on the idea of students training fellow students, a structure we hope will serve to establish the mentoring role we envisioned for the Instruction Assistants when the Research Assistance Program becomes fully staffed with undergraduate students.

After the completion of the workshop, ongoing training (both in-person and via the Canvas training modules) continues for those students working on the Research Assistance

Desk. The shared experience helps connect the students working in different capacities and provides them an opportunity to see the interconnectedness of their work. It cannot be emphasized enough that training is an ongoing and evolving practice. We consistently provide updates about new library resources, and changes in policies and procedures via in-person discussions as well as through a shared electronic mailing list.

IMPLEMENTATION OF THE PROGRAM

When the Research Assistance Program began in late fall 2014, research consultations in the Learning Commons were available on a drop-in basis between 10:00 a.m. and 8:00 p.m. most weekdays and from 2:00 p.m. until 8:00 p.m. on Sundays. On average, one Research Assistant would staff the desk for a two-hour shift, but scheduling efforts discouraged shifts longer than four hours. Most of the service provided during that first semester was the result of drop-in requests, but an online consultation request form was available for students who wished to make an appointment. Online requests were vetted by librarians and, when appropriate, distributed to a shared Research Assistant listserv seeking volunteers to meet with the requesting students. There were occasions when the perceived depth of knowledge required for a research consultation necessitated referral to a subject librarian in which case the consultation would then be transferred to the Reference Department. Research Assistants worked directly with the student to determine a mutually beneficial time to meet in person, either at the Research Assistance Desk or at another location in the library. During the spring 2016 semester, the Research Assistance Desk was staffed approximately 40 hours per week by a staff of 10–12 Research Assistants working two- and three-hour shifts. Research consultations were also performed by Research Assistants outside of those scheduled hours as needed.

We developed a Research Jumpstart worksheet (see Appendix 11–3) that consists of a detailed list of suggestions, resources, and research strategies. This worksheet is completed by a Research Assistant and later shared with the student. Typically, concepts addressed during a research consultation include developing a research topic, searching for sources for a paper or project, and evaluating research resources.

Research Assistants are compensated for the time required to prepare for a scheduled research consultation in addition to the consultation itself. During the first year of the program, Research Assistants were supervised by Teaching and Learning Librarians. During year two, a supplemental layer of supervision was added by a representative of the Reference Department to help provide some continuity both with our cross-training initiative and an added connection to the Libraries' shared public service focus. However, primary supervision continues to be handled by Teaching and Learning Librarians.

EVALUATION OF THE PROGRAM

Since the implementation of the Research Assistance Program, our Research Assistants have recorded statistics into a Qualtrics online survey form. Librarians determined that quantitative data would be necessary to understand the initial needs of the Research Assistants within the Learning Commons space. To meet that goal, the Qualtrics survey was embedded in the Canvas learning management system site established for the Research Assistants' ongoing training which also houses relevant instructional documents, meeting materials (e.g., handouts, agendum), and general staff announcements. On the first page of the survey, the Research Assistant is asked to indicate, after each reference interaction, the mode of interaction (e.g., in-person, telephone, e-mail, instant message/chat, or other) and the question's subject area, as well as the specific question. The second page of the survey form asks whether the question was resolved, why it may not have been (if applicable), and to what library resource (or subject librarian) the unresolved question was referred (if any). The final questions ask the transaction's total duration, the level of difficulty (gauged by the amount of time spent on the question), and the Research Assistant's name. Overall, these eight questions were designed to take minimal time to complete, roughly about a minute or less.

During the period between fall 2014 and the end of fall 2015, the Research Assistance Program has recorded a combined 763 transactions. From these data, we know 26 Research Assistants answered 762 reference and research-related questions covering 39 unique disciplinary subjects, including health and natural science, humanities, social science, fine art, and more (Figure 11.3).

Research Assistants documented the largest number of consultations as falling under a general/interdisciplinary subject category, which happens to primarily consist of introductory level undergraduate courses and common Learning Commons space questions. Intentionally, the drop-in transactions at the Research Assistance Desk are designed to be quick or just-in-time reference and research help; however, there is no established time

Linguistics Folklore Computer Science Informatics	2
African Studies Latin American, Iberian, and Latino Studies Global Studies Communication and Culture Library and Information Science Economics	3
Biology Music Religious Studies Psychology	4
Theater and Drama Government Information—Federal, State, Local Documents	5
Public and Environmental Affairs Political Science	6
English and American Literature	7
Education	8
Anthropology	9
History	20
Business	23
No Subject Listed	218
General / Multidisciplinary	412
Grand Total	**761**

Figure 11.3 Consultations by subject, fall 2014–fall 2015.

limit. Out of the 568 research consultations with recorded durations, the vast majority, 359, were resolved or referred in less than five minutes. The second highest recorded duration consisted of 99 consultations lasting between five and 15 minutes (Figure 11.4).

Research consultations that are arranged by appointment have been shown to be an option not as commonly used by undergraduates. From the Qualtrics assessment, 52 percent (or, 397) of reference/research interactions, out of the total number recorded, are between the hours of 12:00 p.m. and 4:00 p.m. (Figure 11.5).

Notably, the morning and evening hours between 10:00 a.m. and 9:00 p.m. remain substantial enough to justify keeping a relatively similar schedule moving forward. However, because we recorded an interestingly low number of eight consultations taking place after 9:00 p.m. and only five consultations occurring before 10:00 a.m. during the assessed period of 2014–2015, we intend to revise our Research Assistance Desk hours to 10:00 a.m.–8:00 p.m., Monday through Thursday, eliminating Fridays and weekends when demand for such services dropped precipitously.

More broadly, our data indicate that research consultations take place more during the fall semester than during the spring semester, and, further, research consultations tend to occur earlier rather than later in the semester (Figure 11.6).

Although this trend aligns with findings by O'Kelly, Garrison, Merry, and Torreano (2015), who discovered "that consultation numbers quickly increased during the early part of the semester and then followed a predictable pattern that coincides with the academic cycle," suggesting downturns in statistics toward the end of the semester, these

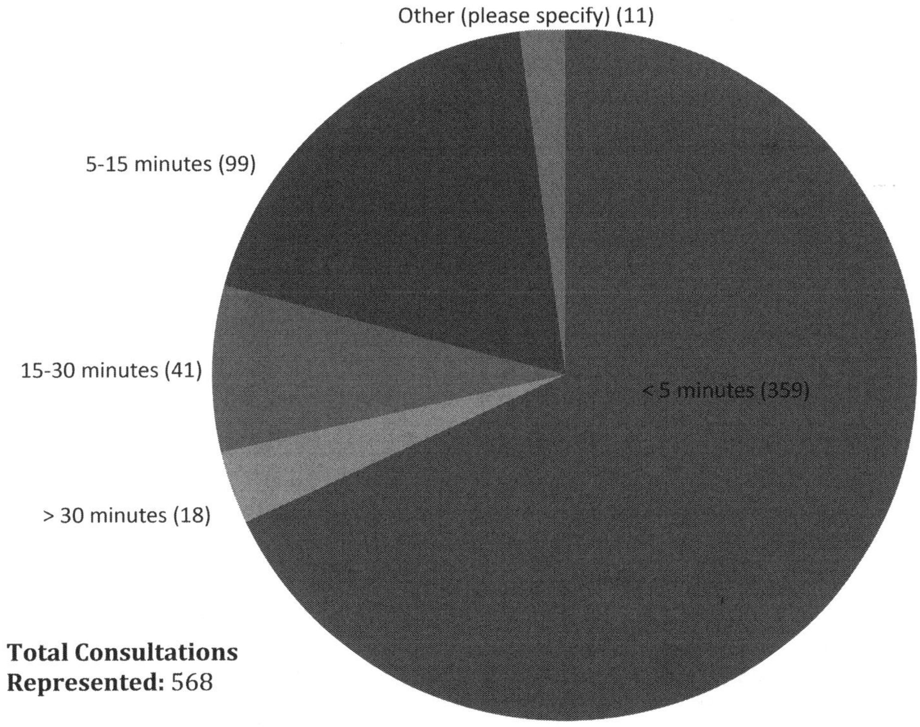

Figure 11.4 Time spent per consultation, fall 2014–fall 2015.

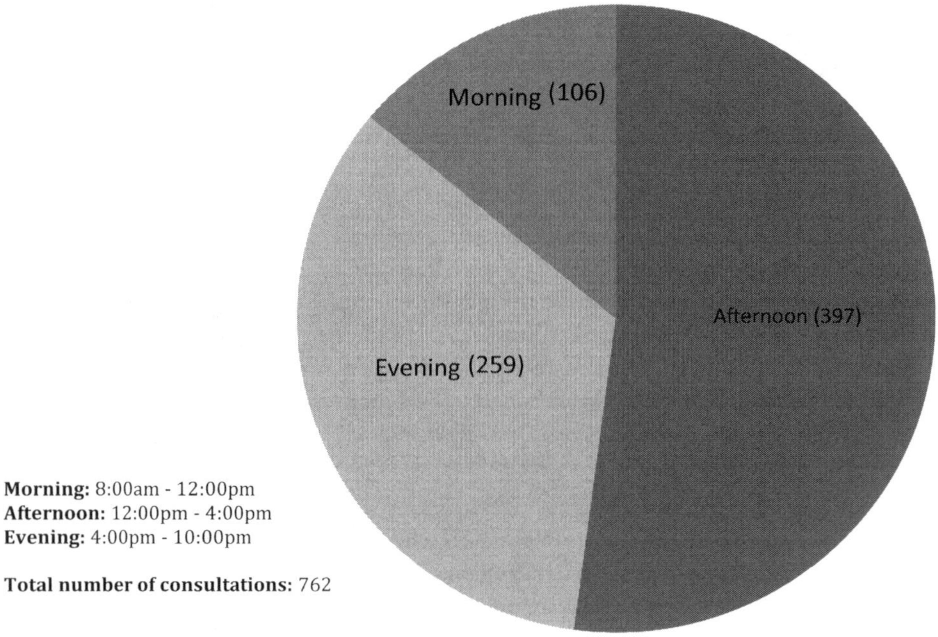

Figure 11.5 Consultation time of day, fall 2014–fall 2015.

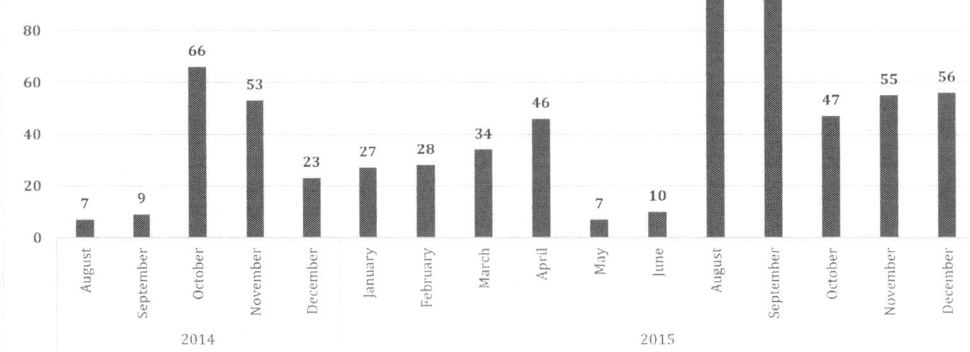

Figure 11.6 Consultations by month, fall 2014–fall 2015.

statistics represent only the first year of offering the program and will likely be more informative over time (p. 171).

These initial findings align well with the projected intention of the Research Assistance Desk in that it would primarily serve as a just-in-time research and reference service and that assistants would, in most cases, refer users to other resources or subject librarians with more specific questions, as well as scheduling more in-depth research consultations with another Research Assistant at a later date.

Qualitative feedback from an anonymous open-answer Qualtrics survey given to the Research Assistants indicated that simple, directional questions frustrated the majority of them and that they did not feel as though they were meaningful, in-depth research assistance. In support of their perspectives, out of 568 Qualtrics responses, well over half, 476, or 87.9 percent were recorded as "very easy" or "easy." And, of the 763 consultations, 147 were recorded as unresolved and referred, with 60 percent referred to University Information Technology Services consultants who shared the Learning Commons service hub space. The data, or lack thereof, do support the idea that undergraduates may not be consistently seeking out help within the Learning Commons, particularly from the Research Assistance Desk. A lack of marketing and partnerships and/or the physical location of the desk could perceivably be the cause.

Furthermore, a separate Learning Commons environmental space study seeking knowledge of the services offered was conducted with approximately 375 randomly selected student respondents. Overall, about 87 percent of undergraduate respondents answered they were either "satisfied" or "very satisfied" with the Learning Commons in general (in contrast to "very dissatisfied," "dissatisfied," or "neutral"). Despite their satisfaction with the space, 69.2 percent of the same undergraduates responded they did not know the Learning Commons offered a Research Assistance Program prior to taking the survey, and 91.7 percent answered they had not used the research assistance service at all. In comparison, 76.9 percent of respondents were aware of the technology center consulting services, and 61.4 percent had used that particular service. In sum, the data sorely highlight the lack of knowledge undergraduates have about the Learning Commons Research Assistance Desk. Qualitative data also highlight the fact that the Research Assistance Desk is not yet meeting its full potential.

We also seek continuous reflection from our Research Assistants after the intensive training has ended and the on-the-job training continues. We require a self-assessment reflection document to be completed by each Research Assistant after his or her first research consultation (see Appendix 11–4). This provides the student with an opportunity to reflect on the process and also allows us to have an idea of where the Research Assistant may require additional training and follow-up.

IMPLICATIONS AND LESSONS LEARNED

Encouragingly, many of our Research Assistants have specifically commented, in individual or group meetings, that peer-to-peer work has been both effective and fulfilling. One response to an anonymous survey distributed to the Research Assistants stated,

> I think the benefit of the peer-to-peer model is that students feel more comfortable working with someone who is clearly closer to them in age. I've had many students come to me after meeting with a librarian and express a certain level of frustration—either because they didn't find the librarian helpful or they didn't understand what the librarian was trying to share with them.

Another Research Assistant relayed, "the most appealing aspects of the peer-to-peer service model is the proximity in experience, since we. . . remember the difficulties of navigating databases and lend a sense of empathy to our interactions with patrons." As members of the Teaching and Learning Department, we regularly ask our student employees to reflect on what they believe is successful with regard to their work at the Research Assistance Desk, as well as which aspects about their work as a peer mentor are more challenging. One Research Assistant responded that the "main challenge is the frustration that the desk is not meeting even half its potential as a resource for students. I have no doubt that more students would utilize the research desk if only they knew about it." However, the fact that the 763 consultations gathered from our initial assessment have taken place despite the lack of marketing indicates the desk has certainly provided a beneficial service worth continuing and improving.

There is undoubtedly more data to gather with respect to undergraduate student satisfaction with research assistance experienced. Additionally, we are planning the implementation of queue management software in summer 2016. The software will help us organize waiting lines for students utilizing our drop-in services. It will also provide more granular student-level data to inform us about student use of Learning Commons services, such as the Research Assistance Program, that we hope will provide further insight into expanding and improving upon our burgeoning research assistance service.

More than a year has passed since the Learning Commons began offering a handful of services staffed primarily for and by students. In addition, the space's recently fashioned partnerships are still gathering their bearings and deciding on a vision and shared orientation for student employees. The combination of a new space and trialing service models suggests that establishing assignment-driven, information literacy instruction in the form of peer-to-peer research assistance has been a positive achievement in and of itself. In fact, our recorded transactions and assessment measures have shown our research assistance service to be a relative success, with little initial marketing or fanfare. This, all things considered, is remarkable and attests to the success of the new Learning Commons being a desirable campus destination for students. As a result, peer-led research assistance in the Learning Commons is currently a consistent and dependable component of the space's service hub offerings, but has the potential to become a more critical amenity.

More intentional training, stronger marketing efforts, and increased assessment will help transition valuable peer-assisted, assignment-driven information literacy into an essential service at Wells Library. In order to move forward, the Learning Commons will need to market the convenience and practicality of the services offered, with the Research Assistance Desk being no exception.

NEXT STEPS

Murphy (2014) found that formal instruction and seeking research help from full-time librarians resonated little with college student respondents in how they learn about the library and its resources. In order to remain relevant, academic libraries need to provide practical and approachable services that provide an obvious purpose. Murphy provided the perspective with supporting evidence that college students mimic how adult learners engage in informal learning in a work environment. In other words, the resources, services, and programs that academic libraries offer should ideally support informal learning opportunities conveniently or students will persist through alternative means—usually their peers. As the Learning Commons partners and staff reflect on the current challenges we face, the factor of convenience that Murphy's study highlighted comes to the forefront.

The lack of adequate signage, for example, in the Learning Commons is neither convenient nor accessible to undergraduates. Rather, it demands more effort in finding where to go and more time deciding which service(s) will best fit their need. Better or additional signage is an obvious answer, but marketing and partnerships are credible, too.

Partnering with external campus units and departments could also help create more practical opportunities for student employees, thereby elevating the current culture of the research assistance position. With approximately 20 Research Assistants at any given time during the academic year, a librarian's ability for mentoring students and developing projects is challenging at best. As many of the Research Assistants have multiple library jobs and conflicting availability, we become less successful at facilitating meaningful experiences beyond opportunities like our research assistance service. We would like our student staff to gain multiple forms of library experiences before they graduate. In our case, a potential avenue of partnership exists with the Department of Information and Library Science. The potential also exists to develop a practicum or paid internship to give graduate students more dedicated and meaningful work experiences like mentoring undergraduate Research Assistants.

We have discovered that orientation and training efforts for all public service student employees could be more consistent and structured. The student employees might benefit from an ongoing training program that incorporates reference, instruction, and outreach aspects, in addition to a substantial component on peer mentoring. From our own observations, we believe that our graduate student Instruction Assistant mentors increasingly become far removed from the affective dimensions of the undergraduate experience—the anxiety, frustration, and overall intimidation that many undergraduates, particularly first-year students, experience throughout the research process. The undergraduate Research Assistants would also benefit from a training regimen that includes in its user-centric focus the relational value of students guiding students (or, in another sense, peer-assisted learning)—"help[ing] student mentors understand why they are doing what they are doing and to recognize its value through their own learning and development" is integral to a peer-to-peer approach (Bolton, Pugliese, and Singleton-Jackson, 2009, p. 25). As the program evolves, we hope to have the Research Assistance Desk staffed exclusively by undergraduate students. We anticipate shifting the mentoring role away from the graduate student Instruction Assistants and placing experienced undergraduate Research Assistants as mentors to less experienced Research Assistants.

Peer mentoring at the Learning Commons Research Assistance Desk involves continuous assessment and evaluation and is an active learning experience for both the learner and the Research Assistant. Just as in the foundational peer-to-peer mission of constructively evaluating and recommending ways to improve weaknesses, both parties are improving the necessary skills to prepare for future academic, professional, and personal endeavors (Reese-Durham, 2005). In the case of the Learning Commons, improving an undergraduate's knowledge of library resources and trying to guide their effective application of the research process are as important as the Research Assistant's ability to acquire critical reference and instruction experience. Embedding peer-assisted information literacy teaching and learning opportunities in academic library services has incredible potential to profoundly and positively impact student learning outcomes. By experimenting with peer-assisted models, we are working to collaboratively integrate information literacy competencies in a service model that supports student success while practically preparing our student employees for their future professional careers.

REFERENCES

Association of College and Research Libraries. (2015). *Framework for information literacy for higher education.* Retrieved from http://www.ala.org/acrl/standards/ilframework

Bolton, T., Pugliese, T., & Singleton-Jackson, J. (2009). Advancing the promotion of information literacy through peer-led learning. *Communications in Information Literacy, 3*(1), 20–30. Retrieved from http://www.comminfolit.org/index.php?journal=cil

Indiana University. (2015a). *IU factbook.* Retrieved from https://www.iu.edu/~uirr/reports/standard/factbook/2015–16/Bloomington/Fast_Facts/Fast_Facts

Indiana University. (2015b). *Principles of excellence.* Retrieved from http://president.iu.edu/initiatives/principles.shtml

Indiana University Bloomington Libraries Department of Teaching and Learning. (2015). *Teaching and learning.* Retrieved from https://libraries.indiana.edu/teach

Murphy, J. A. (2014). Library learning: Undergraduate students' informal, self-directed, and information sharing strategies. *Partnership: The Canadian Journal of Library and Information Practice and Research, 9*(1), 1–20. Retrieved from https://journal.lib.uoguelph.ca/index.php/perj/index#.V4gEMLgrKUk

O'Kelly, M. A., Garrison, J., Merry, B., & Torreano, J. (2015). Building a peer-learning service for students in an academic library. *portal: Libraries & the Academy, 15*(1), 163–182. doi:10.1353/pla.2015.0000

Reese-Durham, N. (2005). Peer evaluation as an active learning technique. *Journal of Instructional Psychology, 32*(4), 338–343.

Wiggins, G. P., & McTighe, J. (2005). *Understanding by design.* Alexandria, VA: Association for Supervision and Curriculum Development.

APPENDIX 11–1: SAMPLE RESEARCH CONSULTATION REQUEST: TRAINING DOCUMENTATION

How would you prepare to help this student?
"I have a 12-page research assignment for X104. I need 3–5 peer-reviewed sources and I don't know where to start!"

Questions to consider:

- What questions might you ask the student to better understand the task and the student's needs?
- What knowledge and skills does the task require?
- How will you know the student has gained the needed knowledge/skills?
- Discuss in pairs: ask for assignment sheet or details; look into whether Course Guide exists.
- Consider what process student will need to go through and what knowledge/skills they'll need (e.g., what is "peer-reviewed," how will sources be used).

APPENDIX 11–2: SAMPLE RESEARCH CONSULTATION REQUEST: FURTHER TRAINING DOCUMENTATION

The student provides more information about the assignment: they are to create an informative poster about a specific aspect of global warming (e.g., government policy, political debates, science education, economic effects).

Use backward design to help you prepare for the consultation.

- What does the student need to know or do? (*Learning outcomes*)
- How will I know they know or can do what is needed? (*Assessment*)
- What activity/activities will help them gain the needed knowledge/skills? (*Sequencing/scaffolding*)

Discuss in pairs: ask for assignment sheet or details; look into whether Course Guide exists.

Consider what process students will need to go through and what knowledge/skills they'll need (e.g., what is "peer-reviewed," how will sources be used).

APPENDIX 11–3: RESEARCH JUMPSTART WORKSHEET

1. NAME/E-MAIL of Researcher:
2. NAME/E-MAIL of Library Consultant:
3. DATE/TIME of Consultation:
4. COURSE Name/Number:
5. Research TOPIC or Assignment DESCRIPTION:

- Suggested research strategies (e.g., narrowing your topic, developing a research question, brainstorming search terms):
- Recommended resources + citations, call numbers and locations, or links (e.g., books, articles, websites, government documents, films):
- How to find more information (e.g., tips for accessing relevant databases):
- Whom to contact for further assistance (i.e., to go more in-depth with your research, contact a subject librarian):

APPENDIX 11–4: RESEARCH ASSISTANT SELF-ASSESSMENT DISCUSSION WORKSHEET

Please fill out the following self-assessment worksheet *after* your first research consultation.

1. What were your biggest concerns as you prepared for the research consultation?
2. Describe three aspects of the consultation that you think went well and why. Responses can range from preparation of research materials, communication with the student, research assignment/project content, student response, and so on.
3. Describe three things that you wish you would have done differently. Explain why and what you might do differently the next time you provide a research consultation.
4. Share an idea for the research assignment/project for this consultation OR how you might change the research assignment/project for the consultation you gave.
5. Write down any general thoughts or observations that you would like to share with your colleagues.

12

The Peer Research Assistants at the Michigan State University Libraries

Emilia R. Marcyk and Benjamin Oberdick

When Michigan State implemented new Engagement Centers in its campus residence halls, they seemed like a natural venue to expand services outside the walls of the library. However, it took multiple attempts to find a service model that fit both the needs of the students and the Michigan State University (MSU) Libraries. In this chapter, we will discuss how a struggling program that sent librarians to the residence halls to provide reference assistance evolved into the robust peer-learning program, the Peer Research Assistants, which exists today.

INSTITUTIONAL CONTEXT

Michigan State University (MSU) is a large, land-grant, research university. As of fall 2015, its student population was 39,143 undergraduates and 11,400 graduate and professional students for a total student population of 50,543 (MSU, 2015a, para 4). Our students represent all 50 U.S. states; 15 percent are international students; 18.1 percent are students of color; 51.6 percent are women, and 48.4 percent are men (MSU, 2015a, para 4). The main campus is located in East Lansing, a medium-sized city adjacent to Michigan's state capital, Lansing.

As part of its mission to serve undergraduate students, MSU implemented a new housing strategy during the 2007–2008 academic year (MSU, n.d.a, p. 1). Based on the urban planning concept of the "urban village," the new strategy organized campus residence halls into neighborhoods, which would serve as hubs for academic, social, and health support for undergraduate students (MSU, n.d.a, p. 1). As of this writing, there are five campus neighborhoods (MSU, 2015b, para 4). Each consists of three to eight residence halls, a team of coordinators for academic and extracurricular programming, and numerous student services and activities.

The centerpiece of each neighborhood is the Engagement Center (EC). The ECs serve as a central hub for student support across four "key developmental areas": academic, health and wellness, intercultural, and residential (MSU, 2016, para 4). ECs are typically housed in a centrally located residence hall within each neighborhood. Both on- and off-campus students can go to any of the five ECs for services ranging from math tutoring and writing help to fitness classes and health clinics. The services are aimed primarily at undergraduate students, though graduate students may use them as well. Some of the guiding principles of the EC model include a student-centered approach and rigorous assessment to meet the "needs and interests of students within each neighborhood" (MSU, n.d. b, p. 1).

The Peer Research Assistant (PRA) Program, the cornerstone of the MSU Libraries' outreach initiative to the residence hall ECs, falls within the area of academic development. Of the stated goals of the neighborhood system, the PRA Program most directly helps students:

- Develop and practice the perspectives, motivations, and skills, which promote academic success
- Become active and engaged learners
- Become both independent and interdependent learners (MSU, 2015b, para 2)

While having library services in the ECs seemed like a natural fit, it took the MSU Libraries two years of experimentation to find a service model that worked for the library and the students we were trying to reach.

BACKGROUND OF THE PROGRAM

The MSU Libraries began providing reference assistance to patrons in the ECs soon after MSU first instituted the neighborhood initiative. The Head of Reference at the time thought there would be benefits to having reference services available closer to where students lived. In the first service model, librarians, rather than students, worked two- to three-hour shifts in the ECs up to three times per week. During fall 2011 and spring 2012, 18 reference librarians provided reference services in three ECs. Over these two semesters, librarians spent 16 weeks in the ECs, and received approximately 32 questions. While working in the ECs, reference librarians tried to partner with the Writing Center to help patrons who were seeking writing assistance. This proved to be a good source of the limited number of questions the librarians received. After answering only 32 questions with this service model, the Head of Reference switched to an appointment-based model, in which librarians only worked in the ECs when a student scheduled an appointment, rather than waiting through long shifts with no one to help. The Libraries tried the appointment model for fall 2012 and spring 2013, but it proved even less successful than the prior model; students made fewer than 20 total appointments during the two semesters, and even when appointments were made, students often did not show up at the scheduled time. The Head of Reference decided that the Libraries needed to take a different approach to maintain services in the residence hall ECs.

Literature on library reference and instruction outreach describes similar problems faced by librarians trying to provide services to students in residence halls. Other libraries have struggled with students feeling intimidated or surveilled by librarians in their dorms, or report general confusion from students about the role of the librarian in that context (Harley, Dreger, & Knobloch 2001; Nims, 1998; Pietraszewski & Smith, 2004; Strothmann & Antell, 2010). The literature shows a few successful programs that integrate peer assistance into residence halls in some form, from Barnes and Peyton (2007), who collaborated with Resident Assistants at Mississippi State University, to Riehle and Witt (2009) who tapped student assistants to teach well-received information literacy sessions in residence halls at Purdue University. While we did not engage in any extensive study to determine the reasons that our students were not asking questions, it became clear from the low number of questions that our outreach to the ECs needed to change.

In fall 2013, the Head of Reference proposed that the MSU Libraries switch to a peer-assisted learning model, and hire undergraduate students to provide reference and research services instead of librarians. Many other campus units and departments used students to provide assistance in the ECs, including the Writing Center, Math Learning Center, and Economics Help Room. Since many students already go to the ECs for academic help and tutoring, using peer assistants seemed like a promising idea for extending reference services outside the walls of the library, while continuing to support the neighborhood initiative.

The Head of Reference approached us with the idea for the new reference services model, and the PRA Program was born. The program would be supervised by the EC Services Coordinator, a 40 percent appointment that was added to the Coordinator's existing job duties.

In the early planning stages, we explored the literature on peer-assisted learning and found a particular quote from Lee Williams (2011) that would form the foundation for our PRA Program philosophy:

> there is no aspect of the collegiate experience. . . that cannot benefit from the involvement of a peer who explains, in language often more accessible, a difficult concept. A peer can talk with students about relationship violence, parking tickets, study skills, self-advocacy, library resources, and motivating a resistant student organization, in ways even the most knowledgeable professionals cannot. (p. 99)

Williams underscores that there is a different, separate benefit that students might derive from talking to a peer rather than to a librarian, even if a librarian is more technically proficient at finding and using information, and applying information literacy concepts. While we expected PRAs to know and use library resources effectively, we thought their ability to network with other students, to be friendly and approachable role models, and to use language that was accessible to their peers would be equally important as traditional reference skills. In addition, we set the following goals and scope for PRA service:

- Find books, articles, and other information sources by using library and other appropriate resources
- Refer patrons to appropriate subject specialists for more advanced help
- Refer students to additional avenues of reference assistance (24/7 chat/IM, e-mail, phone and Reference Desk) when patrons need more immediate help

With a vision and philosophy for the PRA Program in mind, we looked for students to hire. We began by talking to the MSU Libraries' Human Resources Department to see if it had current library student assistants whom they thought would be a good fit for the new program, and spoke to supervisors in other library units with a high quantity of student assistants. We interviewed a number of students for the PRA Program, all of whom were employed by other units and departments in the Main Library or the Business Library, and hired five to work for the pilot program in the fall of 2013. All of the students we hired added the EC's work to the positions they already held in the Libraries and none of them quit their other library jobs. We were able to offer PRAs one to three shifts (three to nine hours) per week, generally not enough to replace existing jobs. However, we felt that the position was still attractive since we paid students at the second highest student pay rate of more than $11 per hour. The high pay rate for the positions reflected the level of responsibility and the duties PRAs would be expected to complete in the ECs. PRAs work solo, and need to be trustworthy, self-motivated, and competent in order to fulfill the Libraries' mission in the ECs of helping students with their basic research needs.

The PRA interviews covered the students' experiences working for the Libraries, their knowledge and awareness of library search tools and resources, and their ability to operate on their own at a location outside the Libraries. Targeting library student employees who already had some necessary skills and general comfort with library resources proved to be a winning strategy. It was much quicker to get these students up to speed providing basic reference and research help to patrons in the ECs than it would have been if they had no prior knowledge or experience.

Initial funding for the program came from money added to the Libraries' student employee budget. The PRA Program came into existence in cooperation with, and in support of, the MSU neighborhood plan. During the summer of 2013 when we were planning the new PRA Program, a budget was proposed based on having PRAs in four ECs, four days of the week, for three hours each time. The funding for this new program was added to the student budget and was dispersed once the pilot began in October 2013.

TRAINING AND PREPARATION OF PRAs

By design, PRAs are not meant to duplicate the exact experience of working with a librarian, but they still need to represent the Libraries in a positive way and hopefully encourage students to return to ask further questions or use other library services. Though the initial group of PRAs had basic familiarity with library resources, training would also introduce them to some of the core tenets of customer service, such as asking effective questions and conducting a basic reference interview.

A week before sending students out into the ECs in October 2013, we held a two-hour information and training meeting with the newly hired PRAs. Of the initial group of PRAs, all had jobs that interfaced with the public, so they were accustomed to answering library-related questions in either the Main or Business Libraries. However, none of these students had any official customer service training through the Libraries or any experience answering research questions from patrons. Therefore, some initial training was necessary to get PRAs ready to work with patrons on a deeper level.

The initial two-hour training consisted of two parts: (1) the duties and expectations that we had for students working in the ECs and (2) basic reference and customer service skills. Aside from logistics such as where and when to work, a large topic for the first part of the meeting was going over how to collect data about each question received while on the job. PRAs use the statistical tool DeskTracker, the same tool MSU librarians use for their reference interactions. PRAs learned how to tell the difference between directional and reference questions and what kinds of information we wanted them to record in the DeskTracker form. In addition to DeskTracker, we gave PRAs guidelines for submitting a nightly shift report.

For the second part of the meeting, we covered the following customer service and reference topics:

- The reference interview: We discussed and demonstrated the types of questions we often receive from patrons and how it can often take some time and work to "discover" the patron's real

question. We focused on helping PRAs ask multiple, targeted questions in order to drill down to the patron's actual information need. After a discussion, we had the PRAs practice interviewing the facilitator. We imitated patrons with specific research questions for each PRA and they practiced helping us with our research need.
- Major databases: The goal was to have PRAs help patrons with basic reference questions, so we wanted them to focus on using the library catalog and large databases, such as ProQuest research library (later Summon, once the Libraries implemented a discovery tool) to help patrons. In order for the PRAs to be comfortable using these resources, we talked them through basic search techniques, refining searches, using facets, and other important things to keep in mind when helping patrons search. After we talked about these resources and did a demonstration, PRAs were given a worksheet with some sample patron questions and asked to use these resources to answer the questions.
- Common assignments: We highlighted and discussed some of the common assignments we encounter from students in our own reference interactions. For example, the vast majority of MSU's 8,000+ first-year students take the same writing class during their initial semesters, and we anticipated these students being heavy users of the EC services. We gave the PRAs example copies of two recurring First-Year Writing assignments, and discussed with them how to help a student with those assignments. These assignments require students to find very specific types of resources and information, so we talked the PRAs through finding these sources. PRAs then brainstormed in groups how they would go about helping the patron and shared their strategies with the group.

We also created a training/informational LibGuide to collect useful links and resources that the PRAs might need during their shifts. The guide serves as a comprehensive reference for PRA policies and procedures; it reviews key resources for PRAs to use when helping patrons, explains and details data collection policies, and information about safety at each EC location. The guide also contains contact information in case PRAs need to reach each other for shift coverage, so is only available to students currently employed by the program.

In subsequent semesters, training has evolved and expanded. For the 2015–2016 academic year, training consisted of two meetings each semester, one at the beginning and one at the end, to be supplemented by online training modules.

The current training sequence now includes the following elements:

- Beginning of fall semester (two hours): It included the same elements covered in the initial training meeting (logistics, collecting statistics, reference interview, major library resources, and common assignments). Returning students are encouraged to share their experiences, offer advice, and work with the new PRAs during group activities.
- End of fall semester (one hour): PRAs debrief and provide feedback about their semesters, and EC Services Coordinator shares program successes.
- Beginning of spring semester (one hour): It includes a discussion of the reference interview and referrals in greater depth. We created an activity using real reference questions received through chat. Students worked in groups of twos and threes and discussed strategies for answering the question, what additional information they would need from the patron to provide a complete answer, and when they would make a referral to a librarian (see Appendix 12–1).
- End of spring semester (one hour): It's the same as fall semester-end meeting, including acknowledgment of graduating seniors.

To supplement in-person meetings, we designed a series of online modules covering various aspects of reference (see Appendix 12–2). Four of these modules launched during

Module Name	*Overview*	*Format*	*Tools Used*
Do You Have Enough Information?	Helps PRAs think about how much information they need from a patron to develop an effective search strategy	Choose your own adventure game, text-based	Twine (free, open source interactive fiction software)
Introduction to the Reference Interview	An introduction to the importance of the reference interview and open/closed questions	Choose your own adventure game, text-based	Twine (free, open source interactive fiction software)
Advanced SearchPlus (local name for Summon discovery tool)	An overview of advanced features of the libraries' discovery tool	Videos with captions and transcripts, PDF with screenshots	Camtasia (video), SnagIt (screenshots), Microsoft Word (PDF)
Brainstorming Search Terms	How to create an effective search from a patron question	Interactive tutorial and quiz	Adobe Captivate

Figure 12.1 Online training modules supplemented in-person training and gave PRAs tasks to complete during quiet shifts.

the fall 2015 semester, with plans to release further modules in subsequent semesters. In future years, these modules will remain on the PRA guide where PRAs can work through them at their own speed. We also plan to incorporate relevant modules and videos created by other libraries. PRAs complete the modules during quiet shifts and report when they finish each module in their shift report. The modules typically take less than 15 minutes to complete. Using modules in addition to face-to-face meetings allowed us to introduce PRAs to more advanced reference or customer service topics.

We select topics for online training modules based on reference training we had as graduate assistants and new librarians. Professional standards, such as the Reference and User Services Association (RUSA) "Behavioral Guidelines for Providers of Reference," and feedback and questions from the PRAs themselves also inform our topic choices. Even though we use professional standards, we are aware that most PRAs are not planning to become librarians, and might not have the same intrinsic investment in professional standards that a librarian might. With that in mind, we break down concepts like the reference interview into more manageable chunks. For example, one module asks PRAs to determine if they have enough information to help a patron and is built like a game, where the player collects points for each additional piece of information they learns from the virtual patron. Another walks the PRAs through the process of choosing open-ended and closed questions using a shoe saleswoman as an example, and prompting them to think of applications for the reference interview outside of the library. We plan to create additional modules in the future, since feedback from the PRAs indicated that they found them useful, and even enjoyable to complete.

IMPLEMENTATION OF THE PROGRAM

In the fall 2013 semester, we implemented a five-week pilot program, which would deploy PRAs to work three-hour shifts, for a total of six to nine hours per week for each

PRA. PRAs represent the Library at the ECs a total of 48 hours per week, or three hours per night, four nights a week, in four campus locations. Starting in spring 2014, PRAs worked throughout the semester, typically for 14–15 weeks (excluding the first week of classes and ending before finals). Shifts are from 6 p.m. to 9 p.m., Sunday through Wednesday. These days and times fall in line with the timing of other tutoring and academic support services offered in the ECs, especially the Writing Center. Since fall 2013, we have employed six to eight PRAs across the four EC locations.

The day-to-day experience differs slightly, depending on the location. All PRAs have a designated space within the EC, where they arrive with their own laptop and set up a sign explaining who they are. In two locations, students are able to share a room within the EC with consultants from the Writing Center. In other EC locations, students have a regular reserved table where they work right next to the Writing Center.

During a typical shift, students answer on average one directional or reference question, though there are some shifts where students are asked no questions and others where they are asked more. Students are expected to help patrons perform basic library searching through the discovery tool or the library catalog. For questions that require more in-depth searching or subject-specific resources, PRAs are asked to refer patrons to the appropriate librarian. There is no formal referral mechanism though we encourage the PRA to give the patron contact information and directions for making an appointment.

The final piece of the PRAs' daily duties is keeping two different sets of statistics: one for the Libraries and one for the ECs. They record each question they are asked and answer given in DeskTracker. The PRAs also collect student ID numbers of each student they help. This database is maintained by the ECs, and is entirely separate from Library statistics.

Since PRAs work outside the library, after normal business hours, supervision is a challenge we address through several measures of accountability: the statistics maintained in DeskTracker, the daily shift report, and visits during the semester. Statistics collected in DeskTracker simultaneously allow the EC Services Coordinator to evaluate PRA work by periodically reviewing questions received and answers given and track the number and types of questions for assessment purposes. Each PRA must submit a summary of her or his shift at the end of each night. The report consists of an e-mail sent directly to the Coordinator. PRAs are expected to include the hours they worked, how many questions they answered, and any observations they have about the EC that day. Most communication is conducted through either e-mail or text, though the EC Services Coordinator does visit each location several times during the semester to check in, see how the semester is going, and field any questions or concerns. Choosing from a pool of candidates who are already known to be reliable has helped maintain the success of the program without daily in-person contact from the supervisor.

EVALUATION OF THE PROGRAM

PRAs receive feedback during individual meetings in the ECs during their shifts. We regularly review the data entered by the PRAs to see what questions are being asked and how the PRAs are answering the patron questions. For the most part, the PRAs answer questions appropriately, and accurately categorize reference and directional questions. When we make rounds to talk with PRAs during their shifts, we discuss the questions they have received and the assistance they provided. This is an opportunity to identify any trends in the ECs and to recognize any common problems the PRAs have when working with patrons. Many PRAs also use the daily shift report to ask us questions. If there is general confusion about something, we e-mail the PRAs as a whole to help clarify the issue and also try to meet with the PRA individually during one of their shifts to talk about it.

Another way that we have assessed the program is by looking at the number and type of questions PRAs are asked in order to understand trends. PRAs record three pieces of data for each question they are asked: whether it was a reference or directional question, a description of the question they were asked, and a description of the answer they gave. Directional questions are defined as questions that do not need any specialized knowledge or library resources to answer; these are typically questions like "who are you?" or "where is the Writing Center?" Reference questions are defined as questions that use library resources (e.g., "how do I find an article on female airplane pilots?"), require more than a one or two sentence answer (e.g., "explain to me what a PRA is"), or require other specialized knowledge (e.g., "how do I cite this book in MLA?").

While the program has grown overall during the last five semesters, some semesters have seen fewer questions than others, and the pattern is not consistent. Fall 2015 saw a large increase in both directional and reference questions over previous semesters, a distinct contrast to spring 2015, which saw the fewest questions since the program began. In fall 2015, we expanded our efforts to promote the program at student fairs and through social media, though we cannot say that this led to more questions (see Figure 12.2).

Keeping track of the number and types of questions asked helps us decide how to staff the ECs and shapes the training for subsequent semesters. PRAs receive questions across many disciplines and topics, just as a reference librarian in the library might (see Figure 12.3). Students ask about brand analysis, color theory, and the history of dyno-technicians, to name a few recent examples. PRAs also explain the peer research program to students who

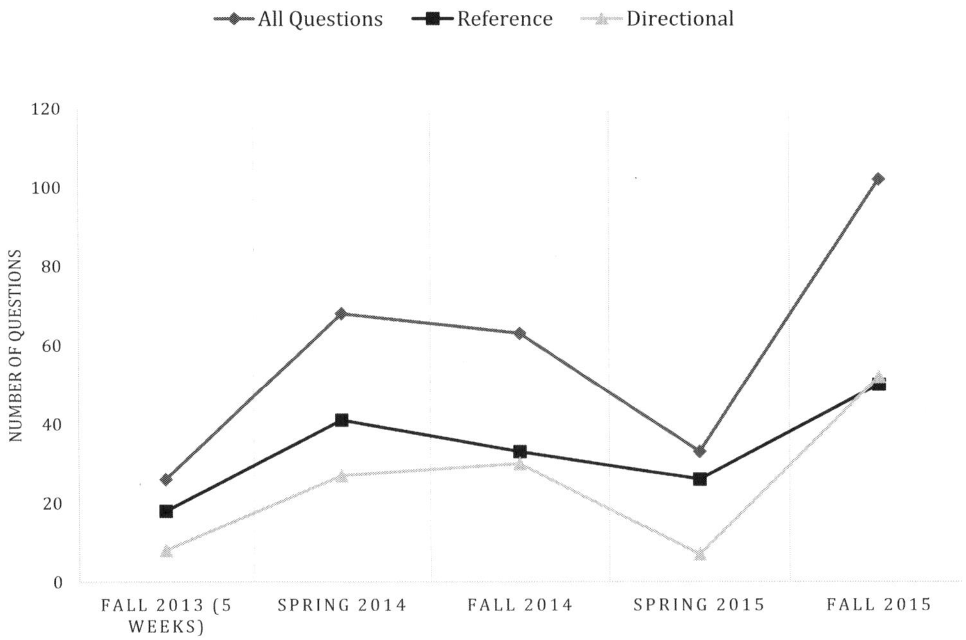

Figure 12.2 Total questions by semester.

ask why they are in the ECs. We encourage PRAs to give students who ask a full summary of the services they provide, since this can lead to return business later in the semester. Anecdotally, we have heard reports from PRAs of students who stop by early in the semester and ask about the program and return later for help with a research-intensive assignment.

Broken down further, the types of reference questions that PRAs receive fall into six large categories:

- Specific topic: questions about specific research topics (besides First-Year Writing)
- First-Year Writing: questions from self-identified First-Year Writing students or questions about known First-Year Writing assignments
- Information about PRA: questions about the purpose and function of the PRA Program (e.g., what is a PRA? How can you help me?)
- General searching: questions that the PRA answered using a library database, but didn't specify a particular subject (i.e., how do I search for articles?)
- Citation: citation styles or how to cite a particular piece of information
- Other: questions that don't fall into any of the other categories.

These statistics are self-reported by the PRAs, and while most do an excellent job describing the questions they are asked, some may occasionally provide an incomplete or inaccurate description that might affect the distribution of questions in Figure 12.3.

Over the last five semesters, we have seen one promising trend emerge. Aside from topical reference questions, the largest group of questions comes from students enrolled in a First-Year Writing (WRA) 100-level class, Michigan State's First-Year Writing seminar. In fall 2015, the PRAs received 15 reference questions from patrons who identified themselves as WRA students; questions from these students have also been a large category for the previous two semesters. Most WRA students complete one or two papers that require them to find popular, scholarly, and sometimes trade articles from or about their major or

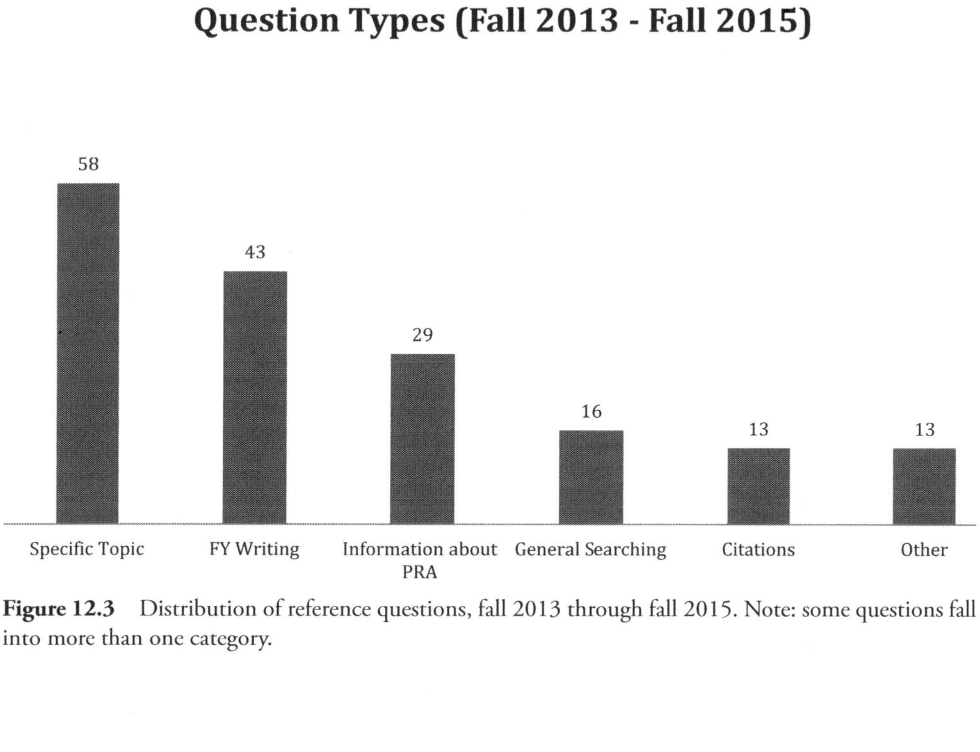

Figure 12.3 Distribution of reference questions, fall 2013 through fall 2015. Note: some questions fall into more than one category.

future profession. Both of us work with WRA sections who come to the library for information literacy instruction and have used our knowledge of typical assignments to prepare PRAs during training. Since we spend time preparing the PRAs to help WRA students and they seem like a natural audience for the program, it is encouraging to see a high number of those questions. The high incidence of WRA questions may also be due to the fact that first-year students at MSU typically live in the residence halls, where the ECs are located.

Overall, PRAs have been particularly successful meeting the most important goal of the program: helping students "find books, articles and other information sources by using library, and other appropriate resources." As the statistics show, PRAs answer a wide range of questions and generally use appropriate library resources to do so. Referrals, either to subject specialists or to other library services, are harder to track, since we do not have an official referral system in place and don't ask PRAs to track referrals in the data they record. Further research will be necessary to determine whether the PRAs effectively refer questions that they cannot handle on their own.

IMPLICATIONS AND LESSONS LEARNED

The PRA Program has made a very positive impact on the library presence in the ECs. During the four semesters that librarians worked in the ECs, they received a total of 52 questions. By comparison, PRAs answered 102 questions in fall 2015 alone and have answered nearly 300 questions total in the five semesters the program has been in place. Based on numbers, we feel that the program has been successful and hope to continue it for the foreseeable future. The program also has value beyond numbers of questions asked; individual PRAs are able to make connections with other students and talk about the program in their classes. PRAs who work in the Writing Center at their EC location are able to jump into Writing Center consultations where the student needs additional help locating information for his or her paper. Anecdotally, some of the PRAs have been able to disseminate information about the program through word of mouth to their peers, which has resulted in additional students seeking them out in the ECs. They are familiar with existing student networks and give the library a friendly and relatable face, which is valuable for helping students feel comfortable asking for help or using library services in the future.

As is unfortunately all too common for library programs, the PRA Program could benefit from better publicity. One of the most common directional questions from fall 2015 was asking the PRA to explain their job, despite advertising at numerous orientation fairs, posters around campus, and social media pushes. However, this is not a problem unique to this particular program, and we are sure that many libraries will identify! Instead of creating even more general advertising, we have found that marketing the PRAs to specific campus groups who already serve undergraduates has been the most effective way of growing the program.

Some of the most successful PRAs are those who have done a good job integrating themselves into the Writing Center process. We have observed that students who come to the Writing Center sometimes have questions more appropriate for the PRAs, such as help locating articles for a paper. PRAs are perfectly positioned to help Writing Center staff with these kinds of questions. Greater integration with the Writing Center across the board would likely lead to more questions. Even if the general undergraduate population does not understand what PRAs do, buy-in and understanding from the Writing Center could lead to more direct referrals and collaboration.

For other libraries interested in starting a peer research or reference program, we found it helpful to integrate into existing programs and infrastructure. Does your university have multiple writing help locations where you could send a student? Are there locations where students already go for academic help or tutoring besides the library? Though the neighborhoods and ECs are particular to our institutional context, there may be existing services at your institution where you can integrate.

We also found that it is important to train peer mentors to be ambassadors for the library and for the PRA Program. We ask students to introduce themselves to other nearby Writing Center staff and look for opportunities to talk about the program with other students. Students also talked about the program if they were taking a class with a number of first-year students or in classes where library-based research was the primary focus. We mention the program during information literacy sessions for WRA, since these students are a growing percentage of the patrons the PRAs encounter and are an ideal target audience as many are unfamiliar with library research and often live in the residence halls.

NEXT STEPS

The future of the PRA Program will hopefully see greater integration into existing EC resources, especially the Writing Center and an online training sequence that PRAs complete during their initial semester. Increased communication with the WRA coordinators about the program could also help draw more patrons, perhaps as a follow-up to their library instruction session. In the future, there may also be a better way to trace referrals to subject specialists or other library services, likely by adding an optional "referral" field to the existing DeskTracker form.

Beyond that, feedback and observations from the PRAs themselves will help shape the future of the program and enable us to adapt to needs that we can't foresee now. While we are the library subject matter experts, the PRAs understand firsthand what it's like to be a student here and now, and their ideas can help us form a responsive and relevant program to meet evolving student needs.

REFERENCES

Barnes, N., & Peyton, G. (2007). Reaching out to the net generation on campus: Promoting the MSU Libraries in the residence halls. *Public Services Quarterly, 2*(4), 47–68. doi:10.1300/J295v02n04_03

Harley, B., Dreger, M., & Knobloch, P. (2001). The postmodern condition: Students, the web, and academic library services. *Reference Services Review, 29*(1), 23–32. doi:10.1108/00907320110366750

Michigan State University. (n.d.a). The evolution of Neighborhoods that are uniquely MSU. Retrieved from http://neighborhoods.msu.edu/sites/default/files/upload/docs/5.The%20Evolution%20of%20Neighborhoods2.pdf

Michigan State University. (n.d.b). *Planning principles.* Retrieved from https://web.archive.org/web/20160819134511/http://www.neighborhoods.msu.edu/sites/default/files/upload/docs/3.%20Planning%20Principles.pdf

Michigan State University. (2015a). *MSU facts.* Retrieved from https://msu.edu/about/thisismsu/facts.htmlhttps://msu.edu/about/thisismsu/facts.html

Michigan State University. (2015b). *Neighborhoods background.* Retrieved from http://neighborhoods.msu.edu/background

Michigan State University. (2016). *Neighborhoods.* Retrieved from http://www.neighborhoods.msu.edu/

Nims, J. K. (1998). Meeting students on their own turf. *Research Strategies, 16*(1), 85–89. doi:10.1016/S0734-3310(98)90009-X

Pietraszewski, B. A., & Smith, M. M. (2004). Enabling the roving reference librarian: Wireless access with tablet PCs. *Reference Services Review, 32*(3), 249–255. doi:10.1108/00907320410553650

Reference and User Services Association. (2013). *Guidelines for behavioral performance of reference and information service providers.* Retrieved from http://www.ala.org/rusa/resources/guidelines/guidelines behavioral

Riehle, C. F., & Witt, M. C. (2009). Librarians in the hall: Instructional outreach in campus residences. *College & Undergraduate Libraries, 16*(2–3), 107–121. doi:10.1080/10691310902958616

Strothmann, M., & Antell, K. (2010). The live-in librarian: Developing library outreach to university residence halls. *Reference & User Services Quarterly, 50*(1), 48–58. Retrieved from https://journals.ala.org/rusq/index

Williams, L. B. (2011). The future of peer education: Broadening the landscape and assessing the benefits. *New Directions for Student Services, 2011*(133), 97–99. doi:10.1002/ss.388

APPENDIX 12–1: EXAMPLE WORKSHEET USED DURING TRAINING

This exercise addresses searching skills, the reference interview, and when to refer questions.

Scenario

Patron question: What is the best way to search for an online research article related to nursing? I am having trouble finding an article when I type in my keywords. . .

Answer these questions with your group:

- What context has the patron already given you about their question (if any)?
- What additional information do you need from the patron to help them? What questions might you ask them?
- What steps would you take to answer this question? At what point would you refer the question to a librarian?

APPENDIX 12–2: PRA TRAINING MODULES

Modules are expected to take less than 15 minutes, and PRAs complete them during quiet periods while they are working.

- Do you have enough information? [http://staff.lib.msu.edu/marcyk/pra/enough]

  A game in which players collect points as they find out more information from an imaginary patron. The game introduces the concept that patrons rarely articulate the full extent of their question when they first ask. Built using Twine [http://twinery.org/]
- Reference interview introduction [http://staff.lib.msu.edu/marcyk/pra/refinterview_intro.html]

  A brief introduction to the reference interview and using open and closed questions. It includes a few practice scenarios. The tutorial uses the example of a shoe saleswoman to introduce the concept of asking effective questions and finding out what a patron really wants. Built using Twine [http://twinery.org/]
- Search terms [http://staff.lib.msu.edu/marcyk/pra/searchterms]

  A scenario in which the player must select keywords, brainstorm synonyms, and construct a search. Built using Adobe Captivate 8
- Advanced SearchPlus

  These materials were created or gathered in response to PRA questions about using various aspects of SearchPlus, the MSU Libraries' discovery tool. Videos were built using Camtasia Studio 7, PDF created in Microsoft Word using screen shots captured with SnagIt 11
  - Using the "My Research" Button (PDF with screenshots) [https://goo.gl/hhIky8]
  - Saving Citations in SearchPlus (video with transcript) [https://mediaspace.msu.edu/media/Saving+Citations+in+SearchPlus/1_6lo3mzns]
  - SearchPlus Filters (video with transcript) [https://mediaspace.msu.edu/media/SearchPlus+Filters/1_l8kwa5i1]

13

Peer Reference Services at Southern Illinois University Carbondale

Joshua Vossler

This chapter aims to document how Morris Library instituted a Peer Mentor Program in order to maintain Information Desk hours during evenings and weekends. Peer Mentors are selected using a point-based system. Training is a graduated process emphasizing on-the-job experience and frequent supervisor feedback. Once training is complete, Peer Mentors often work alone at the Information Desk, fielding directional and research questions and coding those interactions for internal library statistics. Assessment of the Peer Mentor Program is conducted through informal supervisor feedback and a reflective writing assignment.

INSTITUTIONAL CONTEXT

Southern Illinois University Carbondale (SIUC) is a public research university with an enrollment of roughly 18,000 students (14,000 undergraduates and 4,000 graduates) and employs 850 full-time faculty members. Nearly half (8,000) of our students are first-generation college students, most of them Illinois natives (13,000), and nearly all of our students (17,000+) are under the age of 25. The student body is 52 percent white, 30 percent black, and 11 percent Hispanic. We admit 79 percent of undergraduate applicants, and our six-year graduation rate is 47 percent for whites and 32 percent for minorities. The Peer Mentor Program at Morris Library aligns with the university's strategic plan to "Provide every student with support services that promote their successful integration into the academic, social, and cultural community of the University" by allowing us to keep the Information Desk staffed and operational during evenings and weekends, when many of our students prefer to use the library (Southern Illinois University Carbondale, 2013).

Morris Library is SIUC's main library. We are a member of the Association of Research Libraries and hold more than three million physical volumes. The library staff consists of three administrators, 19 faculty librarians (14 tenure-track, five non-tenure-track), 42 professional staff, and 61 support staff. Because of ongoing reductions in subject librarian positions, many liaisons are currently assigned six or more departments. The reduction in subject liaison librarians has also affected staffing at the Information Desk, which serves as a combined service point for library reference and SalukiTech, our computer support unit. The Information Desk sits on the first floor, 20 yards to the right of the library's front entrance. The semicircular desk houses four work stations: one staffed by SalukiTech, with the remaining three stations dedicated to the library. The Information Desk opens 30 minutes after the library opens and closes one hour before the library closes. These hours vary throughout the year, but during the semester the Information Desk is open Monday through Thursday, 8:00 a.m. to 11:00 p.m., Friday 8:00 a.m. to 8:00 p.m., Saturday 10:00 a.m. to 6:00 p.m., and Sunday 11:00 a.m. to 11:00 p.m.

Building and maintaining productive relationships with six or more academic departments is a nearly impossible challenge all on its own and does not leave much time in the day for our librarians to work at the desk. As of 2015, the average librarian spent six hours per week at the desk, down from as many as 12 or 15 hours per week in years past. This reduction in hours has been dealt with by reducing redundant desk staff (where once we had three members of the reference team working at the same time, especially during busy shifts, now we have two or even one), and leaning more heavily on our Peer Mentors.

BACKGROUND OF THE PROGRAM

Morris Library has employed student workers since time immemorial, but the Peer Mentor Program emerged from a specific confluence of events and decisions that culminated in the mid-1990s. By then, the ranks of librarians had been dwindling for 30 years. In particular, two waves of retirements reduced our numbers. In the aftermath of each retirement, many of those newly empty positions vanished, never to be reopened. Though the staff was reduced, library administration made it a priority to maintain Information Desk hours. Librarians at SIUC hold faculty status and therefore have many varying roles and responsibilities; it was not equitable to simply assign librarians to work 20 or more hours per week at the desk to keep it open, and administration was unable to hire additional staff. It did not help the matter that internal statistics—in keeping with national statistics—showed a decline in reference questions (Association of Research Libraries, 2013). It was difficult to build a convincing argument to hire more professionals when the Information Desk, one of our most visible services, was increasingly approached with questions about basic software problems, printing, directions, and library policy: questions a bright undergraduate could be trained to answer. Though library staff had concerns that the quality of our reference services would suffer, we concluded, after conversations about quality versus quantity and the possible drawbacks of reduced desk hours, that it was essential the desk remained open—and that student assistants could help meet that need.

The goal for the Peer Mentor Program has been to maintain service point hours in the face of eroding librarian positions while minimizing the impact on our ability to provide quality reference services. My predecessors decided, and I concur, that Peer Mentors should perform two roles at the Information Desk. Their primary role is to work alone at the desk during evenings and weekends; essentially, to supply the staffing needed to keep the desk open. Their secondary role comes into play during regular work hours, when they work alongside one or more members of the reference team.

In terms of skill, whether working solo or alongside a librarian, a Peer Mentor should be able successfully field nearly all questions they encounter regarding library policy, procedures, and directions. They are also expected to be able to handle basic research questions. For example, a Peer Mentor should be able to assist a first-year English composition student with locating a few articles for a research paper. Anything more complex or subject-specific, however, is to be referred to the appropriate subject librarian, even if that librarian is not immediately available. It is better to give no answer than to give a poor answer.

For better or worse, less than 30 percent of the questions we encounter at the Information Desk (as of the 2014–2015 academic year) can be classified as reference transactions, at least according to the Association of Research Libraries definition: "a reference transaction is an information contact that involves the knowledge, use, recommendations, interpretation, or instruction in the use of one or more information sources by a member of the library staff" (Reference and User Services Association, n.d.). Properly trained Peer Mentors should therefore be able to answer no less than 70 percent of the questions they encounter, and possibly more. To keep track of the number and types of questions we encounter at the Information Desk, we employ RefTracker, an online reference management system. Data from RefTracker show that nonreference questions predominantly fell into four categories: assistance with the printers, explanation of library policy or procedures, directional, and requests for office supplies. Peer Mentors can be trained to answer almost all of these questions inside of a single semester.

The Selection Process

As Head of Reference and Instruction, I oversee, as well as participate in, the library's reference and instruction programs. Although supervision of student workers is shared among all of the Information Desk staff, I am responsible for hiring decisions. To ensure that I make the best decisions possible, I employ a six-step process to select students to become Peer Mentors. My thinking is the more care I take in the hiring process, the more headaches I avoid down the line. The steps are designed to identify candidates who possess three characteristics: scholastic excellence, customer service ability, and critical thinking skills. There are of course any number of other desirable characteristics an ideal Peer Mentor ought to possess, but I consider these three to be the fundamentals. I have four Peer Mentor positions, and hiring tends to happen in batches of two or three at a time, usually in the fall, to replace Peer Mentors who graduated the previous spring. However, should a Peer Mentor depart during the semester, I move to fill the empty position as soon as possible, but sometimes have to wait for suitable applications to come in.

Step 1: The winnowing. The library is among the most desirable places of employment on campus, and we collect student employment applications on a rolling basis, so we usually have 50 or more applications on hand at any given time. I define my first criterion, scholastic excellence, as a GPA of 3.5 or higher (high school GPA is also acceptable, if the student has not yet earned grades at the university), and I do not consider applicants with anything lower. I will consider upper-division students, but I prefer to hire first- and second-year students. They have the potential to stay in the position for three to four years, giving the highest potential return on investment. I insist on a high GPA not only because I believe that Peer Mentors should be academic role models, but also because a student who is struggling with school should not be saddled with the additional stress and responsibility that a job, even a supportive library job, necessarily comes with. This criterion excludes more than 90 percent of the initial pool, usually leaving me with no more than a handful of candidates. At this point I look over the hours each of the remaining applicants indicated he or she is available to work and exclude any applicants who decline to work evenings or weekends, which leaves me with the pool of applicants who qualify for an in-person interview.

Step 2: The interview. Once applicants are selected for an in-person interview, I assess customer service ability and critical thinking skills. Customer service ability is the hardest criterion to quantify. As evidence for customer service ability, I accept work experience that involved customer service, and if that is lacking, I also accept a personable manner. I am not thrilled with this approach, however. Because a student has experience with customer service it does not necessarily follow that the student was good at it, and because a student can be charming during an interview—when she has something to gain—does not mean she will be charming to a frustrated patron at 9:00 on Sunday evening. These concerns notwithstanding, this approach has so far worked out. Students with previous customer service experience seemed to know what they were getting into and had one less thing to learn, which made training easier. Students who lacked customer service experience, but who were pleasant and likeable during the interview, have also done well.

Step 3: The worksheet (see Appendix 13–1). After the interview, I assess critical thinking using a worksheet of research questions that students are asked to complete and return within 24 hours.

Students are encouraged to share their thought process and are told how they think and what they do is just as important as getting the right answer. The answers to all of the questions can be found using our most basic library resources—I do not expect any student to have the abstruse knowledge of a subject librarian, but I do expect them to be able to think through a problem. I find that the garbled citation question is the most illuminating. While I maintain that I would be willing to hire a student who turned in a worksheet with evidence of excellent critical thinking but incorrect answers, the situation has never presented itself. In practice, student performance on the worksheet has fallen into two categories: excellent and poor. I have yet to see a worksheet that falls somewhere in between.

Step 4: References. I am not seeking nuance here. Not all students have had jobs before coming to college, and even those who do, have at most two years of customer service experience. The reference check basically comes down to the binary question of "Is this person easy to work with?" If the answer is yes, I keep the student on the list. If the answer is no, I drop the student from consideration. More often than not, though, references are generally positive. If the student lacks references, I offer the benefit of the doubt and keep the student on the list.

Step 5: Ranking. I do not entirely trust myself to make a gut decision about whom to hire; I prefer to make an evidence-based decision. To that end, I use a point system. One point for being likeable in the interview, one point for completing the worksheet correctly, one point for a glowing reference (neutral or generally positive references are not awarded points). In the case of a tie, the higher rank goes to the student with the higher GPA.

Step 6: Offers. The most common source of conflict between the Peer Mentor and the supervisor has been scheduling. Some students agree to take the position hoping that night and weekend shifts will be temporary, which of course they are not. As an attempt to avoid that problem, I reiterate the schedule expectations as part of my offer of employment: "Dear blank, I am offering you the position of Undergraduate Desk Assistant. If you agree to this position, you will be expected to work 15 hours per week, almost exclusively during evenings and weekends. Are you still interested in the position and this schedule?" Combining the acceptance of the job with the expectations for the schedule emphasizes the inextricable relationship between the two.

TRAINING AND PREPARATION OF PEER MENTORS

Effective training hinges on the supervisor's ability to see the library from an outsider's perspective and the willingness to help the new employee acclimate. The expert's curse—the inability for an experienced person to connect with, and teach, inexperienced people—affects us all and increases over time. As we become more familiar with our libraries and job responsibilities, we forget what it was like to be a neophyte. Peer Mentors, despite being among the brightest and most dedicated students we have, are beginners. For many of them, this is their first job. They are facing tremendous change. If we hope to train them effectively and retain them until graduation, it is critical that we take their needs as beginners into consideration.

To that end, I train Peer Mentors using a graduated approach. They start by shadowing. Our Information Desk is an outward-facing half-moon with three stations. Due to reduced staffing, it is rare for more than two of these stations to be occupied. I place the new Peer Mentor at a vacant station with the directive to observe and ask questions. It is important for the Peer Mentor to start learning about the job as soon as possible, but my real goal is for the Peer Mentor to begin to develop rapport with the reference team and me. I want Peer Mentors to feel like they are a part of the team, and for work to be a friendly, positive environment. The new Peer Mentor ought to be comfortable before anyone starts asking too much from them, especially anything stressful, such as emergency desk coverage on a Friday evening. Once an hour or so, I ask them to spend 15 or 20 minutes reading about library policies and RefTracker code definitions. We code desk interactions according to three broad categories (basic, reference, referral) with a handful of subcategories under each one. For example, if there was a referral, was it to SalukiTech or a librarian or somewhere else? Once they have gotten through it all—about seven pages of material—I quiz them on the content. After each patron interaction they observe, I ask them how they would code it and to explain the rationale behind their coding decisions.

After the first 15 or 20 hours of work, depending on how quickly the Peer Mentor is catching on, I assign a worksheet for them to complete during low traffic periods when there are few patron interactions to shadow (see Appendix 13–2). The worksheet functions as a self-guided tour. It requires Peer Mentors to locate and describe physical items and locations throughout the library, and it quickly builds familiarity with the library building and main collections. If they get any of the questions wrong, either myself or another member of the reference team gives them feedback about where they went wrong and, if necessary, walks them through the entire problem. Given how conscientious the Peer Mentors usually are, I have found that I need to emphasize that the worksheet is a learning tool and that they are expected to do their best to work each problem, but they do not need to be perfect. Even so, some of the Peer Mentors can become overwrought when they encounter a problem they cannot figure out. The only real drawback of the worksheet is that it takes regular care and feeding. Collections move around, items are weeded, and so forth, so someone from the reference team needs to complete and update the worksheet at least once a year, if not each semester. Despite that cost, it is worthwhile and Peer Mentors tell me that they did not always enjoy the worksheet but appreciated how much they learned from it.

The worksheet and the initial shadowing take about two or three weeks if the student works 12 or 15 hours each week. Starting around the third week of their employment,

Peer Mentors field reference questions under close supervision of myself or another member of the reference team and receive feedback after each interaction. They also begin to code interactions for RefTracker, also with supervision and feedback. Once they seem to be able to handle the majority of questions to everyone's satisfaction (I also take the student's self-reported confidence levels into account), they start to field questions with only light supervision and periodic feedback, although a member of the reference team is always present at the desk while students are training.

The initial training period is capped off by having Peer Mentors work two or three solo shifts during low-traffic times with a supervisor out of sight but available for support. Peer Mentors are encouraged to keep a log of problems they encounter and are informed that these initial solo shifts are meant to help us figure out where their strengths and weaknesses are and are part of the training process. After these shifts, we meet to discuss the experience and identify areas for further training. I try to emphasize that additional training is part of the process, and is not in any way remedial. As with the worksheet, Peer Mentors are anxious to be seen as competent and can be easily demoralized if they think they are performing below expectations. Once the additional training is complete, I consider the Peer Mentors to be trained and add them to the weekly Information Desk schedule. Due to staffing needs, at least half of their shifts will be solo, but I make an effort to schedule a few shifts each week alongside myself or another member of the reference team in order to receive continued training, regular supervision, and, most importantly, social contact with myself and others in the department.

IMPLEMENTATION OF THE PROGRAM

Peer Mentors field questions, enforce library noise policies, code interactions in RefTracker, and occasionally perform light clerical duties. Some express interest in attending library school, and I encourage them to assist with one-shot library instruction sessions, online chat reference, or anything else they show interest in learning about. Peer Mentors work at the desk 15–17 hours per week, usually spread across four or five shifts. They encounter as few as one question per hour, and up to 25 questions per hour during peak times. On weekdays, if Peer Mentors have shifts, they work alongside one or two other members of the reference team. On the weekend and on weekday evenings, they work the desk alone. I try to keep Peer Mentor shifts under four hours to prevent burnout, but staffing needs sometimes dictate longer shifts.

In terms of the questions they encounter while working the desk, RefTracker data show that Peer Mentors answer the same types of questions as librarians, but spend less time on each one: 12 percent of librarian desk interactions last more than a minute, as opposed to 2 percent of Peer Mentor desk interactions. This is as it should be. Peer Mentors answer general questions and the occasional basic reference question, but refer anything more complicated or time-consuming to someone on the reference team. The method of referral varies. If the librarian in question is available, the Peer Mentor escorts the patron to the librarian's office for immediate assistance. If the librarian is unavailable, the Peer Mentor sends the librarian an e-mail with a summary of the patron's needs and contact information. Some of our patrons are reluctant to give out their contact information, and in those cases, the Peer Mentors hand out a copy of the librarian's business card. However, Peer Mentors do not often encounter questions that require a referral. I suspect that their youth functions as a deterrent to being approached with complex, subject-specific questions.

In the past, when the desk was quiet, we used to ask Peer Mentors to perform other tasks. They would sort documents, staple handouts, or clean up spreadsheets. I do not do that anymore, at least not when I have a choice: I want to send the message that they are here to assist patrons, not to be gofers. I also worry that if I bog them down with tedious chores, it will inspire them to find better jobs, and I want to retain my Peer Mentors through to graduation. Instead of keeping Peer Mentors working constantly throughout their shifts, I let them use downtime to complete homework, provided they avoid becoming too engrossed. Patrons are understandably reluctant to approach a sprawling undergraduate study nest bristling with textbooks, markers, and charging cables. In the absence of homework, I allow pleasure reading, mobile device use, or puttering around on the web with the workstation computer. Videos, headphones, and anything that is distracting to the Peer Mentors or to patrons around the Information Desk are all strictly prohibited. We have a fairly standard dress code: no hats, clothing should be clean and free of offensive language or symbols, and under no circumstances should it be indistinguishable from pajamas.

Everyone has a hand in helping Peer Mentors grow, but I handle the direct supervision. To that end, I make a point of spending time with Peer Mentors during their solo shifts, maybe once or twice a month, to visit with them and have what amounts to an informal status update. My goal is to build rapport with the Peer Mentors, and I find that regular conversations—as opposed to conversations that only occur in relation to impending discipline—are the best method available, even if it requires a time investment on my part. By maintaining consistent lines of communication, I can address potential problems before they arise and, if necessary, deliver disciplinary messages in a way that comes across as guiding rather than punitive. For memos or more urgent communication, I rely on a combination of text messaging and e-mail. Peer Mentors arrive at the university acculturated to treat a text message as being inherently more urgent than e-mail, and tend to respond to them quickly.

EVALUATION OF THE PROGRAM

All in all, we consider the program a success if the Peer Mentors keep the Information Desk running on evenings and weekends. It does this, ergo the program is successful. Beyond that, assessment is informal, formative, and ongoing. It is a fairly straightforward matter of offering feedback after interactions in which the Peer Mentors excelled, erred, or could have done something differently, but I like to approach it with two goals in mind. First is to help the Peer Mentors understand what went well or needs improvement. This is not challenging: it is a matter of taking the time to explain what I liked or disliked about the interaction, and being patient while the Peer Mentor asks questions. Peer Mentors are bright people; they usually catch on pretty quickly if given the chance. Second is to maintain a positive work environment. This is a bit harder. Pointing out positive things is not as easy as pointing out the negative, so I have to make a special effort to praise Peer Mentors when they do well. Beyond that, the only other thing I do is to frame mistakes as learning opportunities whenever possible. When Peer Mentors graduate, I ask them to write a letter to the next student who will hold that position. They are instructed to write whatever they like, but I also give them a few prompts:

- What did you enjoy most about being a Peer Mentor?
- What was the most valuable thing that you learned from being a Peer Mentor?

- If you could go back in time and give yourself advice about being a Peer Mentor, what would you say?
- How did being a Peer Mentor influence your schoolwork?

These letters are passed to the next students hired, lending continuity to the program. They make for entertaining reading, but they also help me see the position from the Peer Mentor's perspective. Previous letters have focused on three main topics: where to get help for common problems, opportunities for personal and professional growth, and the locations of the best bathrooms in the library. I have learned from all three, but the first two have been especially informative.

By learning what Peer Mentors consider to be common problems—and their solutions—we have been able to improve our training materials. For example, one Peer Mentor wrote about how helpful circulation managers were during nights and weekends, especially when nobody on the reference team is in the library. The student added that it can be daunting to approach a manager from a different area of the library, but stressed that they are friendly and happy to help with problems, even if those problems are outside of that manager's primary area. Although we instruct Peer Mentors to seek out night and weekend managers when necessary, it was helpful to learn that they might feel reluctant to do so and take steps to reduce that reluctance.

By finding out what Peer Mentors consider the best opportunities for personal and professional growth, we have been able to deliberately offer more of those opportunities to future Peer Mentors. For example, Peer Mentors have cited two learning experiences they especially valued, but that are not part of their normal duties: teaching and sitting in on presentations given by candidates for open librarian positions. We now routinely offer Peer Mentors the opportunity to observe instruction sessions, and, if they have the interest, to eventually team teach with a librarian. We also invite Peer Mentors to attend candidate presentations. As with teaching, though, attending these presentations is also completely optional.

IMPLICATIONS AND LESSONS LEARNED

The Peer Mentor Program has affected our practice in a variety of ways, but three stand out. One, it allows us to offer tiered service. Peer Mentors can field the steady stream of basic questions, freeing the reference team to focus on more complex reference questions without interruption. This has been a fantastic division of labor. It is not just efficient; it also helps everyone's morale—both the reference team and Peer Mentors—to have backup available, ready to step in if needed. I only have enough student hours available to schedule Peer Mentors for about three hours per day, but those are the hours—when Peer Mentors work alongside the reference team, as opposed to when they work alone during evenings and weekends—that I feel like the Peer Mentor Program really shines and results in an overall increase in the quality of our service. Two, the program has allowed librarians to limit their time at the desk to an average of six hours per week, leaving more time for them to spend on teaching, collection development, and liaison activities. Three, in addition to their training, Peer Mentors bring their experience as SIUC students with them. They are able to answer questions dealing with the realities of student life from an insider's perspective, which even the most dedicated reference librarian cannot match. For example, I have overheard Peer Mentors field questions like "Which floor of [a particular dormitory] has the quietest places to study on the weekend?" I know that dormitories exist, but I have not been inside one in at least 15 years, and certainly not at this university. Without Peer Mentors, I am not sure I would even know whom I should refer that question to, much less answer it myself. But my Peer Mentor answered it with confidence. However, that same confidence can be a problem sometimes. I would love to make Peer Mentors better at discerning between questions they can answer correctly and questions they should refer to a professional. To be fair, knowing when to refer a question is something that we could probably all stand to improve upon. RefTracker shows librarians and Peer Mentors in a dead heat in this respect: they both refer less than 1 percent of the questions they receive to a subject specialist. I would be happier if I saw something closer to 3 or 4 percent, and that will be an area of interest for the future.

If I could offer unsolicited advice to other libraries that are considering the creation of a Peer Mentor Program, I would recommend doing three things differently (better) than us. One, Peer Mentors should spend at least half of their time working alongside someone from the reference team. I have only been able to manage a couple of hours a week (out of 17) for most of my Peer Mentors, because I rely on them to staff the desk during undesirable weekend and evening shifts. By the time those shifts have all been covered, there is little time left over. Not only is the Peer Mentor/subject librarian combination useful for efficient reference work, the more Peer Mentors work alongside librarians, the more opportunities they have to develop professional relationships and to learn more about the library.

Two is to use a staggered hiring and training approach. It might seem counterintuitive, but if you have funding for six positions, consider hiring only two to begin with. Hire in spring, so you can see how well they do their first semester and to make sure they are going to stick around. I hired a promising student in the first three weeks of the fall semester, only to have her withdraw from the university two weeks later. Had I waited until spring to do my hiring, I could have probably avoided that problem. Then, next spring, hire two more, and the following spring, the last two. Sure, it might take just over two full calendar years before you will be up to full strength, but your program will be easier to sustain from that point on. Three, avoid hiring a less-than-ideal student if you have a weak candidate pool. Instead, save that position for a student you really want to keep for three or four years. Further, when students tell you who they are or what they want, believe them. If an otherwise promising student is reluctant to work a shift you know you will need that student to work, do not hold out hope for a compromise. Just do not hire that student. Hold out and hire one who actually expresses desire for that shift.

NEXT STEPS

Our Peer Mentor Program is working exactly as hoped, so the future will probably be more of the same, possibly a lot more. If we grow to six or more Peer Mentors, which could happen in the next year or two, I plan to revisit the idea of creating online training materials. Our training methods have been working, but readily scalable they are not. Two years ago, I considered implementing a standardized, scalable Peer Mentor training system. I was going to make a course in Desire2Learn, the learning management system we use at SIUC, which contained all of the policies and foundational skills our Peer Mentors need to master. New Peer Mentors would be required to complete the course with an A before I would permit them to work solo shifts. I was also considering a supplemental course for veteran Peer Mentors to complete each semester to remind them of lesser-used but important policies such as what to do in case of a tornado.

But then reality asserted itself. SIUC is in a protracted period of turmoil. Leadership throughout the university has been churning and we face ongoing budget cuts. As a result, our services have been in a state of flux. The speed and magnitude of change have made it counterproductive to invest time building standardized training materials. They will go out of date before they can be deployed. If the Peer Mentor Program grows much larger, however, we are going to need a scalable online training program nonetheless. Peer Mentors require significant training, and my reference team members all have a variety of other responsibilities. Because of the ongoing change, those training materials will have to focus on elements that will remain stable, such as the reference interview. Elements that are likely to change, such as library hours, printing procedures, and library services, will have to be omitted from online training, but even a partial reduction in the training time will be welcome.

In the future I also intend, if at all possible, to hire students who will graduate at staggered times. The semester after I arrived, all of our Peer Mentors graduated. This created a small emergency, and I had to go on a hiring spree. I was able to hire three quality Peer Mentors, but that was more luck than anything. I do not want to put myself in that position again if I can help it. The Peer Mentor Program has required ongoing care and feeding, but it has yielded a variety of benefits. For the library, it has allowed us to maintain reference desk hours in the wake of significant budget cuts. When Peer Mentors work overlapping shifts with librarians, it has facilitated a tiered service model, which raised the quality of our reference services. For the Peer Mentors, it has provided their first professional work experience, and about a quarter of them have expressed plans to attend library school after graduation.

Finally, apart from those fairly concrete advantages, there has been another less tangible advantage that has benefited both Peer Mentors and librarians: it has brought bright, curious young people into regular contact with the reference team. We have been energized by their enthusiasm, and they have had the opportunity to learn from experienced professionals. Even if the budget quadrupled overnight and I did not need Peer Mentors to maintain reference hours, I would keep the program going for that reason alone.

REFERENCES

Association of Research Libraries. (2013). [Graph illustration of service trends in ARL libraries, 1991–2012]. *ARL statistics 2011–2012*. Retrieved from http://www.arl.org/storage/documents/service-trends.pdf

Reference and User Services Association. (n.d.). *Definitions of reference*. Retrieved from http://www.ala.org/rusa/resources/guidelines/definitionsreference

Southern Illinois University Carbondale. (2013). *Pathways to excellence: A strategic plan*. Retrieved from http://chancellor.siu.edu/strategic-plan/index.html

APPENDIX 13–1: HIRING WORKSHEET

Instructions: In addition to completing the answers to this quiz, be sure to include your PROCESS. That is, what steps do you take and where do you look? We are less interested in whether your answers are right or wrong than we are in understanding your thought process.

Question #1: A patron is looking for a 2010 article on FAA fatigue research. He believes it is in Aviation Psychology and Applied Human Factors, volume 2, issue 1, pgs. 87–98. What is the title of this article? Do we have access to it?

Question #2: A patron is doing a paper on cigarette smoking and needs two books and two scholarly articles on the history of the industry, and can't wait—these materials need to be available today.

Title and call numbers for two books:

1.
2.

Article and journal title for two articles (also indicate whether they are print or web):

1.
2.

Question #3: Does Morris Library have any DVDs or videos on electric cars?

APPENDIX 13–2: TRAINING WORKSHEET

Instructions: Using the information provided in the column "Title of Item," determine each item's call number, the floor it is held on, and its color (to the best of your ability). *Warning 1:* The online catalog might lie to you. Confirm all three pieces of information in person. *Warning 2:* The information we provided you might be less than 100 percent correct, which reflects the kind of challenges you will face at the Information Desk. Critical thinking is required at all stages of the research process.

Title of Item	***Call Number***	***Floor***	***Color of Item***
A Patch of Ivy			
Acta Horticulturae (no. 647)			
Child Behavior Therapy (1980 v. 2)			
Christian Science Monitor Weekly—latest issue			
Come with Me (Clure)			
Communicating Professionally: A How-to-Do-It (1998)			
Delia's Tears			
Dinotopia: A Land apart from Time			
Don Quichotte in Koln			
Encyclopedia of Pop Rock and Soul (1989)			
Fighting Lady: A Drama of the Pacific			
Hydraulic Intrusion by a High-Speed Traversing Water Jet			
Journal of Bryology (2008)			
Journal of Portfolio Management (1995 (fall) volume 22)			
Journal of Weather Modification (1987)			
Mind and the World Order			
More Prayers			
Only a Miracle: A Christmas Opera			
Portraits of Greatness (1961 edition)			
Practicing What We Preach			
Proceedings of the American Catholic Philosophical Association (2008)			
Rules of the Game: The Complete Illustrated (NOT OVERSIZE 1990)			
Schools for the New Needs			
Side Effects of Drugs (v. 7)			
Solar Heating and Cooling of Residential Buildings: Design of Systems			
The Drama Review: TDR (2001 volume 45)			
The Joy of Science: An Examination of How Scientists Ask			
Vegetation Mapping: From Patch to Planet			
What Color Is Your Parachute (2013)			

14

Undergraduate Research Assistants at Hope College

Jessica Hronchek and Rachel Bishop

In response to changing desk traffic and shifting librarian responsibilities, Van Wylen Library at Hope College made the decision to change its Research Desk model to one in which undergraduate Research Assistants primarily staff the desk and research librarians are available on call. To best support this modification, the Research Desk supervisors implemented an improved hiring procedure, an updated training program, and a new referral process for research questions at the desk. Initial assessment shows that the model generally works, though we continue to try to improve Research Assistants' judgment on when to refer questions to librarians and to foster a collaborative dynamic between student Research Assistants and librarians.

INSTITUTIONAL CONTEXT

Hope College is a private liberal arts institution in Western Michigan. It is a residential campus of approximately 3,400 undergraduate students with over 35 majors in disciplines ranging from dance and philosophy to nursing and engineering. Its student population draws primarily from the Midwest, with 69 percent of students coming from Michigan and an additional 20 percent from surrounding states, but others come from throughout the United States and from over 30 countries. Hope is a school where undergraduate research has a strong tradition, and faculty–student collaborative research is an established part of the curriculum in all disciplines. For example, Hope receives more science grant funding for undergraduate research than any other liberal arts college in Michigan. At the College's annual Celebration of Undergraduate Research and Creative Performance, over 300 students present posters on original research projects they produced the previous year. Students frequently have the opportunity to work alongside faculty through summer research programs and regularly coauthor papers with faculty. Building on this strength, our recently established collegewide strategic plan outlines a goal for all students to have some sort of individualized experiential learning opportunity that supports their major and vocational interests. Parallel to this focus is Hope's mission to cultivate leadership and service traits within our students. Both of these are areas in which the Library can serve a key role through curricular partnerships, internships, and student employment.

BACKGROUND OF THE PROGRAM

Since at least the 1990s, Van Wylen Library has employed undergraduate assistants on the Research Desk, which is staffed all hours that the Library is open. These students worked collaboratively with research librarians, co-staffing during business hours and evenings and providing solo coverage during the quieter times of late nights and most of the weekend. Because of the independent nature of this job, these Research Assistants were traditionally hired based on their strong research skills and received on-the-job training shadowing librarians.

Beginning in 2014, the research and instruction team began to reconsider the current model for Research Desk services. We noted two major trends that became the rationale for changing our approach. The first was the decreasing traffic to the physical Research Desk. Though patrons still seemed to greatly prefer a personal visit to the desk as opposed to a distance reference communication (e-mail, chat, text, and phone are all available), the overall number of questions received at the desk was declining substantially, and the majority of questions were categorized as directional, technology-related, or basic lookup or item access questions, most of which could be capably fielded by student Research Assistants. Less than a quarter of interactions were considered to be research questions.

The second trend was a shift in focus of the research and instruction team. The members of this group increasingly found that their time was devoted to course-focused instruction, prescheduled individual research consultations, and efforts to increase campuswide integration of information literacy. Librarians were beginning to experience burnout from having large blocks of time committed to sitting at a quiet desk when their time could be devoted to other initiatives. Because of this, the team began to investigate if an on-call desk service model would allow for better use of librarian time. Could student Research Assistants be trained in a triage model that allowed them to independently handle most simple queries and refer more complex research questions to a librarian? This model wouldn't be jarring within the broader context of our Library. Most of the other service points, including the Circulation Desk, a Media/Technology Desk, and a Writing Center, employ undergraduates as the primary face greeting patrons, with librarians or paraprofessionals providing assistance as needed. In reviewing best practices at other institutions, we found several other examples of libraries that had implemented the triage model of service, one in which student assistants help their peers with most basic questions, such as directions, printer problems, and known item searches, while referring more complex research questions to librarians (Massey-Burzio, 1992; Sonntag & Palsson, 2007; Stevens, 2013; Peters, 2015).

Given the factors described earlier and the close proximity of librarians' offices to the desk, the department decided to experiment with an on-call model. Librarians would continue to staff the desk the same number of hours as before but could stay in their offices. Student Research Assistants would staff the desk all hours that the Library was open and handle most basic questions but would consult with a librarian for more complex research queries.

In addition to allowing for more flexibility in librarian workload, this decision also had the potential to capitalize on the strengths of peer learning. By training Research Assistants who were comfortable and confident navigating library systems, they could serve as ambassadors of Van Wylen Library to other students, both during and outside of their work time. Some students visiting the Library may be more comfortable asking a fellow student a question than asking a librarian, opening the door to research conversations that might not happen otherwise (Cotton, Kilner, & Oliver, 2014). In reaction to this decision, the student co-supervisors identified three areas of initial focus: improving hiring practices, cultivating a teamwork-based culture and referral model, and increasing the level of formal training to replace the informal on-the-job learning previously relied upon.

The Research Desk at Van Wylen Library has always relied heavily on recommendations for the Research Assistant positions. Since we only hire students who are sophomores or older, we contacted departments where we knew that the faculty would have early evidence of students' research abilities. We also solicited recommendations from the Phelps Scholars, a diversity program at Hope in which students from a range of backgrounds live together during their freshman year, are placed in the same First-Year Seminar sections, and participate in other research, community service, and group activities together. We recruit from this group of students in order to ensure a diverse face for the Research Desk in the hope that this would encourage students of all backgrounds to feel comfortable asking for help.

We try to do most of our hiring at the end of spring semester, in preparation for the fall semester and to assist with summer coverage. Because of the popularity of off-campus study, we sometimes need to hire for the spring semester to keep the 11 to 12 students needed to staff the desk all hours. Most Research Assistants, once hired, remain with us until graduation. We try to maintain a balance of sophomores, juniors, and seniors to avoid a large influx of inexperienced assistants at any one time. Though we don't hire explicitly for disciplinary balance, we usually end up with a wide mixture of majors.

Based on conversations with another institution that had moved to a peer-assisted research model, we decided to make the application process more complex in order to narrow down to particularly motivated students. After receiving a list of student recommendations from faculty, we contacted these students and asked if they were interested in applying, providing them with the required application materials. A few students contacted us directly with interest in the position, and we included them in the application process. In addition to filling out a general application and schedule, we asked students to provide an example of a recent research paper and a statement describing why they wanted to work at the Library Research Desk. During the follow-up interview, we asked them to describe their research process for their example paper, including the aspects of research in which they felt most confident and where they had difficulties. We also asked them to come prepared to demonstrate their favorite library research tool, so that we could get a sense of what they were already comfortable doing. This interview process gave us the opportunity to ask leading questions and establish their general level of comfort with the Library. These research-focused questions were paired with questions designed to ascertain their customer service experience and reliability as independent workers (Appendix 14–1). The application method helped us feel confident in the cohort of students we were hiring under the new model.

In addition to revising our hiring process, the team also spent time fleshing out documents that clarified the overall mission of the desk and our vision for the referral model. We were very concerned with maintaining an excellent level of library service and also creating a culture where our research assistants were very comfortable teaming with librarians. This had been easy to cultivate when librarians sat with students for the majority of shifts. We didn't want to lose this connection because of both physical and figurative office doors. Our new and revised documents included the following:

- A new Research Desk mission statement (Appendix 14–2)
- A document clarifying the types of questions we wanted Research Assistants to feel very comfortable answering on their own and the types of questions that warranted a librarian referral

- Methods for the referral process to librarians (whether in person or via email when a librarian isn't in the building)
- Best practices for creating connection and contact between Research Assistants and librarians

TRAINING AND PREPARATION OF RESEARCH ASSISTANTS

Formalized training was an important element for the new desk model. As mentioned earlier, previous Research Assistants were trained through a much more organic process. After hiring, they attended a brief group orientation on general employee policies and walked through a training checklist with the librarians who worked the desk with them. The training checklist consisted of a list of every element that was included in the job, from printer maintenance to searching our catalog and databases. Because multiple librarians were involved in the training of each new student, we used a checklist to keep track and make sure that every item had been covered verbally once. After that, they learned on the job by shadowing librarians.

For the new model, we implemented a multilevel training program intended to provide exhaustive coverage and repetition of the primary skills needed for the desk. It involved an expanded orientation session for all Research Assistants, a training checklist for new students, weekly practice sessions with different assignments for new and returning students, librarian mentors, librarian-led workshops on more advanced research skills, and a group meeting at mid and end semester (Figure 14.1). Some of these ideas, as well as some of our hiring practices, came as a result of conversations with Grand Valley State University Libraries, which had recently moved to a peer research consultation model at its new library (O'Kelly, Garrison, Merry, & Torreano, 2015).

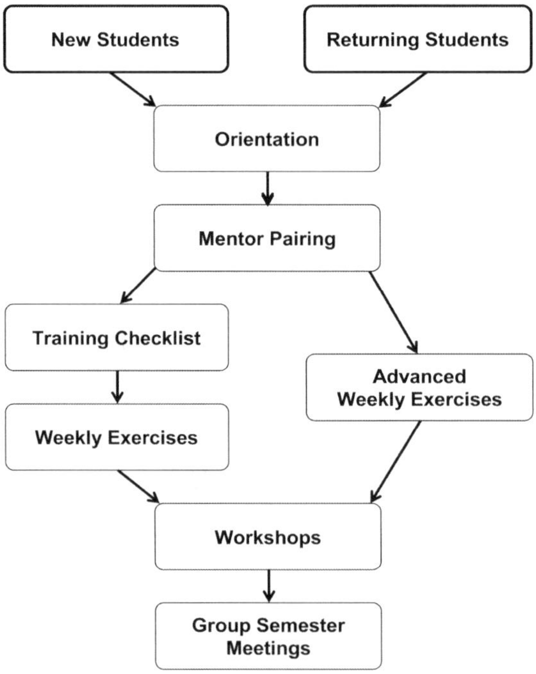

Figure 14.1 Research Assistants training workflow.

Research Assistants Training Workflow

For a number of years, new and returning research assistants were required to attend a two-hour orientation at the beginning of the year that primarily focused on employee policies. The new orientation was lengthened to three hours and included the following: ice breaker exercises, a discussion about Library mission, practice on the reference interview and referral model, and policy overview (Appendix 14–3). After general icebreakers, we shared the Research Desk mission statement as well as the Van Wylen Library mission statement, and we talked about the Research Desk's place in the overall structure of the Library. The students broke into groups and considered what the mission statement meant to them and what it meant to them to be student ambassadors for the Library and for good research. We then discussed the kinds of questions that typically came to the desk and described what questions could be handled by Research Assistants and what questions merited a referral. We talked about the art of the reference interview, emphasizing the importance of asking good questions, and brainstormed the kinds of questions they could ask. We then gave them sample research questions and had them create and perform mock research interviews in pairs. Almost all of the questions were of the type that needed to include a librarian, so they practiced the referral process. The meeting ended with an overview of desk employee policies and a summary of the training plan for the rest of the semester.

We retained the training checklist because it was a good way to ensure that each new Research Assistant received a basic orientation to all the elements of the job. This ranged from printer and fax supplying and troubleshooting to an introduction to basic research tools and to Library policies and emergency procedures. Much of this material was repeated in an online Research Desk Manual created in LibGuides. In addition to being instructed on all of the items on the checklist, we also asked students to read through the manual and refer to it as needed. This initial checklist training took place over approximately the first two weeks that students worked, led by whichever librarian happened to be on call with each new student. Each student had their own copy of the checklist that was kept in a binder at the desk so that they and all the Research and Instruction librarians knew what remained to be completed.

The first piece of follow-up training was weekly practice exercises that the students completed on their own (e.g., see libguides.hope.edu/palsampletraining). These exercises focused on the known item searches that we wanted our students to be comfortable navigating: looking up books in our catalog and discovery tool and finding them on the shelf, helping students navigate our link resolver from databases and discovery tool, and locating items from citations. Students also practiced developing good keyword searches, exploring subject specific databases beyond the discovery platform, and creating basic citations in several formats. Both new and returning student assistants had exercises to complete, and we plan that every semester students will have exercises that serve to refresh key skills and offer more advanced practice. The exercises were outlined using a LibGuide, and answers were submitted via printouts, e-mails, Google Forms, and the online quiz-making tool classmarker.com. We continue to explore better ways to centralize these exercises, such as transitioning to our campus course management system, a tool that students are likely more familiar with.

These assignments were submitted to and graded by librarian mentors. The mentor arrangement was created to ease the training workload on the Research Desk supervisors and to encourage the kind of engagement that came more organically when students and librarians sat together on the desk. It also afforded the supervisors more insights into each student's strengths. The twelve Research Assistants were divided between four Research and Instruction Librarians (two of whom are the Research Desk supervisors). We asked mentor librarians to get to know their mentees and provide continuing education for these students as areas of need arose through questions and feedback gathered from the training exercises. This was done as each librarian saw fit, through formal or informal meetings with individual students, even through social activities outside of the Library in some cases. The librarians met on a regular basis to discuss the performance of the student assistants, to talk about any issues, and to review and assess our structure.

Each of the four research librarians also offered a workshop during the course of the semester. Workshops ranged in focus from a particular skill or tool (like searching for music scores or navigating LexisNexis) to broader sessions on the major database interfaces, and the conceptual framework for search strategies. Research Assistants were required to attend at least one of these workshops each semester, which gave us the opportunity to work with smaller groups of students on additional research skills. It also allowed librarians to share skills in their areas of expertise.

Finally, we held check-in meetings with the entire group of students twice during the semester. The end-of-semester meeting was a social gathering with food and crafts, to help encourage community among the Research Assistants. For our mid-semester meeting, students came with questions and experiences from the Research Desk, which we discussed as a group. This group conversation was particularly helpful as it allowed us to see that students were still not clear on what the referral model should look like. We were able to clarify this and provide follow-up communication after the meeting reminding them of the triage goals.

During this meeting we also highlighted a couple of areas that we wanted to focus on for improved service at the desk, particularly in chat reference. Because Research Assistants staff the desk all hours the Library is open, we have them serve as the first point of contact for most of our chat reference, referring complex research questions to librarians. As a part of our initial orientation we provided Research Assistants with training on best practices in chat reference, particularly with respect to professionalism and etiquette (Appendix 14–4). Because our chat service saves all transcripts, throughout the semester we consulted the transcripts to evaluate these interactions. We would occasionally point out a mistake to an individual Research Assistant, but we mostly used this information to create follow-up training that would benefit all Research Assistants. During the mid-semester meeting, we selected one particularly good chat transcript and shared it with the group, and had Research Assistants identify the features that made it a quality reference interaction. We then shared a couple of fake chat transcripts that highlighted some of the problems we had occasionally noted and had students evaluate these as well. The problems we tried to feature included:

- A lack of professional language
- Not answering chat questions punctually
- Incorrect answers stemming from not getting enough information from the patron
- Just providing links without trying to teach the patron how to find things for themselves
- Not referring patrons with complex research questions to a librarian

During the second semester a similar transcript evaluation exercise was incorporated into the weekly training exercises and was assigned and completed using an online forum in our content management system.

IMPLEMENTATION OF THE PROGRAM

The Van Wylen Library hires 11–12 Research Assistants to staff the research desk for all 94 hours that the Library is open. During this time, students are scheduled to work 90- to 120-minute shifts, and most students work eight to ten hours a week. The desk is located close to the main entry of the primary campus Library, making it an easy stop for patrons first entering the building with questions. Other service desks in the Library will refer questions to the Research Desk, depending on the nature of the inquiries.

Although the Research Desk and research librarian offices are in close physical proximity to each other, it is essential that communication continues to occur between the Research Assistant and the on-call librarian in order to maintain a supportive working environment as well as to encourage and foster consistent referrals during normal business hours. One way we work to accomplish this is by a greeting system during shift changes; when research librarians are scheduled to be on call at specific times during the week, at night, and on weekends, Research Assistants are instructed to locate the on-call librarian at the beginning of their shifts, and, in turn, librarians greet the student assistant upon their shift changes. In addition, librarian mentors sometimes work with the student assigned to them during the course of a shift as time permits.

The manner in which referrals happens will depend on the type of question as well as the time of day. Librarians are on call during business hours, three hours per evening, Monday through Thursday, and three hours on Sundays. If a research question comes to the desk when a librarian is on call but not at the Research Desk, then the Research Assistants are encouraged to ask the librarian to come out. The desk contains two stations with swiveling computers; the students sit at the computer closest to the door, and the on-call librarian can either take over a prestarted search on that terminal, work with the patron on the second terminal, or invite the patron back to her office for a consultation-style meeting. Generally, we encourage librarians to handle these questions on the desk, because this provides additional training opportunities for Research Assistants. If a research question occurs during a time when librarians are not in the building, Research Assistants work with the patron to try to meet their information need, and then they are responsible for documenting each research transaction by referring the patron to librarians via e-mail. In these e-mails, they provide the patron's e-mail address, summarize the question and the help that they provided, and offer any suggestions on what additional assistance they think the patron might need.

In addition to answering patron questions, other duties on a given shift might include working on training exercises to either improve or refresh their knowledge of library tools and research skills or completing any long-term projects assigned to them by librarians. They also refill the lab printers and tidy and maintain the stapler and supply table. Research Assistants who work when the Library closes are also responsible for teaming with student workers from other areas of the Library to perform the closing sweep. When not assisting patrons or performing these additional duties, they are allowed to do their own homework or reading.

Initially there was some concern among Library staff members when the librarians decided to redirect their time by moving toward an on-call model at the Research Desk. With a little education and communication about the intention for serving the academic community in a more proactive approach as well as our confidence in the skills, intelligence, and character of our student workers, most Library staff understood the necessity for the healthy evolution of our service model. We communicated through staff meetings how we envisioned the on-call model would work and encouraged colleagues to provide feedback on its impact as the semester progressed.

EVALUATION OF THE PROGRAM

At the end of the fall semester we polled the Research Assistants to get their opinions and to assess the effectiveness of our training program and the on-call model in general as it related to their confidence levels as peer mentors. We asked them to rate their feelings on the helpfulness of various training components including the beginning of the semester orientation, our mid-semester meeting, the checklist, the weekly practice exercises, our mentor program, and the workshops we provided. In addition, we asked them to express their views of our on-call system, how well supported they felt by the on-call model, how our training program helped them, and in what areas the program could be stronger. We received an excellent response rate as 11 out of our 12 students completed the survey. From our results, we learned that, out of all the training components we offered, students valued both the beginning-of-the-semester orientation and our mentor programs most. Students also favorably ranked the checklist training and our mid-semester meeting, but had mixed opinions on the helpfulness of the weekly practice exercises. The librarian workshops were not scored as highly as these other components.

When asked about the adequacy of our training program, many students mentioned that, although they felt more confident about the research process, they would have benefited more if a librarian had spent some one-on-one time with them, especially during the beginning of the semester, to go over the specific exercises and to model a reference interaction. In the words of one assistant: "I feel that the first year employees are missing out on a critical piece of training when the librarians are not at the desk. While they are on call and accessible, it feels like the new students are being cheated out of the close mentorship with the librarians." This demonstrated to us that perhaps the artificially created mentoring relationships were not as effective as the organic ones that had emerged when librarians staffed the desk. Some students mentioned that the training exercises were too extensive and could have been given during the workshops. In general, however, Research Assistants felt very supported by the librarians and that, aside from some students needing more one-on-one attention at the beginning of the semester, most students felt that the new on-call model worked very well.

One problem identified through the feedback we received from our Research Assistants was that they were confused about when to answer a question independently and when to refer a patron to a librarian. Ironically, the extensive level of training students received emerged as a contributing factor in the lack of referrals to on-call librarians. One student summed it up very well while answering the question—How comfortable do you feel reaching out to the on-call librarians during your shift?—to which they responded "Pretty comfortable about asking but still unsure of when they should be involved because sometimes I feel confident enough to answer the research question but then I reflect on the situation later and I can't help wondering if I should have asked a librarian to help." Other students shared that they felt concerned that they were "interrupting" the on-call librarian when they came to get us, so we had to continue to remind them that this wasn't the case.

In our conversations about this issue both during the planning period and throughout the semester, we frequently described it as "having our cake and eating it too." We wanted to have excellently trained Research Assistants who felt comfortable and confident in their own research abilities, but we also wanted them to call on librarian expertise regularly so that patrons still had access to librarians via the Research Desk and not just through prescheduled appointments. We wanted Research Assistants who were always learning more about library-based research and eager to share this knowledge with their peers, while also realizing that they were not mini-librarians. We think this balance is important because our institution prides itself on having close engagement between students and faculty in the learning and research process, and this includes interactions between students and faculty librarians. Also, it has been shown through studies like Project Information Literacy that students sometimes think that librarians are only available to help with certain kinds of research problems and we want to be clear that we are there for all stages of research (Head, 2013). We want this outreach to occur at all of our access points, both course-based library instruction and the Research Desk. This concern for cultivating student assistant independence while maintaining a level of librarian oversight comes up regularly in libraries transitioning to a triage model (Miles, 2013; Sonntag & Palsson, 2007; Peters, 2015). Having just begun our transition to this new model, we are still learning, and in the future, we will continue to evaluate, assess, and adjust our structure to best serve our students, be they patrons or assistants.

One assessment that we had hoped to do was to send a survey to patrons who had been referred via e-mail to librarians during times when a librarian wasn't in the building. This seemed to be an easy way to collect feedback on our Research Assistants' performance when they weren't collaborating directly with a librarian and to measure the success of the combined peer/librarian service offered through virtual referrals. However, we received very few desk referral e-mails from our Research Assistants, too few to warrant a survey. End-of-semester analysis of our desk statistics showed that during the night and weekend times, there were only 37 questions recorded as research-oriented, which is one explanation for the lack of referrals. A second reason is likely the uncertainty our Research Assistants felt when a question necessitated a referral. In the future, we need to decide if a more formal measure of patron satisfaction should be taken to assess all Research Desk encounters.

IMPLICATIONS AND LESSONS LEARNED

Just as Hope College holds a high regard for close faculty–student collaboration along with the creation of independent lifelong learners, the Library staff also tries to create a balance between collaboration and leadership for our Research Assistants. Our recent attempts at increasing the responsibilities of our student workers through our on-call model have proved that our students are bright, capable, very willing to learn, and helpful in guiding their peers in their areas of research. The hiring criteria, and more specifically the essays we initiated, seem to have been a successful tool in weeding out those students who are only interested in working here on a superficial basis, ensuring a group of students who truly desire to help and educate their peers.

Our student assistants seem to be learning the triage model, responding favorably to our support of their efforts. Feedback we received from some included:

> Quote 1: I feel really comfortable because I feel that the librarians are always there and willing to help.

Quote 2: Because of how accessible the librarians are, I am always comfortable asking for help. Also, I do know the extent to my knowledge and the scope of work, so if there is anything that is beyond me, I feel comfortable asking the librarian for assistance or explanation.

Moving forward, we think that the on-call model is a positive mechanism for helping our Research Assistants gain confidence in communicating with and assisting other students. It has also benefited Research and Instruction Librarians in giving them more flexible time to work on other outreach projects when the desk is quiet. The challenge we face is a continued desire to find balance between empowering our students to be confident and capable peer educators while keeping librarians an accessible part of "just in time" research support. For the institution contemplating this model, we encourage you to have conversations about what responsibilities you want your students to have, what the tipping point will be for a referral to a research librarian, and how you plan to train your students clearly in this model. This should include good training in the art of the reference interview and helping peer assistants ask good questions. One of the more challenging things for students to catch is that a complex need can be buried behind a simple patron question.

NEXT STEPS

By aligning the Research Desk's goals with the missions of the Library and the College as well as with our strategic plan, we have developed an intensive and supportive structure that has nurtured and created a self-confident student work force. At the same time, we realize the necessity of balance, so in the future we plan to be more vigilant in our endeavors of providing a solid physical presence to encourage Research Assistants as well as to clarify the sometimes conspicuously hidden depths of inquiry that tend to dwell within a seemingly innocent research question. Our goals are really to elevate not only our patrons' knowledge, but more so, to increase the curiosity and scope of our student assistants' repertoire. This requires allowing them to tackle the kinds of advanced searching that teaches them these skills while reminding them that the burden of responsibility does not fall entirely on them. We intend on doing this by spending more individualized time with each of our Research Assistants in addition to the formalized training sessions and workshops. This will help them become increasing aware of the support we provide through this gentle guidance process so that they continue to thrive and grow as the intelligent young adults that they are. One way to achieve this is through the adaption of our on-call model to a slightly modified form. Librarians will be encouraged to not only check in at the beginning of each shift but to spend more time with each Research Assistant during their shifts in order to answer their questions, model reference interactions, and encourage increasing librarian referrals. They have the liberty to move back to the on-call model when there is less traffic in the Library.

We continue to fine-tune the training program, particularly the training exercises, to create a greater variety of assignments, some of which they will continue to do independently and some of which will require engaging with a librarian to complete. The hope is that this will both model what a good Research Assistant and librarian collaboration can look like and increase their information literacy skills in more nuanced ways. For example, they may dialogue about asking better questions or engage in a problem-based approach to learning how to construct effective searches. We are very dedicated in our commitment toward this end, and, more importantly, we are extremely proud of our capable Research Assistants who have time and time again helped to provide excellent service at Van Wylen Library.

REFERENCES

Cotton, Y., Kilner, A., & Oliver, J. (2014, January). Partners in learning. *CILIP Update,* 42–44. Retrieved from http://www.cilip.org.uk

Head, A. J. (2013). *Learning the ropes: How freshmen conduct course research once they enter college.* Retrieved from http://projectinfolit.org/images/pdfs/pil_2013_freshmenstudy_fullreport.pdf

Massey-Burzio, V. (1992). Reference encounters of a different kind: A symposium. *Journal of Academic Librarianship, 18*(5), 276–286.

Miles, D. B. (2013). Shall we get rid of the reference desk? *Reference & User Services Quarterly, 52*(4), 320–333. Retrieved from https://journals.ala.org/rusq/index

O'Kelly, M. A., Garrison, J., Merry, B., & Torreano, J. (2015). Building a peer-learning service for students in an academic library. *portal: Libraries & the Academy, 15*(1), 163–182. doi:10.1353/pla.2015.0000

Peters, T. (2015). Taking librarians off the desk: One library changes its reference desk staffing model. *Performance Measurement & Metrics, 16*(1), 18–27. doi:10.1108/PMM-11–2014–0038

Sonntag, G., & Palsson, F. (2007). No longer the sacred cow—No longer a desk: Transforming reference service to meet 21st century user needs. *Library Philosophy and Practice.* Retrieved from http://digital commons.unl.edu/libphilprac/

Stevens, C. R. (2013). Reference reviewed and re-envisioned: Revamping librarian and desk-centric services with LibStARs and LibAnswers. *Journal of Academic Librarianship, 39*(2), 202–214. doi:10.1016/j.acalib.2012.11.006

APPENDIX 14–1: INTERVIEW QUESTIONS

1. Why do you want to work at the Research Desk?
2. Tell us more about the research process you went through while doing the research example you provided us—what were your pitfalls/challenges and/or successes?
3. What do you consider your biggest research strengths? What about your research weaknesses?
4. Show us your favorite library resource tool. Demonstrate how it works and what you like about it (pretend that we don't know anything about this resource).
   - Ask follow-up questions about their activities and what they show us.
5. This job requires excellent customer service skills. Describe a situation in which you had to deal with a person who was difficult. How did you overcome the challenge (i.e., class project, job).
6. This job requires you to work closely with librarians. Can you describe a work or school experience in which you had to collaborate with others? Are you comfortable asking for help when you aren't sure how to proceed?
7. This job requires you to open/close the library on your own, requires you to be on time for shifts, and generally requires a lot of independent responsible work—could you tell us an example of having similar responsibilities in another setting?
8. Questions?

APPENDIX 14–2: RESEARCH DESK MISSION STATEMENT

The mission of the Research Help Desk is to provide access to relevant research materials and educate patrons on effective research processes in order to promote and facilitate the intellectual and cultural development of the Hope College community.

The goals of the Research Help Desk are:

1) Provide a helpful and friendly atmosphere to encourage open dialog about users' information needs.
2) Meet the information needs of users while empowering them to develop their own research skills and strategies.
3) Inspire curiosity about research both within and beyond the academic setting.
4) Work in close collaboration with each other as well as with other library staff to provide the best services to our patrons.

APPENDIX 14–3: ORIENTATION SCHEDULE

ORIENTATION

(*Food and drinks provided at the beginning and throughout*)

1) Team-building exercises—Have everyone share their favorite summer activity, favorite thing about the library, and what they are excited about this semester.

2) Mission statement review
   - Introduce library's mission and the Research Desk mission and talk about them
   - Diagram of the library's departments, their functions, and where we fit
   - Short video of library staff describing the value of student library employees
   - Break into small groups and ask each group to talk about the mission and what it means to be a student "ambassador" for the library

   BREAK—Also a chance for students to get their picture taken for the Research Assistant photo board

3) Research interview/referral training
   - Warm up with humorous video.
   - Describe the goals of this training—to be able to ask good questions and make referrals—specifics research skills will be taught later.
   - Go over a handout that summarizes the question types we receive at the desk, what types they will be trained to answer well, and what types they should refer to a librarian.
   - Describe what referrals will look like, depending on when a librarian is on call and when we are out of the building
   - Brainstorm on the board a list of good questions you can ask to conduct a good reference interview.
   - Jessica and Rachel model an example research question and reference interview. One plays the part of a patron and the other a research assistant.
   - Break into six pairs (trying to pair new students with an experienced one), give each pair a question and have them create a role play of a good reference interview and referral. Come back together and ask some groups to perform them.
     BREAK

4) Work policies
   - Time sheets, schedule, substitute requests
   - Dress code, etiquette
   - Chat etiquette, handout and summary of professional chat
   - Safety
   - Library closing training

5) Description of future training
   - On-desk training exercises
   - Checklist
   - Mentor assignments
   - Workshops
   - Team-building activities (mid and end of semester)

APPENDIX 14–4: CHAT REFERENCE TIPS FOR RESEARCH ASSISTANTS

Be more formal with your chat language.

- Remember, this is a stranger you are talking to, not a friend.
- You are representing the library, and those on the other end may assume they are talking to a staff member.

Remember to give a greeting and "sign off."

- Avoid jumping right into answering the question without some kind of acknowledgment.
- Phrases to try:
  - **Best Practice!** Give your name: "Hi this is Jessica" (just first name is fine).
  - "Hi XX" (if they give their name).
  - "Thank you for your question."
  - "I'm happy to help you with this."
  - "Just a moment while I look up the answer to your question."
  - "I'm happy to help you with this. Can you tell me a little more about your topic/the assignment/what you're looking for?"

If it's a really short question (like "what are the hours tonight?"), it can be tough to give a greeting. However, immediately follow up with a sign off, like;

- "Is there any other question I can help you with?"

Other sign-off phrases to try:

- "Let us know if there is anything else we can help you with."
- "Feel free to follow up on chat, askalibrarian@hope.edu, or in person if you have more questions."
- "You're welcome!" (if they thank you).

Important! Try to avoid leaving a question unanswered.

- *It's OK to not know the answer yourself!* We don't expect you to know everything, but you should be able to point the patron toward additional help.
- Examples:
  - "I'm going to transfer you to a librarian for more help with your question. Just a moment."
  - "I don't have the answer to your question, and there is not a staff member available right now. If you give me your e-mail address, I'll have a librarian follow up with the answer shortly" (then e-mail the transcript to askalibrarian).
  - "It looks like we have the article, but I'm not able to access it either. Could you give me your e-mail address? I'll have a librarian double-check this citation and get back to you."
  - "This sounds like an interesting and complex research question. I'm happy to try to get you started, but we could help you even more if you scheduled a research appointment with a librarian (http://www.hope.edu/lib/ask/consultation.php) or e-mailed your question to askalibrarian@hope.edu for more follow-up."

Index

Note: Page numbers in *italic* indicate a figure or table on the corresponding page.

About the Editors and Contributors

Clinton Baugess is a Research and Instruction Librarian at Gettysburg College's Musselman Library. His primary responsibilities are coordinating the library's information literacy instruction program; serving as a liaison to the German Studies, History, and Psychology departments; and working closely with students in the Peer Research Mentor Program in the Research and Instruction Department. He also supports Musselman Library's undergraduate internship and digital scholarship programs. He earned his MLS from Indiana University Bloomington.

Rachel Bishop serves on a team of research and instruction librarians at Hope College, a small liberal arts institution in Michigan. She is a co-supervisor of student research assistants collaborating on student hiring and training for the library's Research Help Desk, and she has worked on the successful implementation of the library's current reference service model. Her interests include instruction, mentoring, student research behaviors, and all things related to student empowerment as she also heads up the User Services Committee at the library. She received her MLIS from Wayne State University in Detroit, Michigan and her MA in Clinical Psychology from the Center for Humanistic Psychology in Detroit Michigan.

Ellen V. Blumberg is the Student Engagement and Information Commons Librarian at the University of Texas at San Antonio Libraries. She has coordinated the Libraries' Peer Research Coaches Program since 2013. She also directs all the student engagement efforts for both the main campus and downtown campus locations and promotes collaborative initiatives with the Libraries' academic partners to support student success. She earned a BA in Psychology from Indiana University and an MLIS from the University of Texas at Austin.

Brett Bodemer fulfills multiple roles at the Robert E. Kennedy Library at California Polytechnic State University in San Luis Obispo. As the College of Liberal Arts Librarian, he supports the instructional, consultation, and collections needs of that college. As Coordinator of the Digital Research, Scholarship and Creative Activities Hub, he coordinates both general reference and specialized research help for GIS, statistics, and data visualization. He has successfully fostered reference and instructional programs that leverage the skills and insights of undergraduate peer assistants since 2009.

Michael Courtney, the Outreach and Engagement Librarian at Indiana University Libraries, connects the Libraries' resources and services to the academic priorities of various campus communities and student audiences, including first-year students, distance learners, international students, transfer students, graduate students, and others; he also serves as the collection manager for the Undergraduate Core Collection. As an active participant in the instructional initiatives of the Teaching and Learning Department, Mike provides leadership and direction for librarians and graduate instruction assistants in the effective design and teaching of information literacy education. In addition, Michael is responsible for coordinating the libraries' distance education services and their collaboration with distance education programs across the university system.

Annie Donahue is the Director of the UNH Manchester Library where in addition to her administrative duties she contributes to collection development, reference, and instruction activities. Her research focuses on collaborations between teaching and library faculty, assessing student learning, and integrating information literacy within the curriculum. She shares her scholarship through journal articles and coauthored book chapters as well as through regional, national, and international conference presentations.

Kim Donovan is the current Director and Writing Specialist for the Center of Academic Enrichment at UNH Manchester. She has been a college instructor and learning center professional since 2000, and is a doctoral candidate in Composition and TESOL at the Indiana University of Pennsylvania.

Tyler A. Dunn is the Lead Access Services Librarian at Palo Alto College in San Antonio, Texas. In addition to overseeing circulation, reserves, and interlibrary loan, she teaches library instruction and practices collection development as the subject librarian for the behavioral sciences. She also coordinates the college Children's Library, which includes planning summer camps and literacy programs. She previously worked in several Library Assistant positions in the Public Services division of University of Texas at San Antonio Libraries. She received her MLS from the University of North Texas.

Anna Esty (now Assogba) serves as Research Librarian for Student Outreach in the Faculty of Arts and Sciences at Harvard University. She received her MLS from Simmons College. Prior to Harvard, she worked as a Library Assistant, Serials, at Berklee College of Music. She has published in *Computers in Libraries* and *The Chronicle of Higher Education*, and, in collaboration with her colleague Fred Burchsted, has contributed to a biographical section introduction in the *Guide to Reference in Genealogy and Biography*.

Carolyn Gamtso is the Head of Reference and Instruction at UNH Manchester Library. She is interested in creative information literacy initiatives and enjoys working with faculty to design interactive, experiential student workshops. She collaborates with UNH Manchester's Center for Academic Enrichment to train writing tutors in information literacy skills and helps to oversee the college's Research Mentor Program. Carolyn's research interests include faculty/librarian classroom collaborations and peer tutoring in the library. She has shared her scholarship in the area of library instruction at local, regional, national, and international conferences, and she has coauthored several articles and book chapters that discuss information literacy projects and practices. Carolyn earned a BA in English from the College of the Holy Cross, an MA in English from Indiana University, and an MLIS from the University of Rhode Island. She is an alumna of the Association of College and Research Libraries (ACRL) Immersion Program (Teaching Track, 2003).

Alexis Gomez, Library Coordinator at Pickering Educational Resources Library at Boston University, received her BA in Psychology from Harvard College with a minor in the History of Science. She worked as a cataloging assistant, lab assistant at the library User Research Center, Peer Research Fellow, and Library House Outreach Program Assistant Coordinator at the Harvard Library during her college years and is looking forward to pursuing an MLIS and a career in academic libraries.

Jessica Hronchek is a Research and Instruction Librarian at Hope College. In addition to general education instruction, she serves as the liaison to the visual and performing arts departments, providing information literacy instruction and collection development support in these areas. She is a co-supervisor of student Research Assistants at Van Wylen Library, focusing on training. Her research interests include information literacy and research behavior in the creative arts. She received her MLS and MA in Art History from Indiana University Bloomington.

Patricia Iannuzzi began her tenure as Dean of the University Libraries at the University of Nevada, Las Vegas (UNLV), in February 2005. Iannuzzi has a 35-year career as a librarian and educator, in administrative and faculty positions in libraries at the University of California, Berkeley; Florida International University; Yale University; and Tufts University. An international leader in information literacy, Iannuzzi chaired the national, multi-association task force to establish student learning outcomes, Information Literacy Competency Standards for Higher Education (2000). In addition to her robust publication history, Iannuzzi also speaks and consults worldwide on the topics of information literacy learning outcomes, research-based learning, and 21st-century competencies.

Ramona Islam, Curricular Design and Research Librarian at Harvard University and an education doctoral student at Lesley University, received her MLS from Kent State University and a master's degree in Educational Technology from Fairfield University. Ramona is a past editorial board member and current peer reviewer for *College & Research Libraries*, and her professional writing has appeared in the *Journal of Library Administration*, *College & Research Libraries*, the Association of Research Libraries *SPEC Kit* series, and *Urban Library Journal*.

Mallory Jallas is a Research and Instruction Librarian at Gettysburg College's Musselman Library. She is the co-coordinator of the library's Peer Research Mentor Program in the Research and Instruction Department. Her work focuses on information literacy instruction, reference service, and library marketing. She received her MS in Library and Information Science from the University of Illinois at Urbana–Champaign.

Jan H. Kemp, Assistant Dean for Public Services at the University of Texas at San Antonio, received her MLS from the University of Texas at Austin and master's degree in Business

Administration from Texas Tech University. She has held administrative positions at Texas Tech, North Carolina State University, and Lamar University. Active in ACRL, she is currently a co-convener of the ULS Evidence-Based Practices Discussion Group. Her recent research interests have included chat reference and textbook lending services. She coauthored a paper on chat reference that won the Beta Phi Mu/Library Research Round Table Research Paper Award in 2015.

Vegas Longlois is an AmeriCorp member at ImpactAlabama, where she coaches high school debate for students in Birmingham schools, conducts free vision screenings for preschool students, and files taxes for low-income families. She served as a Peer Research Fellow within the Harvard Library House Outreach Program in 2015–2016. In 2016, she received a BA in Folklore and Mythology with a secondary in Global Health from Harvard University and a citation in Spanish.

Reed Lowrie manages reference services at Cabot, Lamont, Tozzer, and Widener Libraries at Harvard University. He has a master's degree in English Literature from the University of Chicago and an MLS from the University of Illinois. He has worked in public services in academic libraries (Dartmouth College, University of Chicago, Harvard University) for over 20 years. He has published professionally in *Journal of Family Practice, Magazines for Libraries*, and the *New England Map Organization Newsletter*.

Emilia R. Marcyk is the Instructional Technology and Information Literacy Librarian at Michigan State University, where she develops instructional content, leads information literacy sessions for the First-Year Writing program, and supervises undergraduate Peer Research Assistants. She received her MS in Library and Information Science from the University of Illinois at Urbana–Champaign, and is an alumna of ACRL Immersion Program (Teacher Track, 2015). She has published and presented previously on innovative online tools for student reference assistant training and the value of chat reference services.

Pamela Martin is the Coordinator for Outreach and Peer Learning at Utah's State University's Merrill-Cazier Library. She oversees the Library Peer Mentor Program, teaches library instruction sessions, and engages with student groups and student employees across campus. Martin's research interests include information literacy, peer learning, and staff management. She recently served as the President of the Utah Library Association.

Theresa McDevitt is the Government Information/Outreach Librarian at Indiana University of Pennsylvania Libraries. She has worked with residence hall peer educators to increase student awareness of the benefits of using library services, resources, and spaces for many years.

Rosan Mitola (editor) is Outreach Librarian for the University of Nevada, Las Vegas, where she collaborates with campus groups to integrate library collections and services into co-curricular educational experiences for students. She oversees the Mason Undergraduate Peer Research Coach Program that contributes to student engagement through outreach and peer-assisted learning in library instruction. Her primary research interest is co-curricular contributions to student success. Mitola has presented and published on developing a professional development workshop program for student employees.

Benjamin Oberdick is the Head of Information Literacy for the Michigan State University Libraries (MSUL), where he leads a team in providing information literacy instruction for students in a First-Year Writing class. He also provides reference services for MSUL patrons and established the Peer Research Assistant Program at MSU which employs undergraduate students to provide research assistance for students in the residence halls. He is a three-time alumna of ACRL's Immersion Program (Teacher Track, 2010; Intentional Teacher Track, 2012; Practical Management Track, 2014) and also the former chair of the ACRL's Instruction Section Peer-Reviewed Instructional Materials Online (PRIMO) Committee.

Kate Otto is the Learning Commons Librarian at Indiana University Bloomington's Herman B Wells Library, where she works with campus partners to provide services that support primarily undergraduates in their efforts to achieve academic, personal, and professional success. She is an alumna of ACRL's Immersion Program (Teacher Track, 2015) and a content creator for the K-State-led New Literacies Alliance curricular project. Kate has presented on the value of extending First Year Experience programs beyond the freshman year and on community partnerships increasing the relevance of digital humanities projects.

Erin Rinto (editor) is Teaching and Learning Librarian at the University of Nevada, Las Vegas, where she coordinates the library instruction component of the English Composition Program. She publishes and presents on the topics of information literacy instruction and assessment in the context of First-Year Writing courses and the implications of peer-to-peer learning in the library environment. Rinto is an active member of the ACRL Instruction Section Teaching Methods Committee and an alumna of ACRL's Immersion Program (Program Track, 2013).

Genevieve Schaack is Dean of Students at Wellsprings Friends School, a small, alternative high school in Eugene, Oregon. Her passion for teaching began as an undergraduate when she was employed as a peer tutor at the University of Oregon's Mathematics Library. She is currently pursuing her master's in Public Administration with an emphasis in education policy from the University of Oregon.

Meggan Smith is a Research and Instruction Librarian at Gettysburg College's Musselman Library. Her primary responsibilities are coordinating the library's reference services; providing information literacy instruction; serving as a liaison to the Biology, Education, and Health Sciences departments; and co-coordinating the Peer Research Mentor Program at Gettysburg College. She earned her MLIS from the University of Pittsburgh.

Malaika M. Turner is the Associate Director for Residential Living and Well-Being, where she supervises full-time residence directors in the Office of Housing Residential Living and Dining, and administrators in the Center for Health and Well-Being. She also oversees student peer programs, namely, the Academic Success Mentor Program, which was created to assist first-year and transfer students, within the residence halls, make meaningful connections to university and experience academic success. Malaika completed her doctorate at Indiana University of Pennsylvania, where her topic was "Technology's Impact on the Learning Experience of At-Risk Digital Natives."

Joshua Vossler is Head of Reference and Instruction for Morris Library at Southern Illinois University Carbondale, where he supervises the library's Information Desk and leads the instruction program. He presents and publishes on the application of creativity and humor to information literacy instruction, as well as instructional videography. He has facilitated workshops on incorporating humor and story into library instruction, and his instructional videos have been recognized by ACRL's Instruction Section Innovation Award (2012, with John Watts) and PRIMO (2015, 2011), and in 2016, he won (with Christina Heady) Best Publicity/Marketing Film at the ARL Film Festival.

John Watts (editor) is Teaching and Learning Librarian at the University of Nevada, Las Vegas, where he works with faculty and students to integrate the library into the general education curriculum. He presents and publishes on the topics of creativity in information literacy instruction and student learning outcomes assessment. Watts has facilitated invited workshops on incorporating humor and story into library instruction as well as workshops for teaching faculty on student learning outcomes assessment and research assignment design. He was a facilitator and curriculum designer for ACRL's Assessment in Action program and Intersections of Scholarly Communication and Information Literacy Task Force, and a corecipient of the ACRL Instruction Section Innovation Award.

Jenny Wong-Welch is the STEM Librarian at San Diego State University. In addition to her responsibilities of providing research assistance and library instruction for the College of Engineering and the departments of Astronomy, Physics, and Mathematics/Statistics, she is the Director of build IT @ SDSU Library, a student-run makerspace designed to foster creativity and innovation by providing an infrastructure for DIY learning of technology. She has presented and published on the role of libraries as makerspaces on the academic campus and the library's ability to use the process of creating to make information literacy more tangible.

Janelle Wertzberger is Assistant Dean and Director of Scholarly Communications at Gettysburg College's Musselman Library. She provides leadership and vision for the scholarly communications and library publishing program. She manages the institutional repository, *The Cupola: Scholarship at Gettysburg College*. She supports the research of undergraduate students and faculty and participates actively in the digital scholarship and information literacy instruction programs. She is also involved in the design and implementation of library programs and learning series, which support the curriculum, expand understanding of diversity and inclusion, encourage critical thinking, and enliven the imagination.

Annie Zeidman-Karpinski is the first Kenneth M. and Kenda H. Singer Science Librarian at the University of Oregon. She provides reference for any question that comes her way, mentoring and instructing when she's allowed, and collection development for Human Physiology, Mathematics, and Computer and Information Science departments. She is passionate about not being boring as well as learning how to improve her interactions with the students and colleagues she has the privilege of interacting with informally and formally. She has written about using chat for reference, Math librarianship, how video games belong in instruction and libraries, and how to get meaningful performance-based classroom assessments.